Cacti of Texas
AND NEIGHBORING STATES

A Field Guide   by Del Weniger

UNIVERSITY OF TEXAS PRESS AUSTIN

First Edition, 1984

Requests for permission to reproduce material from this work should be sent to Permis-
sions, University of Texas Press, Box 7819,
Austin, Texas 78713.

Library of Congress Cataloging in Publication Data
Weniger, Del.
    Cacti of Texas and neighboring states.

    Includes indexes.
    1. Cactus—Texas—Identification.
2. Botany—Texas.   I. Title.
QK495.C11W36   1984
583'.47'09764   83-26015
ISBN 0-292-71085-2
ISBN 0-292-71063-1 (pbk.)

Cacti of Texas and Neighboring States

Contents

Acknowledgments   vi
Introduction   vii
What Is a Cactus?   1
Key to the Genera of the Cacti   6
Genus *Echinocereus*   9
  Key to the Echinocerei   10
Genus *Wilcoxia*   79
Genus *Peniocereus*   82
Genus *Acanthocereus*   85
Genus *Echinocactus*   88
  Key to the Echinocacti   91
Genus *Lophophora*   137
Genus *Ariocarpus*   142
Genus *Pediocactus*   146
Genus *Epithelantha*   152
Genus *Mammillaria*   155
  Key to the Mammillarias   159
Genus *Opuntia*   228
  Key to the Opuntias   231
Glossary   341
Index of Scientific Names   347
Index of Common Names   354

Acknowledgments

This book is made possible largely by
the contributions to *Cacti of the Southwest*. All acknowledgments listed there
thus apply here. I also wish to mention
the added help of Mr. Kenneth Heil.
The photographs of *Echinocereus
kuenzleri* and of *Echinocactus whipplei*
var. *intermedius* and var. *heilii* were
taken and contributed by him.

Introduction

This is a field guide. Its purpose is to make possible the identification of the cacti growing in the five states covered. It therefore contains a distillation of the descriptive material from my previous book, *Cacti of the Southwest*, published by the University of Texas Press in 1970, as well as the photographs and keys from that book.

The lesser scope of this guide, together with the desire to make it small enough for handy field use, has made it necessary to leave out the wealth of historical and taxonomic information for which the earlier book was well known. Anyone interested in those aspects of the cacti should refer to it.

It has proved very difficult to deal with the cacti without becoming ensnared in the taxonomic confusion which exists concerning them. It has been impossible to note here all the different names used for the various forms, yet I desire to give the reader some reference from which to start in tracing synonyms. Lyman Benson's exhaustive treatment, *The Cacti of the United States and Canada*, has appeared, and since it purports to be the bible of cactology, I have included for each form any different name he has chosen. Since his taxonomic notes are usually very complete, anyone who wishes to pursue the matter further may trace out any synonyms through them. I have included references to any new opinions published since my earlier book which seem significant to me.

In the United States there has long been a tendency to break down the treatment of cacti into state studies. States are artificial areas and their boundaries have nothing to do with plant distribution, but it has been impossible to ignore them. The present study, however, includes all the forms of cacti presently known to be growing in five states: Arkansas, Louisiana, New Mexico, Oklahoma, and Texas. These five states make up a unit much more logically considered, cactuswise, than any one of them individually.

The cacti are listed by their recognized scientific names, immediately followed (where such exist) by all of the common names by which the cactus is known in various localities, including the Spanish and sometimes the Indian names. Spellings of these common names show the local variations found in the literature.

Each entry contains a description, updated from the original one of the species, the known range of natural distribution in rather general terms, a discussion of unusual or interesting features, and a color photograph of the plant, in most cases in bloom. More detailed information can be found in my *Cacti of the Southwest*.

A few of the photographs were made in the plant's natural location, but in most cases this proved to be impractical. Most cacti bloom only a few days out of the year, and it was obviously impossible to be in a canyon of the Texas Big Bend on precisely the days when each cactus chose to bloom.

Much effort, therefore, has gone into the work of locating the various forms in the wild, then bringing them in and growing them in such congenial environments that they have bloomed, so that they could be pictured at the right moment. The soils and backgrounds visible in the pictures are, therefore, not usually the natural environments of the plants. In fact, the colors of these have often been chosen to contrast with and make as clearly visible as possible the spines and other characters of the cacti. This means that no conclusion about the environments of these plants can be drawn from these pictures. Unless otherwise stated, the photographs are from my own collection. Measurements given in the photograph captions are the plant body sizes of the specific plants pictured and do not, unless otherwise stated, include flowers. In most cases this size is smaller than the maximum size achieved by the species.

In organizing this presentation, one of the biggest problems was the delineation of the genera. The widest possible range of opinions is held today by the different authorities in the field on the limits of the genera in the Cactaceae. It seems that the present extent of the knowledge of the cacti does not enable anyone to give as definite a list of cactus genera as can be made for many other plant groups. There are several very different systems of genera, each very logical in the light of a certain set of assumptions. The reasons for my adopting a very conservative system are set forth in *Cacti of the Southwest*.

Within the genera no attempt has been made to organize the species into tribes or sections, since this sort of thing—as, for instance, various proposals for the genus *Opuntia*—seems still to be based on conjecture, and I find little newer and more solid evidence for any of the various contradictory proposals already made.

Cacti of Texas
and Neighboring States

What Is a Cactus?

Before going directly into the description of the various cacti we might pause to consider, for those who have not concerned themselves about these things before, how a cactus differs from other plants, what is so special about it, and what are some of the problems the uniqueness of its form and physiology bring to it in its natural situation and to us if we desire to raise it.

Mostly because of certain flower characteristics, it is quite often assumed that cacti are related to the rose family. From here one can go as far as one's imagination chooses to range, presuming with some that the roses of the West Indies changed in order to adapt to more arid conditions and so gave rise to the Pereskias and through them to all cacti. This is an enchanting story, and I am sure that the cactophiles are pleased with the idea that their favorites might be descendants of the rose, but I am not so certain that the rose enthusiasts are as sympathetic to the idea of appending the cacti to their queen of the flowers. Most agree that the cacti are a young group, maybe 20,000 years old, and an equally big problem is how they could have developed their extreme and fantastic adaptations in such a comparatively short time.

Be that as it may, the cacti are here, and one needs to know how to recognize them. This task is complicated by the fact that most of the obvious characters by which one thinks to recognize them are shared by some plant or other somewhere in the world. This is true of such things as large, fleshy stems, vicious spines, and reduction of leaves, which to an amateur mean cactus every time. There are other plants showing all of these characteristics, some of them to almost the extent the cacti do.

It is a failure to recognize this fact that accounts for the popular articles, nursery ads, and many "cactus plantings" containing mention or actual specimens of completely unrelated plants under the banner of cactus. Although they show at least some of the above characteristics, it must be stated that such things as yuccas, agaves, century plants, sotols, and so on are not cacti at all but extremely modified members of the lily family. Ocotillo and allthorn are individual residents of the desert community showing some of the same adaptations but belonging to other plant families. Then there is the whole multitude of African plants paralleling the cacti in almost every feature of stem, rib, spine, and leaf, but all belonging to the huge, worldwide genus *Euphorbia*, which also includes such plants as the poinsettia. We sometimes speak of all these other plants as succulents, setting up the categories of cacti and succulents—although the cacti are also succulent, since the word merely means "fleshy."

How do you tell a cactus? A cactus is always a dicot, and its two seed leaves will distinguish it at once from all those members of the lily family so often called cacti, since they are monocots and have only one seed leaf.

A feature which all cacti have and share with no other plant is the structure called the areole. All cacti have areoles quite liberally scattered over the surface, usually arranged in rows or spirals in the most conspicuous places. These are round to elongated spots from $\frac{1}{16}$ to sometimes well over $\frac{1}{2}$ inch in greatest measurement; their surfaces are hard, rough, uneven, and brown or blackish or else covered with white to brown or blackish wool. These areoles are now considered to be the equivalent of complex buds, and it is from them that whatever spines the cactus possesses grow. The spines, since they come from these areoles, are always arranged in clusters, which is another feature not found on other spiny plants, whose spines are produced singly from some source other than an areole.

Beyond this, for the actual features separating cacti from all other plants, one has to look to the flower. Certain rather technical features of the flower are cited, such as its having sepals and petals numerous and intergrading, having an inferior ovary with one seed chamber, and having one single style with several stigma lobes.

The key to understanding why the cactus is such a strange plant is the understanding of its major problem and how it solves it. This is the problem of water.

The cactus is typically a resident of the desert or else of habitats where, for one reason or another, the water supply is practically nonexistent at least part of the time. This may be because of inadequate rainfall or because the soil is too coarse or too thin to hold much water. The finely branching roots of a cactus absorb water rapidly when it is available, and the plant stores this bonanza of water to the limit of its capacity. The adaptations for great water-storing capacity form the basis for the most obvious peculiarity of the cactus.

The most common means of storing water found in these plants is by the enlarging of the stem into a thick, fleshy column or even a round ball. A cactus adapted this way becomes literally a water-filled column or ball, actually, in large specimens, a barrel of water—from which comes the common term "barrel cactus." The interior of such a cactus is not a reservoir of pure water into which you could dip a ladle, as cartoons sometimes show the thirsty prospector doing, but a mass of soft tissue permeated with water. Except for the supporting framework necessary in larger species, that interior is of about the consistency of a melon's watery pulp. When rain comes, it fills to the maximum with water, and in times of drought this reserve is gradually reduced. Thus, the cactus stem swells and shrinks according to the water supply, and there is always an arrangement of ribs or tubercles which make this change in bulk possible without the whole stem alternately caving in or splitting open.

In a number of the cacti where adaptations for clambering up trees, camouflage in thickets, or something else limits the thickness or size of the stems, the root may become the water-storage organ instead. In these cacti the root may become a carrotlike taproot weighing up to fifty pounds (in the extreme case of an old *Peniocereus greggii* specimen) or a cluster of tubers (as found on *Wilcoxia poselgeri* and some of the Opuntias).

To further preserve water, the leaves of a cactus are reduced or eliminated altogether. The more strictly a desert dweller a species is, the more completely the leaves tend to be reduced or absent. The green stems take over the functions of the leaves. The cacti's compact form is covered with a thick, waxy epidermis which is impervious to water, and even its stomata are equipped with means to reduce moisture loss. There is great variation in the tenacity with which individual cacti hold water, with the most extreme desert forms said to release up to six thousand times less water in a given moment than an ordinary plant of the same weight.

The thick, dry protective covering of the cactus is so deceptive that we seldom think of the soft, delicate, watery interior which it protects, but we may be sure the thirsty denizens of the desert, where water is life itself, are ever conscious of it. As a deterrent to predation, the succulent flesh of almost all cacti is entirely covered with a system of spines so sharp and dangerous and so perfectly spreading and interlacing that neither the browsers nor the rodents can get their teeth between them to bite into the plant. The spines are never poisonous. The water problem, then, is directly responsible for the soft makeup of a cactus and indirectly responsible for its hard, waxy exterior and its often unpleasant but also fascinating array of spines.

The cacti face another closely related problem. How can they survive the baking heat and searing light of their desert habitat? Of course many cacti could not, and these grow only in the shade of thickets or trees, but the others are said to depend on their own spines for shade. The spines achieve their shading effect, somewhat after the manner of a lathhouse cover, by breaking the radiation up into moving strips of endurable duration. Several forms also protect the exposed surface, especially the tender growing area at the top, with a covering of wool or hair, usually white and reflective. One can fairly well judge how extreme a desert situation a species comes from and how much sun it can stand by looking at how extensively this wool is developed or how complete the spine shading is.

With no tender leaves, the compact body of the cactus, within its spiny envelope, is thus remarkably well protected against any of the natural forces or living enemies of its habitat, and it can survive in places where only the hardiest persist. Yet it has one more major problem to surmount. It must reproduce itself. And to do this it must usually produce a flower. Some of the cacti avoid this at all but the most favorable times and depend instead upon very well developed vegetative reproduction, but sooner or later all have to bloom.

The cactus flower is almost always renowned for its size and beauty, said to be for the purpose of attracting insects or other flying forms across the arid distances to pollinate it. At any rate it does not seem to be beautiful for our benefit, because the flower usually lasts so short a period and blooms at such an unfavorable time that we hardly ever catch a glimpse of it, and it usually is "born to blush unseen and waste its sweetness on the desert air."

Most cacti have flowers which open in the worst heat of the day, usually for only a few hours, and then are closed and fading before the cool of the evening begins. In most forms, the flower has its brief life, the reproductive act is completed by insects which scorn the heat, and the life spark is already down within the spiny ovary before the desert cools.

Many tropical and a few of our U.S. cacti reverse this schedule entirely and open their gigantic, wonderfully fragrant flowers at night to be pollinated by night-flying insects or in a few cases by bats. In most cases these species produce their flowers on tall, spiny stems where no ordinary predator could reach them anyway, but they fade as quickly as the others and are usually only sadly wilted remains by dawn. Only the saguaro, whose flowers are inaccessible to almost any predator, and some other forms protected by especially long spines seem able to enjoy the luxury of longer-lasting flowers.

The cactus fruit, which follows the flower, is usually protected at first by spines or wool and grows to become a berry with numerous small seeds. In some cases this dries up and the seeds are allowed to scatter, but in many species the ripe berry becomes fleshy and at the same time loses its spines or rises out of its wool covering. It is never poisonous, and it ranges from sour to very sweet in different species. It is snapped up and carried off by animals and birds, who finally get a meal from the cactus but who pay for it by scattering the seeds far and wide. Some of the sweetest of these fruits are relished by humans. Those of the Opuntias are called tunas, and the strawberry cactus (of which there are several species) bears this common name because the flavor of the red fruits suggests that of strawberries.

In all of its stages, then, the cactus is admirably adapted for survival in an arid environment, with all of these special features most accentuated in the forms inhabiting the more severe desert regions and less markedly developed in those of less extreme situations. But these same wonderful features which make the cactus so successful in the desert bring their own problems with them, limiting it in important ways even in its natural environment and making the tough desert thing one of the most vulnerable of plants when brought out of the desert into cultivation.

Having to restrict their transpiration to a minimum to conserve their stored water, the cacti are limited thereby to very slow life processes and growth as compared with other plants. When looking at a large old cactus one should appreciate the time it took, at this reduced rate, to achieve its bulk. It is often said that a saguaro cactus 1 foot tall is about twenty-five years old, a barrel cactus 1 foot in diameter between twenty and forty years old. The rates of growth vary from species to species, but almost no cactus is over a fraction of an inch tall at the end of its first year, and they all must have long periods of time to achieve their potential size.

Problems arise for a cactus transplanted from the desert into a moist environment. Adapted to hoarding its water, with its stomata small and guarded by various means against the pull of the dry desert air, what can it do in the humid air where it is now? It cannot open and lay its moisture out for the humid air. This is not its way. And since this air does not pull water out of its deep recesses, the flow will be less than it would be in the desert, so your cactus, which you thought would respond with prodigious growth to your kindness in bringing it into the moisture, may actually suffer and grow poorly because it cannot transpire and carry on its life processes here.

I have also mentioned the adaptations of the cactus which enable it to live in the extreme heat and light of the desert. These may also bring severe problems.

The flesh of most cacti is more or less shaded and protected by the spines and a covering of wool or hair. In the forms which grow in extremely exposed places this covering may be developed to protect against temperatures of well over 100 degrees Fahrenheit and some of the most intense light radiation found on earth. The outer tissues themselves, and even the life processes of some of these species, are adapted to such extremes. It seems, for instance, that some of these cacti cannot even begin photosynthesis until the temperature reaches 75 degrees or higher. Everything in them is adjusted for high heat and light intensities.

Air-conditioning has marked the end of many a cactus dish-garden because the plants can hardly carry on photosynthesis in the coolness we maintain, even in a window, and when this is coupled with what is for them little better than darkness, they may not be able to manufacture enough food even to stay alive.

We have seen some of the remarkable adaptations which make cacti so fascinating and have tried to understand the problems these changes are meant to meet, as well as the special problems they can generate for cactus growers. Successful cactus culture consists of recognizing these problems and helping the cactus meet them naturally. One does not have success with cacti by removing them from all their natural problems. More cacti in cultivation have been killed by too much kindness than by anything else.

It is well to recall that there are cacti adapted for almost every sort of environment, from shady rain forest to extreme desert exposure. All the problems of growing cacti mentioned above are less critical for those plants adapted to less severe conditions, and these can be grown much more easily than the most restricted ones; some of them can be treated quite a lot like other plants. But these are generally the less spiny, less succulent forms, which are, therefore, the ones less fascinating to most of us. It is perhaps unfortunate, but unavoidable, that to grow pitahayas and barrels and other remarkable types one has to simulate to a fair degree the extreme environments of their hot, arid homes.

Key to the Genera of the Cacti

The keys which are given here and before the discussion of each major genus are based as far as possible on the vegetative characters of adult individuals, but it appears to be impossible to construct workable keys for the cacti based on these alone. It was found necessary to refer in some cases to the flowers or fruits and sometimes even to the seeds. This means that the keys will be less than satisfactory in certain seasons and will not identify most juvenile forms at all. Those using the keys will need to have before them very nearly complete adult specimens of the living plants.

The keys are artificial and are my own. They are binomial keys, presenting a series of choices between two alternatives. In use, one reads the first choice (*1a*) and compares the specimen in question with the description. If the description at *1a* fits the specimen, one then proceeds to the number given at the end of the description and repeats the process there. If the description at *1a* does not fit the specimen, then the user abandons *1a* and moves on to *1b*, which is the alternate choice. If the specimen matches *1b*, then one moves to the number given at the end of *1b*, and so on. When this process is followed carefully with a mature plant from our area, it should lead to a description, after which a plant name and page number are given. This is the name of the specimen in hand and the discussion of it will start on that page. If at any point the specimen does not fit either the *a* or *b* choice one has arrived at, there are two possible explanations. Either the user has already made a wrong choice somewhere earlier in the process, or else the cactus is not included in the key. Careful reconsideration of all choices should show which is the case. If the user cannot choose between alternatives by studying the specimen, he or she may have to secure a more mature or more complete example in order to key the form.

1a. Stems of mature plants ribbed—that is, the surfaces of the stems covered with vertical or sometimes spiraling ridges which may be completely uninterrupted, undulate, or sometimes almost completely interrupted by grooves between the areoles, but which are never, on mature stems, rows of completely separate tubercles—2.

2a. Plants possessing spines—3.

3a. Stems of plants upright, prostrate, or clambering, with mature stems more than twice as long as they are thick; the flowers produced on the sides of the stems, with the ovary surfaces spiny; the fruit remaining fleshy and indehiscent or sometimes splitting open laterally—4.

4a. Stems not more than about 6 times as long as they are thick, not over 24 inches long, upright or prostrate, but not clambering, often caespitose; the flowers produced from a rupture of the stem epidermis just above an areole

—Genus *Echinocereus* (see key on page 10).

4b. Stems when mature at least 8 to sometimes 100 times as long as they are thick, on old specimens becoming more than 24 inches long, upright or clambering, never caespitose; the flowers produced from within a spine areole—5.

5a. Stems ¼ to 1 inch in diameter; spines ¹⁄₃₂ to ¼ inch long; roots tuberous—6.

6a. Stems ¼ to ⅝ inch thick; ribs 8; spines to ¼ or ⅜ inch long; roots clustering tubers; flowers purplish with short tubes and opening during the day   —Genus *Wilcoxia* (see page 79).

6b. Stems ½ to 1 inch thick; ribs 3 to 6; spines ¹⁄₃₂ to ⅛ inch long; root a single extremely large taproot; flowers mostly white with long tubes and opening at night

—Genus *Peniocereus* (see page 82).

5b. Stems 2 to 4 inches in diameter; spines ⅜ to 2 inches long; roots fibrous   —Genus *Acanthocereus* (see page 85).

3b. Stems of plants upright, never more than twice as tall as they are thick; the flowers produced at the apex of the stem, with the ovary surface scaly or sometimes with hair, but never spiny; the fruit opening basally or laterally

—Genus *Echinocactus* (see key on page 91).

2b. Plants spineless—7.

7a. Flowers large and yellow with red centers; ovary scaly

—Genus *Echinocactus* (see key on page 91).

7b. Flowers small and pinkish; fruit never having spines or scales   —Genus *Lophophora* (see page 137).

1b. Stems of plants smooth or else tubercled—that is, covered with nipplelike projections which may be arranged in spiral rows and which may overlap due to their length, but which are never confluent to form raised ribs—8.

8a. Plants a fraction of an inch to about 6 inches tall; stems depressed, hemispherical, or columnar, but never jointed; the spines straight or hooked but never barbed glochids; the ovaries and fruits naked or with only a few scales on them—9.

9a. Plants spineless   —Genus *Ariocarpus* (see page 142).

9b. Plants spiny—10.

10a. Fruit becoming dry and splitting open

—Genus *Pediocactus* (see page 146).

10b. Fruit remaining fleshy and not splitting open—11.

11a. Flowers produced in the axils of the tubercles

—Genus *Mammillaria* (see key on page 159).

11b. Flowers produced from the tips of the tubercles
—Genus *Epithelantha* (see page 152).

8b. Plants several inches to sometimes 6 or more feet tall;
stems jointed; at least some of the spines barbed glochids; the ovary naked or spiny
—Genus *Opuntia* (see key on page 231).

Genus *Echinocereus* Engelmann

The Echinocerei make up one of the largest genera of cacti, both in number of different species and in number of individuals found growing in the area of this study. Many of its members are collected and grown by cactus fanciers all over the world as great favorites because of the beauty of their flowers as well as of the plants themselves.

The name of the genus is composed of two words: *echinos*, meaning "spiny," which refers to the very spiny covering of the typical members of this genus, and *cereus*, which means "wax candle," a reference to the stately appearance of the stems of the upright species.

The Echinocerei are oval, conical, or cylindrical cacti, always with ribbed stems. The vertical ribs of some species are more or less divided into swellings which may be called warts or tubercles, but these are never completely separated from one another as in some other genera, so the ribs are always an outstanding character of them all.

These cacti are usually very spiny, as their name implies, and these spines may be straight or curved but are never hooked, as is common in some other groups.

The stems of Echinocerei are always low as compared with many of their relatives. Most of them are well under 12 inches long when mature, and the few in the Southwest which sometimes surpass that do not usually exceed 24 inches long. These stems are erect in most species, but in a few they lie partly or entirely prostrate upon the ground.

The plant body of some species remains a single, unbranched stem throughout life. Others cluster or branch sparingly only when very old, but many regularly form clusters of stems almost from the start. In some these clusters are made up of only a few stems, but in a few of them one plant may with age become a huge, caespitose clump of as many as a hundred or more stems. These stems are never divided into joints, however.

The flowers of this genus are borne on the ribs at the spine-bearing areoles, developing just above the uppermost spines of the areoles, where they literally burst through the epidermis of the stem. They may be produced from almost any point on the stem, different species bearing them high or low, but most commonly they appear on the sides of the stems a little below the tips.

The flowers are usually very large and beautiful, so beautiful that many fanciers pick one or another species in this genus as the most beautiful of our native cacti. However, a few of the Echinocerei have small and inconspicuous greenish flowers. The petals of some species remain only partly open, making the flowers funnel-shaped, while those of others open very widely. A perianth tube is always present. The outer surface of the ovary is always spiny and sometimes woolly as well. The stigma lobes are always green on all of our species.

The fruits produced by these cacti are always fleshy and thin-skinned and often edible. Those of some species are considered delicacies. Something of their character may be imagined from the fact that a number of them are known by the common name strawberry cacti. These fruits are also spiny, but the spines become loosened as the fruits mature and may be easily brushed off.

The members of the genus *Echinocereus* inhabit a wide belt of the North American continent from Utah and Wyoming south throughout most of northern Mexico to a little beyond the latitude of Mexico City, and from central Oklahoma and Texas on the east to the Pacific on the west. Within this huge area more than eighty species have been described by various authorities, but many of these so intergrade that later students have combined various ones. The result is that almost every book or article on this genus has at least a slightly different method of listing them, depending upon the taxonomic philosophy of the writer as well as upon her or his knowledge of these cacti. This has caused much confusion and makes it necessary for us to deal with many authors and names in order to know exactly what plant we have before us.

I will attempt to make or follow no formal classification of the species within the genus because it is too large a group and we have in the area of this study only a minority of the forms which would have to be considered in such a classification. Instead, I will group the species in a purely artificial series according to their most obvious characteristics, while concentrating upon describing the various forms properly and calling them, in the light of the most recent knowledge, by their proper names.

The Echinocerei grow mostly in exposed places on dry slopes and hills in the full strength of the southwestern sun. Only a few of them prefer the shade of bushes and trees. With this sun-loving characteristic and their inability to tolerate excess moisture remembered, most of them are rather easily cultivated and are, therefore, popular among collectors. They have a wide range of tolerance of cold, those of the north being very resistant, while many of those of Mexico perish by freezing when brought farther north.

Key to the Echinocerei

1a. Stems upright or sprawling, comparatively thick, being 2 inches or more thick when mature—2.
   2a. Having all three of the following characters: areoles always ½ inch or less apart; ribs always more than 10; radial spines always more than 12—3.
      3a. Flowers small, 1 to 1½ inches long and less than that in width, yellow, yellow-brown, or pinkish-red in color—4.

4a. Areoles elongated; central spines 0 to 3 in number, arranged in a vertical row, and 1 inch or less in length on mature plants—5.

  5a. Plant globose to short-cylindric; radials ¼ inch or less long—6.

    6a. Ribs 12 to 18; radials 16 to more than 20; plant 2 inches or more tall when mature—7.

      7a. Spines varicolored red, brownish, or purplish-red and white   —*E. viridiflorus* var. *viridiflorus.*

      7b. Spines yellowish   —*E. viridiflorus* var. *standleyi.*

    6b. Ribs 6 to 9; radials 8 to 12; plant about 1 inch tall when mature   —*E. davisii.*

  5b. Plant cylindrical; radials to ½ inch long   —*E. viridiflorus* var. *cylindricus.*

4b. Areoles broad oval to round; centrals 3 to 12 in number and not standing in a straight vertical row, but instead spreading outward from the center of the areole—8.

      8a. Radials 12 to 23; ribs hardly tuberculate; centrals 3 to 5 in number on mature plants   —*E. chloranthus* var. *chloranthus.*

      8b. Radials 30 or more; ribs markedly tuberculate; centrals 5 to 12 on mature plants—9.

        9a. Centrals to only ½ inch long; immature plants having flexible hairs instead of spines; flowers greenish-yellow to bronze and with glossy surface   —*E. chloranthus* var. *neocapillus.*

        9b. Centrals ¾ to 1¼ inches long; immature plants having rigid spines from the first; flowers pale pinkish or brownish-red and with a dull surface —*E. russanthus.*

3b. Flowers large and showy, 2 to 5 inches or more in length and width, yellow to purple in color—10.

  10a. Flower tube with long, cobwebby wool and hairlike, bristly spines; spines not recurved against the plant body—11.

    11a. Longest radial spines ⅜ inch or less—12.

      12a. Central spines 0 to 2, porrect and if more than 1, then arranged in a strict vertical row—13.

      13a. Centrals usually missing and ⅛ inch or less long when present—14.

        14a. Size of mature plant stems 3 to 12 inches tall by 2 to 3½ inches thick; flower 3 to 5 inches long and nearly as wide, petals 30 to 50, stigma lobes 8 to 22—15.

        15a. Radial spines 15 to 36—16.

          16a. Spines white to gray or reddish, often with dark tips, but not with the outer parts of the spines conspicuously shiny purplish or black so as to give the plant a shiny blackish aspect   —*E. caespitosus* var. *caespitosus.*

16b. Outer parts of the spines bright, shiny, purplish or black, giving the plant a conspicuous blackish appearance —*E. caespitosus* var. *purpureus*.

15b. Radial spines 12 to 15
—*E. caespitosus* var. *perbellus*.

14b. Size of mature plant stem to only 3 inches tall and 1 inch thick; flowers small, to only 2 inches long and 1¾ inches wide, petals to only 20 in number and stigma lobes to only 8 —*E. caespitosus* var. *minor*.

13b. 1 black central ³⁄₁₆ to ¼ inch long always present
—*E. melanocentrus*.

12b. Centrals 3 to 7 and not in a strict vertical row, but spreading —*E. fitchii*.

11b. Longest radial spines ⅜ to 1 inch—17.

17a. Stems usually caespitose; areoles more than ⅛ inch long, having no central spines over ⅜ inch long—18.

18a. Radials ⅝ to 1 inch long; flower rose-red —*E. baileyi*.

18b. Radials ³⁄₁₆ to ½ inch long; flower pale pinkish
—*E. albispinus*.

17b. Stems usually simple; areoles ⅛ inch or less long, having at least the main central spines ⅜ inch or more long on mature areoles —*E. chisoensis*.

10b. Flower tube with short wool and rigid spines—19.

19a. Spines of the plant body strictly pectinate and recurved against the plant body; areoles oval to elongated—20.

20a. Centrals 2 to 3 in a vertical row; radials slender to medium stout, white to purplish or pinkish and the plant often banded with color, but spines of individual areole not variegated—21.

21a. Flower purple with white zone and green center
—*E. pectinatus* var. *wenigeri*.

21b. Flower orange-yellow with green center
—*E. pectinatus* var. *ctenoides*.

20b. Centrals none; radials stout; spines of individual areoles variegated grays or tans and red
—*E. pectinatus* var. *rigidissimus*.

19b. Spines of plant body spreading outward instead of being pectinate; areoles oval to round—22.

22a. Radial spines 15 to 25; areoles ⅛ to ⅜ inch apart; flower 3 to 5½ inches long—23.

23a. Radials 16 to 25 and to ½ inch long; plant simple or sparingly branched
—*E. dasyacanthus* var. *dasyacanthus*.

23b. Radials 15 or 16 and to only ⅜ inch long; plant

caespitose   —*E. dasyacanthus* var. *hildmanii.*

22b. Radial spines 10 to 15; flower 2 to 3 inches long; areoles ⁵⁄₁₆ to ½ inch apart   —*E. roetteri* (in part).

2b. Never having all three of the characters listed under *2a* or, in other words, having any one or more of the three following characters: areoles more than ½ inch apart; ribs less than 10; radials less than 12—24.

24a. Flowers scarlet-red and lasting up to 4 or 5 days, with the petals firm and their edges entire—25.

25a. Ribs 5 to 9; radial spines 2 to 9; centrals 0 or 1—26.

26a. Spines greatly flattened and usually channeled or furrowed—27.

27a. Spines extremely heavy—28.

28a. Central spine absent; radials 2 to 6; areoles ⅞ to 1½ inches apart   —*E. triglochidiatus* var. *triglochidiatus.*

28b. 1 central present in at least part of the areoles; radials 6 to 8; areoles ¼ to ¾ inch apart

       —*E. triglochidiatus* var. *gonacanthus.*

27b. Spines slender to medium thickness; radials 5 to 7; centrals 0 to 1   —*E. triglochidiatus* var. *hexaedrus.*

26b. Spines round or practically so and slender to medium in thickness   —*E. triglochidiatus* var. *octacanthus.*

25b. Ribs 7 to 15; radial spines 7 to 16; centrals 1 to 6—29.

29a. Plant clustering densely into dome-shaped masses of equal, short stems not usually over 6 inches tall—30.

30a. Centrals 1 to 5; areoles ³⁄₁₆ to ⅜ inch apart; largest central round   —*E. coccineus* var. *coccineus.*

30b. Centrals 3 to 5; areoles ⁵⁄₁₆ to ⅝ inch apart; largest central flattened   —*E. coccineus* var. *conoideus.*

29b. Plant clustering sparingly to form flat clumps of unequal stems up to 18 inches tall—31.

31a. Centrals several—32.

32a. Ribs 8 to 11; radials 7 to 12; centrals usually 3 or 4 and variable in length from ¾ to over 2 inches long; all spines round and medium thickness to heavy, whitish to ashy purplish-gray or reddish in color—33.

33a. Ovary tube with long, flexible hair

       —*E. polyacanthus* var. *polyacanthus.*

33b. Ovary tube with sparse and short wool

       —*E. polyacanthus* var. *rosei.*

32b. Ribs 11 to 15; radials 8 to 16; centrals 4 to 6; spines round and white, yellow, or reddish-yellow in color

       —*E. polyacanthus* var. *neo-mexicanus.*

31b. Central 1   —*E. mojaviensis.*

24b. Flowers purple or yellow with red centers and delicate, lasting only 1 or 2 days, with petals soft and more or less emarginate—34.

34a. Spines opaque; flesh medium to dark or gray-green—35.

35a. Mature spines opaque and varicolored or variegated with shades of brown, gray, and white streaking at least some of them; radials 2 to 12; centrals 0 to 3—36.

36a. Radials 5–12, these slender, round or nearly so, and straight, with the uppermost ones smallest, bristlelike or missing—37.

37a. Stems more or less flaccid, wrinkled, with broad, somewhat tuberculate ribs; central 1, long and curving upward
—*E. fendleri* var. *fendleri*.

37b. Stems firm and not wrinkled; ribs narrow and not markedly tuberculate; centrals 1 to 3, the main 1 porrect and straight   —*E. fendleri* var. *rectispinus*.

36b. Radials 2–6, these white and chalky, stout, flattened, and often curved, with the uppermost ones longest
—*E. kuenzleri*.

35b. Mature spines opaque but not variegated or varicolored; radials 14 to 17; centrals 2 to 8—38.

38a. Lowest radials as long as the lateral ones in the areole; fruits 1¼ to 2 inches long   —*E. lloydii*.

38b. Lowest radials shorter than the laterals; fruits ½ to ⅞ inch long   —*E. roetteri* (in part).

34b. Spines translucent to some degree; flesh light or medium green—39.

39a. Areoles ½ to 1½ inches apart; ribs only slightly tuberculate on mature stems; flowers purple—40.

40a. Ribs 11 to 13; areoles ½ to ¾ inch apart; plant forming a large, regular, hemispherical clump from a single root center; flowers 4 to 5 inches long   —*E. stramineus*.

40b. Ribs 7 to 10; areoles ¾ to 1½ inches apart; plant forming an irregular, sprawling, or prostrate clump, often with adventitious roots; flowers 1½ to 3 inches tall—41.

41a. Stems extremely flabby; becoming prostrate and to 30 inches long; flower with 20 to 35 inner petals in several series and 10 to 12 stigma lobes
—*E. enneacanthus* var. *carnosus*.

41b. Stems sprawling, more or less flabby, and to 15 inches or so in maximum length; flower with 10 to 15 inner petals in one row and 8 to 10 stigma lobes—42.

42a. Stem to 2¾ inches thick, comparatively firm and upright; radials ¼ to ⅝ inch long and straight; areoles ¼ to 1 inch apart
—*E. enneacanthus* var. *enneacanthus*.

42b. Stems 3 to 4 inches in diameter, flabby, and semiprostrate; radials ¾ to 1½ inches long, often curving; areoles 1 to 1½ inches apart   —*E. dubius.*

39b. Areoles ⅜ to ½ inch apart; ribs extremely tuberculate; flowers yellow with red centers   —*E. papillosus* var. *papillosus.*

1b. Stems prostrate and slender, being ½ to 1½ inches thick—43.

43a. Central spine present on all or most areoles and ⅜ to 2 inches long—44.

44a. Stems to only 4 inches long; central spine ⅜ inch long; flower yellow with red center; ribs markedly tuberculate

—*E. papillosus* var. *angusticeps.*

44b. Stems 6 to 14 inches long; central spine ½ to 2 inches long; flower purple—45.

45a. Central spine ½ to 2 inches long, dark in color, and somewhat aimed and curved downward; flower with a dark reddish-purple throat and narrow, pointed petals   —*E. blanckii.*

45b. Central spine ½ to 1½ inches long, yellowish-brown, porrect or turning upward; flower with a white throat

—*E. berlandieri* (in part).

43b. Central spine usually missing, and if present on occasional areoles only ¼ inch or less in length—46.

46a. Radial spines 4 to 6 and some of them ¼ to 1¼ inches long; flower with white throat and narrow, pointed petals

—*E. berlandieri* (immature or stunted growth form).

46b. Radial spines 3 to 6 and only ¹⁄₁₆ to ¼ inch long; flower with white throat and broad, blunt-tipped petals   —*E. pentalophus.*

Echinocereus viridiflorus Eng.
Green-Flowered Torch Cactus, Green-Flowered Pitaya, Nylon Cactus, New Mexico Rainbow Cactus

STEMS Single, or small clusters of up to 6 heads, spherical to columnar, varying from 1 in. sphere to column 8 in. tall by 3 in. diameter; light green to yellowish-green; 13–15 low ribs with shallow vertical grooves between; definite grooves crossing ribs between areoles, tuberculate in appearance.

AREOLES Small, narrow oblong to very elongated, up to about ⅜ in. apart; young areoles covered with short white felt, old ones bare except for small tuft of wool above spines of each areole where flower has developed.

SPINES 12–20+ radial spines, straight, rigid, lying flat on surface of plant or recurving back toward grooves between ribs; may interlock with spines of adjacent areoles; small, very weak upper ones bristlelike, 1/16 in. long; lateral and lower spines ¼–½ in. long; great variation in color, purplish-red or yellow or whitish; upper and lower ones in each areole white, lateral reddish most typical; variations may occur on same plant, often in zones, producing banded appearance. Typically 1 central spine, thicker, more rigid than radials, standing erect in center of areole; often curved upward toward tip, ½–1 in. long; white with reddish tip, half and half, or all purplish-red except for white base; 1–2 auxiliary central spines possible, shorter, 1/16–3/16 in. long, arranged in perfect vertical row. Many plants lack central entirely. All spines have bulbous bases.

FLOWERS Small, lemon-yellow or straw-colored, often approaching chartreuse or bronze; about 1 in. long by ¾ in. diameter, produced on old areoles on sides of stem; outer petals linear, brownish midline with lemon-yellow or chartreuse edges; inner petals longer, a little broader toward rounded tips, lemon-yellow to straw-colored, darker green in midline; edges entire; stamens same colors; style longer than stamens, crowned by 6–10 dark green, fat stigma lobes; each areole of ovary has short white wool, 4–12 white spines to ¼ in. long.

FRUITS ⅜–½ in. long, egg-shaped, greenish, with white wool and spines.

RANGE Eastern Wyoming, eastern Colorado south through eastern New Mexico to El Paso, southeast into Big Bend of Texas.

REMARKS *E. viridiflorus* is most northerly of Echinocerei, growing on bleak prairies and foothills of eastern Wyoming and Colorado in extreme conditions, found occasionally in Texas Panhandle and northeastern New Mexico. It is a small, squat, egg-shaped, withdrawing plant, seldom over 2–3 in. tall. These northern plants have long, up-curving central spines and radials shorter than southern plants. In the south from Socorro and Roswell, New Mexico, into Guadalupe Mountains and Big Bend area of Texas, its appearance is so different that separate varieties are set up, which are often confused with *E. chloranthus*.

Echinocereus viridiflorus var. *viridiflorus*. Larger plant 2¼ inches tall.

Echinocereus viridiflorus var. *viridiflorus* (Eng.)

STEMS As the species, except spherical to conical, up to only about 5 in. high by 3 in. diameter; clustering.

AREOLES As the species.

SPINES As the species, except centrals often missing, never over ½ in. long.

FLOWERS As the species, except usually lemon-yellow; petals somewhat rounded at ends.

FRUITS As the species.

RANGE Eastern Wyoming and Colorado through eastern New Mexico to Santa Fe; east into Oklahoma and Texas panhandles; rare in high plains of northwestern Texas.

REMARKS More hardy northern form of species; small, difficult to locate; easily grown in northern gardens where most cacti do not survive.

Echinocereus viridiflorus var. *cylindricus* (Eng.) Rumpl.

STEMS As the species, except cylindrical and to at least 8 in. tall by 3 in. diameter; seldom clustering.
AREOLES As the species.
SPINES As the species, except 14–24 radials, maximum length to ½ in.; 0–3 centrals, in vertical row, main central to 1 in. or entirely missing or no longer than ¹⁄₁₆–³⁄₁₆ in. auxiliary centrals.
FLOWERS As the species, except often brownish; petals more sharply pointed.
FRUITS As the species.
RANGE Common from southern New Mexico, southeast through Davis Mountains and Big Bend of Texas.
REMARKS *E. viridiflorus* as it appears in its southern range, much more robust radial spines about twice as long as and more interlocking than northern form; central spines extremely variable; large columnar specimens, distinctly reddish of spine and bronze of flower, usually commercially distributed as *E. chloranthus*.

Echinocereus viridiflorus var. *standleyi* (B. & R.) Orcutt (Benson: *E. viridiflorus* var. *correllii*)

STEMS As the species, except becoming cylindrical and growing to 4 in. tall; seldom clustering.
AREOLES As the species.
SPINES As the species, except clear, rather translucent yellow, may be whitish when old.
FLOWERS As the species.
FRUITS As the species.
RANGE South central New Mexico into Texas Big Bend.
REMARKS Flowers indistinguishable from the species; close to var. *cylindricus* in shape of stems and character of centrals; radial spines shorter, more like var. *viridiflorus*; distinct only in clear yellow color of spines.

Echinocereus davisii Houghton

STEMS Globular, single; a dwarf plant, ½–1¼ in. tall when mature; 6–8 ribs, rather high and broken into almost separated tubercles; dark green flesh.
AREOLES Narrow oval to elongated, ⅛–³⁄₁₆ in. long, little wool even when young.
SPINES White, tips dark brown; all are radials, 8–13; upper shortest, slender,

Echinocereus viridiflorus var. *cylindricus*. 4¼ inches tall.

Echinocereus viridiflorus var. *standleyi*. 4 inches tall.

Echinocereus davisii. 1 inch tall.

round, 1/8−1/4 in. long; laterals longer, stouter, flattened, 3/8−5/8 in. long, straight or somewhat curved and recurved against plant.

FLOWERS Straw-yellow, 1 in. long, not opening widely; outer petals narrow, midlines reddish to umber, edges yellowish; pointed and entire; inner petals straw-yellow, linear to slightly broadened above, tips sharply pointed; green filaments, light yellow anthers; light green style crowned by 5 light green, heavy, curving stigma lobes; ovary with 12 white spines, 1/4 in. long on each areole, but no wool.

FRUITS Oval, 3/8 in. long.

RANGE Limestone summits, south of Marathon, Texas.

REMARKS One of two dwarf cacti of Brewster County; grows on same few hills as *Mammillaria nellieae*, underneath moss in crevices of ledges; rarely visible, sends flowers up briefly above moss; restricted to two or three ranches near Marathon. Distinct from *E. viridiflorus* in rib and spine number and spine length, flowers more pointed, has no wool on ovary areoles; long-lived.

Echinocereus chloranthus (Eng.) Rumpl.
Green-Flowered Torch Cactus, Green-Flowered Pitaya

STEMS Cylindrical, to 10 in. high by 3 in. thick, may have 1–2 branches from main stem; 12–18 ribs, low and tuberculate at areoles, broad, shallow furrows between ribs and between tubercles; pale green.

AREOLES Oval to circular, large, up to ¼ in. apart; young have much short white or yellowish wool which disappears with age; old almost bare except for wool on floral areole above spines.

SPINES 12–38 radials, straight, rigid, interlocking; may recurve back slightly; upper 4–6 short, weak, ¼ in. or less; gradual increase in size going around areole; laterals ½ in. long, lower ones to ¾ in.; upper radials white; laterals, lower ones white, yellowish, purple-red, or variegated; great variation in centrals; typical form has 3–6 centrals on mature areoles, spreading from center, not in straight line, stout, rigid, translucent, usually curved; typically 1–2 upper centrals ¼–½ in. long pointing upward, red, or white with red tips; 2 centrals spreading laterally, straight or curved, ¾ in. long, all red or with whitish or yellowish bases; 1 long central below pointing downward, often curved, white, may have reddish tip, stout, rigid, ¾–1¼ in. long; may have extra central or 2; young plants without centrals until 4 in. high, added gradually after that; all spines have bulbous bases, bases of radials covered until very old by wool of areole.

FLOWERS Funnel-shaped, not opening widely, produced on sides of stems; 1 in. diameter by 1¼ in. long, dark green or yellowish-green; outer petals have brownish midlines and green edges; inner petals dark green in midlines with lighter edges, often suffused with brown; petals linear, not broadening, edges entire, tips sharply pointed; light green filaments, cream-colored anthers; long green pistil ends in 8 dark green stigma lobes; ovary areoles have white wool, white spines ¼–½ in. long.

FRUITS Small, greenish, very spiny; about ½ in. long, almost spherical.

RANGE Cook's Peak and near Rincon in southern New Mexico through Organ and Franklin mountains into Texas and Mexico; in Texas from El Paso east to Van Horn; separate variety isolated in Brewster County.

REMARKS Beautiful, tall, slender column of long, rigid, varicolored spines, partly obscuring surface of stem, spreading in all directions, giving unkempt appearance; small green, yellow-green, or bronze-green flowers produced on sides of stems similar to *E. viridiflorus*; localized form growing in mountains northwest and southeast of El Paso. Very difficult to distinguish from *E. viridiflorus* var. *cylindricus*, which grows in same range and is also typically cylindrical, stouter than *E. chloranthus*, with elongated areoles, 1–3 centrals in straight row; species differ in number, shape, size of areoles, length, arrangement of central spines on mature specimens; immature specimens recognized by areoles.

Echinocereus chloranthus var. *chloranthus*. Young plant (left); mature plant, 4 inches tall (right).

Echinocereus chloranthus var. *chloranthus* (Eng.)

STEMS As the species, except grows to only 8 in.

AREOLES As the species, except areoles ⅜ in. apart.

SPINES As the species, except always spiny, never hairy; 12–23 radials, 3–6 centrals.

FLOWERS As the species.

FRUITS As the species.

RANGE Extreme southern New Mexico, into El Paso and Hudspeth counties, Texas, on into Mexico.

REMARKS Typical form of species; restricted range.

Echinocereus chloranthus var. *neocapillus*. Immature plant (center), 1¼ inches tall, flanked by mature specimens.

Echinocereus chloranthus var. *neocapillus* Weniger

STEMS Cylindrical, up to 10 in. high, 2½ in. thick, usually single; 12–18 ribs, low, with distinct tubercles; pale or yellowish-green.

AREOLES Oval, ³⁄₁₆ in. long, covered with much white or yellowish wool when young, bare when old except for very small tuft at upper end of areole where flower is produced; up to ¼ in. apart.

SPINES 30–38 straight, slender radial spines, radiating evenly around areole, often crowded, interlocking with spines from other areoles; upper very slender, ⅛ in. long; length increases around areole; laterals to ½ in. long, lower ones slightly shorter; clear translucent yellow or chalk-white, all of an areole being same color, usually forming bands of yellow and white on older plants; 5–10 centrals, all heavier, straight, spreading in all directions, uppermost ⅛–¼ in. long, slender; rest heavier, ¼–¾ in. long, translucent yellow, often with reddish tip, or all reddish; all spines have bulbous bases; immature plants or new branches have no spines, but have thick covering of white, very fine, flexible hairs, ¼–½ in. long, 40 hairs per areole; when

Echinocereus chloranthus var. *neocapillus*. 3½ inches tall.

plant 1–2 in. tall, spines begin appearing at tip of stem; juvenile hairs often seen on bases of older specimens.

FLOWERS As the species.

FRUITS As the species.

RANGE Small area south of Marathon, Texas.

REMARKS Immature plants very striking, having no rigid spines, covered with much long white hair; when 1½ in. high, yellow or white spines produced; bases of plants often show belt of white wool, with typical spines above; spines of adults very similar to *E. chloranthus*, differ in number; radials obscure surface of stem much more than do those of typical form; centrals more numerous and shorter; major difference is juvenile stage: young plants of typical *E. chloranthus* never have hairs; nearest typical *E. chloranthus* occurs 150 miles northwest; number of spines, spine color, areole shape distinguish this variety from *E. viridiflorus* var. *cylindricus*.

Echinocereus russanthus Weniger

STEMS Cylindrical, to 10 in. tall, 2½ in. thick; almost always branching to form clusters of up to 12 stems; 13–18 ribs, low and narrow with indistinct tubercles; medium green.

AREOLES Round at first, then broadly oval; ⅛ in. long, with white wool when young; ⅛–⅜ in. apart.

SPINES All very slender, somewhat flexible; 30–45 bristlelike radial spines, very crowded, interlocking with adjacent areoles; tuft of small ones at upper edge of areole, ³⁄₁₆–¼ in. long; laterals longer, lower ones ½–⅝ in. long; white or straw-colored; 7–12 centrals spreading in all directions from bulbous bases, upper ones small; slender flexible lower ones ¾–1¼ in. long; centrals with tip, upper half, or whole spine reddish or purplish.

FLOWERS 1 in. long, funnel-shaped, opening to only ½ in. diameter; rust-red, sometimes with darker midlines; all segments linear, ends pointed, but not sharply; bases of all segments lighter, center greenish; pale yellow stamens; long yellowish style; 8–10 green stigma lobes.

FRUITS About ½ in. long, oval to almost spherical; covered with clusters of slender white spines, 10–12 on each areole.

RANGE Small area of southwestern Brewster County, Texas.

REMARKS *E. chloranthus* has 12–23 radials, 3–6 centrals; *E. russanthus* has 30–45+ radials, 7–12 centrals, smaller flowers, more narrow and linear petals, rust or russet-red and delicate; *E. chloranthus* flowers yellow to brown or chocolate, never reddish, petals are firm, opaque, glossy.

Echinocereus russanthus. 4½ inches tall.

Echinocereus caespitosus Eng.
(Benson: *E. reichenbachii*)
Lace Cactus, Purple Candle, Classen's Cactus

STEMS Spherical when very young, cylindrical when mature; typical adult 4–8 in. tall by 2–2½ in. thick; single stem or commonly branched to form cluster of up to 12 upright stems; 10–19 ribs, narrow, definite, divided into distinct tubercles; dark green.

AREOLES Small, oval, quite woolly when young, elongated vertically and bare when older; ⅛–³⁄₁₆ in. long, to ³⁄₁₆ in. apart.

SPINES 12–36 rigid, slender radial spines, lying almost flat, pectinate; top ones very tiny, almost bristlelike, ¹⁄₃₂–⅛ in. long; laterals robust, ³⁄₁₆–⁵⁄₁₆ in. long; lower 1–3 somewhat smaller; spines of adjacent clusters may interlock; white, white with brown tips, yellowish with brown tips, all brown, or outer half black or purplish; spines of any single areole never variegated; no central spine common, or 1 central standing straight out, or 2 centrals, one above the other; these stout, firm, ¹⁄₃₂–⅛ in. long.

FLOWERS Very large, colorful, 2–5 in. tall, 2–4 in. diameter, brilliant purple or rose-pink; flower tube covered with white, cobwebby wool, ¼+ in. long, and clusters of 10–14 very fine, hairlike, white, gray, or black spines, ¼–¾ in. long; outer segments lengthen gradually, with greenish or brownish midlines and pink edges; 30–50+ petals arise from narrow reddish, reddish-brown, or bright green bases and broaden to ¼+ in. wide; upper part purple or rose-pink, edges ragged, often notched; tips vary from erose, rather blunt to almost entire and definitely pointed; filaments reddish at bases, fading above; cream-colored anthers; long reddish or pinkish style, crowned by 8–22 large, dark green stigma lobes; dwarf form with same flower but reduced in size and number of almost all flower parts.

FRUITS Egg-shaped or almost spherical, covered with slender spines and wool; green until splits open.

RANGE Most eastern of Echinocerei; found in hilly, mostly limestone regions from far southeastern Oklahoma to western edge of Brazos River coastal plain, westward wherever proper conditions are found throughout central and western Oklahoma, into southeastern Colorado, over all of northwestern Texas and just into New Mexico; southern limit west through Texas south of San Antonio to Eagle Pass, into Mexico; northwest of Big Spring, Texas, to just east of Carlsbad and Roswell, New Mexico; western limit from Carlsbad north into eastern Colorado.

REMARKS One of most collected, fancied, and best known of all cacti; beautiful body with truly lacy spines, exquisite flowers, produced in profusion; widespread range, common cactus of two-thirds of Oklahoma and all of central Texas. Eastern specimens have 20–30 radial spines; western specimens 12–32, with less wool on growing stem areoles and shorter spines.

Spines of *E. caespitosus* typically not so extremely pressed against the

Echinocereus caespitosus var. *caespitosus*. The white-spined lace cactus, 3 inches tall.

plant or quite so heavy as *E. pectinatus*; on flower tube and remaining on fruit, *E. caespitosus* has much long wool, extremely thin, flexible, hairlike spines up to ¾ in. long; *E. pectinatus* has shorter wool, comparatively thick, rigid spines up to ⅜ in. long.

Echinocereus caespitosus var. *caespitosus* (Eng.)
(Benson: *E. reichenbachii* var. *reichenbachii*)

STEMS As the species.
AREOLES As the species.
SPINES As the species, except 15–36 radial spines, usually interlocking with adjacent areoles; in extreme northwestern part of range individuals with 15–20 radials become majority in some populations.

Echinocereus caespitosus var. *caespitosus*. The brown-spined brown-lace cactus, 5 inches tall.

Echinocereus caespitosus var. *minor*. Largest stem pictured, 2 inches tall.

FLOWERS As the species.
FRUITS As the species.
RANGE 96th parallel in Texas and Oklahoma west to near Del Rio, Big Spring, and Amarillo in Texas; throughout central, western Oklahoma to base of Panhandle; most northwesterly in Alabaster Caverns, Woodward, Shattuck, Oklahoma; Sanford, Palo Duro Canyon in Texas.
REMARKS Typical form of species; largest, most clustering form.

Echinocereus caespitosus var. *minor* Eng.

STEMS As the species, except very much smaller, maximum of only 3 in. tall by 1 in. diameter.
AREOLES As the species.
SPINES As the species, except no centrals.
FLOWERS Small, 2 in. tall by 1½–1¾ in. diameter; pale lavender-pink; 15–25 smaller petals; 8 stigma lobes.
RANGE Stockdale, Wilson County, Texas.
REMARKS Reduction of size and flower parts consistent in any environmental situation.

Echinocereus caespitosus var. *perbellus.* 2 inches tall.

Echinocereus caespitosus var. *perbellus* (B. & R.)

STEMS As the species, except not over 4 in. tall; 13–15 ribs.
AREOLES As the species.
SPINES As the species, except only 12–15 radials; no central.
FLOWERS As the species, except smaller, 2 in. tall and wide.
FRUITS As the species.
RANGE Type locality Big Spring, Texas; found occasionally north in Texas, along western edge of Oklahoma to Majors County, west into New Mexico to Pecos River, into Colorado; pure population found near Muleshoe, Bailey County, Texas.
REMARKS Doubtful variety.

Echinocereus caespitosus var. *purpureus* (Lahman) Weniger
Black Lace

STEMS As the species, except smaller in maximum size, clusters more sparingly.
AREOLES As the species.

Echinocereus caespitosus var. *purpureus*. 3⅓ inches tall.

SPINES 14–22 radials, 0–3 centrals; as the species, except upper part of each spine shiny purplish or glistening black.
FLOWERS As the species, except always purple; 12 stigma lobes.
FRUITS As the species.
RANGE Wichita and Glass (Gloss) mountains of western Oklahoma.
REMARKS Very rare; dark coloration of spines distinguishes from typical *E. caespitosus.*

Echinocereus melanocentrus Lowry
(Benson: *E. reichenbachii* var. *albertii*)

STEMS Spherical to oval when young, becoming cylindrical; single or sometimes 2–3 side branches when very old; maximum 6½ in. tall, 2 in. thick; 10–13 ribs of definite, confluent tubercles; very deep green.
AREOLES To ⅛ in. apart; oval when young to elongated when old; woolly at first, becoming bare.
SPINES 14–20 slender radials lying pectinate close to plant surface; upper ones only ¹⁄₃₂–¹⁄₁₆ in. long, laterals lengthening to maximum of ¼–⅜ in., may interlock; 1 central standing out, perpendicular to plant body, or turned slightly upward, straight, slender, rises from bulbous base, black or mahogany, ³⁄₁₆–⅜ in. long.
FLOWERS 2–3 in. across and tall, rose-pink with reddish centers; petals almost linear or slightly broadening over upper parts, ends more or less ragged, recurving greatly as flower ages; pinkish style, 12–13 green stigma lobes; ovary with cobwebby wool, very black or brown and white, very slender, flexible, hairlike spines ¼–½ in. long.
FRUITS Unknown.
RANGE Very localized in sections of Jim Wells and Kleberg counties, Texas.
REMARKS Found growing under extremely heavy brush in extremely localized situations; very similar to *E. caespitosus,* which, however, does not grow within 100 miles of *E. melanocentrus;* flowers differ. Flowers of *E. melanocentrus* identical to *E. fitchii,* which, however, has 3–7 spreading centrals and its radials not pectinate.

Echinocereus fitchii B. & R.

STEMS Upright, usually single, sometimes 1–2 side branches when very old; 6 in. tall, 2 in. thick; medium to dark green; 10–14 ribs of low, confluent tubercles.
AREOLES Round when young, becoming oval on sides; small, almost touching to ³⁄₁₆ in. apart; woolly when young, becoming bare.
SPINES 20–25 radials, white with brown tips to tan with reddish-brown tips;

Echinocereus melanocentrus. 2 inches tall.

Echinocereus fitchii. 2¼ inches tall.

slender, not pectinate, spreading slightly outward from plant surface; uppers very short, lower laterals ¼–⅜ in. long; 3–7 slender centrals, same color as radials, rising from slightly bulbous bases, ⅛–³⁄₁₆ in. long, spreading to sides instead of standing out in 1 row.

FLOWERS Large, showy, pink, always with dark burgundy centers; 2½ in. tall, 2–4 in. across; flower tube with much cobwebby wool, 10–17 hairlike, yellowish or white, dark-tipped spines to ½ in. long; much variation in petal shape, linear to spatulate, ends blunt or pointed, ragged or entire, usually recurving when flower completely open; long pink style; 12–13 green stigma lobes; fragrant.

FRUITS Spherical to oval, ½–1 in. long; remain green; covered with white wool and spines.

RANGE Along Rio Grande from Rio Grande City northwest past Laredo to Eagle Pass, Texas.

REMARKS Immigrant from Mexico; easily distinguished from other cacti of this group by spines spreading outward; superficial similarity to E. pectinatus, but spines, flowers, ovary with wool and hairlike, flexible spines differ; much variation in spine colors but no banding; easy to grow, with beautiful flowers.

Echinocereus baileyi B. & R.
(Benson: *E. reichenbachii* var. *albispinus*)

STEMS Globose or oblong, becoming cylindrical with age; usually form clusters with up to 30 stems when old; 8 in. tall, 3½ in. thick; medium green; ribs narrow, somewhat tuberculate.

AREOLES Oval when young, very woolly, becoming elongated when older; usually bare when very old, but may retain mass of dirty white or tawny wool at upper edge; ⅛–¼ in. apart.

SPINES 12–28 slender, rigid radials, not pectinate, spreading outward from plant, interlocking with adjacent areoles; uppers very small, weak; laterals become progressively longer, ⅝–1 in. long; 0–5 centrals, often very small, ⅛–⅜ in. long; multiple centrals spread from crowded bases lined up vertically in middle of areole; vary from pure white to yellowish, straw-colored to rust-brown, or rosy-reddish, uniform on individual plant.

FLOWERS Large, showy, 2–3 in. tall, 2¼–3½ in. diameter; fuchsia; petals arise from narrow red bases, upper parts broad, ends ragged or erose; stamens very short, style short for group; 10–21 (most commonly 10–12) dark green stigma lobes; ovary surface covered with much long white wool, 5–15 hairlike, white to rusty spines ¼–⅜ in. long on each areole.

FRUITS Egg-shaped, ⅜–½ in. long; remain green, covered with wool and bristles until split open.

RANGE Restricted to Wichita Mountains of southwestern Oklahoma.

Echinocereus baileyi. White-spined. 4¼ inches tall.

Echinocereus baileyi. Brown-spined, clustering. Largest stem pictured, 2¼ inches tall.

REMARKS One of most attractive of Echinocerei; easily distinguished from its relatives by profusion and length of spines; flowers similar to those of lace cactus but rose-red rather than purple; vast majority of plants have 2–5 unmistakable centrals to ⅜ in. long.

Echinocereus albispinus Lahman
(Not Benson: *E. reichenbachii* var. *albispinus*)

STEMS Densely clustering, cylindrical, 3–6 in. tall, to 1 in. thick; 12–14 narrow, tuberculate ribs.
AREOLES Oval, very woolly when young; wool persists, but very old areoles are bare.

Echinocereus albispinus. Tallest stem pictured, 2 inches high.

SPINES 14−20 radials, not pectinate, deflected evenly outward all around areole; slender, uppers ³⁄₁₆ in. long, laterals ³⁄₈−½ in. long; no centrals; pure white or white with light brown, translucent tips.

FLOWERS Very pale pink or rose-pink, 1½−2½ in. tall, 1¾−3 in. diameter; opening very widely so petals curved backward; petals arise from very narrow, brownish bases, broaden only slightly to maximum width of ¼ in.; upper parts whitish-pink, upper edges very ragged, pointed at apex; white style; 7−11 light green stigma lobes; ovary surface has much white wool, clusters of 12+ hairlike spines to ¼ in. long, in shades of white, grays, tans, browns, to black; flowers usually produced below apex of plant, may appear well down sides of stems.

FRUITS Almost spherical, ½−¾ in. across, green.

RANGE Type locality near Medicine Park, Oklahoma, in eastern end of Wichita Mountains; also northwest of Tishomingo, Oklahoma.

REMARKS Spines are shorter and, while not pectinate, stand out around areole evenly at angle unlike *E. baileyi*; manicured appearance; flowers palest of any related Echinocereus.

Echinocereus chisoensis. 7 inches tall.

Echinocereus chisoensis Marshall

STEMS Columnar, to 8 in. tall, slender, maximum diameter 2 in.; almost always single; 13–16 ribs composed of very distinct tubercles separated by broad valleys; deep green or blue-green.

AREOLES ⅛ in. or less across; circular, woolly at first, becoming oval and naked when older; ¼ in. apart.

SPINES 10–15 very slender, evenly spaced radials parallel to plant body; white or gray below with upper part red-brown or maroon; uppers only ¹⁄₁₆–⅛ in. long, bristlelike; laterals progressively longer, lowers ¼–¾ in. long; 1–4 centrals, 1 porrect, ¼–⅝ in. long, others spreading and shorter, all very slender, straight, from bulbous bases; black or dark red-brown, usually with whitish bases.

FLOWERS Rose, with reddish centers, 2½ in. long, never opening widely, 1–2 in. diameter; long petals, remaining perfectly upright; oblong, deep red bases, upper parts rose, with entire, pointed tips; short white pistil; 10 small green stigma lobes; surface of ovary has some white wool and clusters of 8–14 white to brownish, hairlike spines.

Echinocereus pectinatus var. *wenigeri*. Stem 4½ inches tall.

FRUITS Elongated, 1–1⅜ in. long, ½ in. diameter; red, fleshy when ripe, but covered with wool, bristles; dry, split open when older.
RANGE Chisos Mountains, Big Bend National Park, Texas.
REMARKS Found shielded in clumps of brush, well camouflaged; flowers showing only pale rose of outer petal surfaces.

Echinocereus pectinatus var. *wenigeri* Benson
Comb Hedgehog

STEMS Single, or 2–3 when older; egg-shaped to stoutly cylindrical; to 10 in. tall, 3½ in. thick; distinct, confluent tubercles form 13–18 shallow ribs.

AREOLES Broadly oval, woolly at tip, becoming narrowly oval or elongated, bare when older; to ³⁄₁₆ in. apart.

SPINES 14–20 radials, pectinate; laterals somewhat recurved into grooves between ribs; medium to heavy, very rigid; uppers most slender, short; laterals ³⁄₈–½ in.; 2–3 centrals in vertical row in center of each areole, stout, ¹⁄₁₆–⅛ in. long; all spines white with pinkish or purplish tips.

FLOWERS Very large, 3-colored, 3–5 in. tall and broad; outer half or less of each oblong, broad, blunt petal lavender-pink; white below extending to narrow bases of green petals; whitish stigma; 9–12 large, dark green stigma lobes; ovary surface with some short white wool, 6–18 rigid spines, white or white with dark brown tips, to ⅜ in. long.

FRUITS Spherical, 1 in. diameter; fleshy at first, then bronze or brown until dry and split.

RANGE Local form of Mexican species; narrow band between Del Rio and Sanderson, Texas, along Rio Grande.

REMARKS Uncommon; fewer ribs, more oval, more woolly, more widely spaced areoles, whiter spine coloring, lower maximum number of both radials and centrals, heavier spines than Mexican species. Distinguished from *E. dasyacanthus* by rigidly recurved radials, very short centrals in 1 vertical line; from *E. pectinatus* by flower tube with short wool, short, rigid spines, white zone in flower; from *E. caespitosus* with long wool, long, flexible, hairlike spines on flower, no white zone.

Echinocereus pectinatus var. *rigidissimus* (Eng.) Rumpl.
Arizona Rainbow Hedgehog, Cabeza del Viejo

STEMS Thick, columnar, to 8 in. tall, 4 in. thick; rarely branched, 18–23 narrow, tuberculate ribs.

AREOLES Elongated, to ¼ in. apart.

SPINES 15–23 radials, pectinate, recurved to lie flat on plant surface, very heavy, rigid; uppers small, translucent tan, amber, or gray; laterals, lowers to ⅝ in. long, tan or amber or amber with red tips, sometimes all red giving banded appearance; no centrals.

FLOWERS As var. *wenigeri*, except outer parts of segments fuchsia, often 13 stigma lobes.

FRUITS As var. *wenigeri*.

RANGE Extreme southwest New Mexico, south Arizona into Sonora, Mexico.

REMARKS Distinguished from typical form by heavier spines, larger stem; spines are always all radials, interlocking to hide plant body; prolific bloomer. Distinguished from *E. viridiflorus* var. *cylindricus* by that plant's large size, short spines, and different flower. Var. *rigidissimus* only form of this species to present variegation of spine color on single areole.

Echinocereus pectinatus var. *rigidissimus*. 6 inches tall.

Echinocereus pectinatus var. *ctenoides* (right) and *Echinocereus caespitosus* var. *caespitosus* (left). Note typical ovary wall and fruit coverings.

Echinocereus pectinatus var. *ctenoides* (Eng.) Weniger

STEMS Single or clustering to 6 stems, each heavily cylindrical, to 6 in. tall by 3 in. diameter; 15–16 ribs greatly interrupted by tubercles.
AREOLES As the species.
SPINES As the species, except 14–22 radials, 2–4 centrals; white with very light brown tips, never purplish or banded.
FLOWERS Large, showy orange-yellow, 2½–4 in. long and wide; petals linear to narrowly spatulate, ends erose, upper part with bright orange midline, lower third green, center bright green; greenish-white style, 13 dark green stigma lobes; outer ovary surface has some short white wool, 14–16 short, rigid spines, white with dark brown tips.
FRUITS ½–1⅛ in. diameter, spherical or egg-shaped, green then greenish-brown when ripe, covered with short wool, rigid spines, deciduous when fruit ripens.
RANGE Originally Eagle Pass to Pecos River in Texas, south to Santa Rosa, Coahuila, Mexico, westward into Chihuahua; apparently now extinct in Texas.

Echinocereus pectinatus var. *ctenoides*. 3 inches tall.

Echinocereus dasyacanthus var. *dasyacanthus*. Yellow-flowered. 10½-inch stem.

Echinocereus dasyacanthus Eng.
Texas Rainbow Cactus, Golden Rainbow Hedgehog, Yellow-Flowered Pitaya

STEMS Oval at first, then cylindrical, maximum 14 in. tall, 4 in. thick; usually single, may branch when old; 12–21 narrow, tuberculate ribs.

AREOLES Round with tan wool at growing tip of active stem, becoming oval or elliptical and bare when older; ⅛–⅜ in. apart.

SPINES 15–25 radials spreading outward, interlocking, heavily covering plant surface, rigid, medium thick, uppers very short, laterals to ⅝ in. long; 2–5 robust centrals, ⅛–1 in. long, spreading in all directions, not in vertical row; all white, yellowish, or tan, tips reddish or rust-brown; may be banded.

FLOWERS Very large, showy, 3–5½ in. long and wide, yellow through pink to violet and magenta; very long spatulate petals, ends ragged, notched, or pointed, green bases; long white style; 12–22 large, deep green stigma lobes; long flower tube has some short wool, 7–18 rigid spines to ½ in. and pure white to white with reddish tips on each areole.

Echinocereus dasyacanthus var. *dasyacanthus*. Pink-flowered. 12-inch stem.

FRUITS Spherical, 1–2 in. diameter, covered with spines at first; these are shed and the surface becomes red-brown or purplish when ripe.

RANGE Southeastern New Mexico through southwestern Texas.

REMARKS Largest member of this group, most robust in every feature. Consistent varieties cannot be determined on basis of flower colors or spine thickness; it therefore includes some of Benson's *E. pectinatus* var. *pectinatus*, var. *minor*, and var. *neo-mexicanus*.

Echinocereus dasyacanthus var. *dasyacanthus* (Eng.) Weniger

STEMS As the species.

AREOLES As the species, except always round.

SPINES As the species, except central ³⁄₈ in. or longer.

FLOWERS As the species.

FRUITS As the species.

Echinocereus dasyacanthus var. *hildmanii*. Stems 5 inches tall.

RANGE Southeastern New Mexico and southeastern Texas east to Guadalupe and Davis mountains and to Sanderson, Texas; ranges into Mexico.
REMARKS Common, typical form of species; New Mexico and El Paso specimens bloom yellow or orange-yellow; pink in most of Big Bend; red and purplish in lower, eastern part of Big Bend; full range of colors found south, west of Sanderson, Texas.

Echinocereus dasyacanthus var. *hildmanii* (Arendt) Weniger

STEMS Ovate to tapering cylindrical, clustering to 6–8+ stems, to 10 in. tall, 3 in. diameter; dark green; 12–16 very tuberculate, narrow ribs.
AREOLES Round to oval, woolly when young, then bare; 3/16–1/4 in. apart.
SPINES 15–16 radials to 3/8 in. long, white or gray at bases with maroon or brownish tips; 3–5 centrals 1/8–5/16 in. long, same color as radials to completely maroon or dark red-brown; not banded.
FLOWERS As the species, except 4 in. tall, 3½ in. across, deep orange-yellow;

Echinocereus roetteri. 4¾ inches tall.

15–19 stigma lobes.
FRUITS Not observed.
RANGE Davis and Apache mountains of west Texas to Pecos, Texas.
REMARKS Close to *E. dasyacanthus* but never a rainbow, no banding of colors, fewer spines, dark green flesh always visible, definitely clustering; rare form.

Echinocereus roetteri (Eng.) Rumpl.

STEMS Single, egg-shaped then cylindrical, to 6 in. tall, 3 in. diameter; bluish or grayish-green; 10–13 ribs composed of definite tubercles.
AREOLES Oval or round, some tan wool when young, naked when old; ¼–½ in. apart.
SPINES 8–15 radials including very tiny bristlelike ones at top; upper radials ⅛–³⁄₁₆ in. long; laterals of medium thickness, straight, to ½ in. long, lowermost shorter, weaker; 2–5 stout, straight centrals, ⅜–½ in. long, spreading in all directions; all spines are opaque, ashy brown or maroon, with blackish

Echinocereus lloydii. 12 inches tall.

tips, bulbous bases.

FLOWERS Purple suffused with salmon; 2–3 in. long, not opening widely.

FRUITS Round to elongated, egg-shaped, ½–⅞ in. long.

RANGE Southeastern New Mexico.

REMARKS Extremely rare, obscure; similar to more robust *E. lloydii* but much smaller, nonclustering, flowers and fruits very much smaller; includes some of Benson's *E. pectinatus* var. *minor*.

Echinocereus lloydii B. & R.

STEMS Simple then clustering and branching to 6 stems when old, each of large size before clustering; to 12 in. high, 4½ in. thick, cylindrical, bright green to gray-green; 11–13 broad, interrupted, extremely tuberculate ribs; ¾+ in. deep furrows running down sides of ribs between broad bases of tubercles.

AREOLES Medium to large, oval to circular, much white wool when young, mostly bare with age; ½–⅝ in. apart.

SPINES Ashy gray to reddish-gray when mature, brilliant purplish-red when young; medium stout, round, straight from bulbous bases; 14–17 radials, lower and laterals ½–⅞ in. long; upper radials much more slender, ¼ in. long; 4–8 centrals perpendicular to stem spreading slightly from center.

FLOWERS Large, very beautiful, 3 in. long, 2–3½ in. diameter; much color variation, most commonly scarlet, may be coral-pink; outer petals greenish in midline, entire edges, pointed tips; inner petals long, spatulate, entire edges sometimes notched at tips; 9–14 green stigma lobes; pinkish filaments, extremely small anthers, pinkish or rose; ovary tube bears some white wool, clusters of 7–12 firm, reddish spines.

FRUITS Egg-shaped, 1¼–2 in. long; densely covered with spines which loosen fairly easily when fruit is ripe, fleshy, greenish-orange.

RANGE Tuna Springs, Pecos County, Texas.

REMARKS Similar to *E. triglochidiatus–E. polyacanthus–E. coccineus* group except flowers more purplish, less waxy, less long-lasting than claret cups. Including the New Mexico specimens ascribed to this species would require significantly broadening the description.

Echinocereus triglochidiatus Eng.
Claret-Cup Cactus, Strawberry Cactus, King's Cup Cactus

STEMS Globular to cylindrical; 5–9 broad, rounded ribs with wide, shallow grooves between; 3–18 in. long, often wrinkled, dark to pale green; variable, loose, usually with 12 heads or fewer, occasionally many more on old plants. .

AREOLES Circular, ⅛–¼+ in. diameter; distance apart varies; much white wool when young, usually bare when older.

SPINES Yellowish or red when young, then opaque, ashy gray to almost black when old; vary in number, size, shape: 2–9 radials, 0–1 centrals, ⅜–2½ in. long, slender to very thick, rounded to greatly flattened, angular or channeled, straight or curved.

FLOWERS 2–2¾ in. long, 1–1½ in. diameter, rigid, waxy, remarkable for persistence, often staying open for several days and nights; stiff, blunt petals scarlet-red or orange-red from narrow green or whitish bases; stamens as long as or longer than petals, filaments greenish below, fuchsia above; very tiny fuchsia anthers, same length as style, may partly enclose stigma; 5–11 green stigma lobes; ovary surface has small areoles, each with fleshy scale-like segment, a little white wool, 2–6 slender, white, or white-tipped brown spines.

FRUITS Varying within species; round or oval, ¾–1½ in., somewhat tuberculate to smooth, some spines usually deciduous with ripening; green, green with pinkish cast, or bright red when ripe.

RANGE Texas Hill Country, west through all of Big Bend to El Paso, north through central New Mexico into Colorado and northwestern Arizona.

Echinocereus triglochidiatus var. *triglochidiatus*. 8 inches tall.

REMARKS Firm, long-lasting petals, scarlet-red with no blue pigments, stamens light magenta; called claret cups because of flower coloration; much controversy exists concerning taxonomy of this species.

Echinocereus triglochidiatus var. *triglochidiatus* (Eng.)

STEMS Clustering or branching slowly, 2–12 unequal, loosely clustered stems per plant; cylindrical, dark green, somewhat wrinkled, to 8 in. high, 3 in. diameter; 6–8 (usually 7) broad ribs with slight swellings at areoles, very shallow grooves between.

AREOLES Circular, not large for group, white wool persists; ⅞–1½ in. apart.

SPINES Ashy gray to black, ½–2½ in. long; very stout, ⅛ in. diameter; very much enlarged bases, very flattened or angled, distinct ridges or grooves running length of spines, concave top surfaces; often curved; 2–6 (usually 3) spines per areole, all radials.

FLOWERS As the species, except 1¼ in. long; petals broadest at tips, very blunt.

FRUITS Oval or egg-shaped, 1–1¼ in. long, ¾–1 in. diameter; tuberculate; areoles on upper ends of long, broad tubercles ⅛ in. wide at top, ½ in. wide at base; each areole with pinkish, fleshy scale and 2–5 stout, persistent spines.

Echinocereus triglochidiatus var. *gonacanthus*. 4 inches tall.

RANGE Northern New Mexico from upper Pecos River west to just beyond Arizona boundary, north into Colorado; southern limit near Albuquerque.
REMARKS Handsome cactus, one of New Mexico's finest; very hardy; fiery red flowers.

Echinocereus triglochidiatus var. *gonacanthus* (Eng.) B. & R.
Claret-Cup Cactus, King's Cup Cactus

STEMS Cylindrical, clustering very slowly, sparingly; 7–9 rounded ribs with shallow grooves between; distinct, rounded swellings at areoles; northwestern population 3–6 in. high and 2½ in. thick; population of White Sands National Monument 18+ in. tall, 4½ in. thick.
AREOLES Very large for group, ¼–⅜ in. diameter; much wool when young, lost with age; ¼–¾ in. apart.
SPINES Commonly 1 very heavy curved and twisted central with 6–7 angles, 1–2½ in. long, ⅛ in. thick; 6–8 radials, lower 7 shortest, radiating evenly; upper same size as central or longer; as heavy as or heavier than var.

triglochidiatus, more of them; curved, bent, twisted, conspicuously angled, ridged, furrowed; largest ones with 6–7 flattened surfaces, deep grooves; yellowish, mottled or tipped with black when young, then gray to black.

FLOWERS As the species, except 2½ in. long, petals widening more gradually from narrow bases, tips not as broad; ovary surface has slender white bristles ½+ in. long.

FRUITS Spiny, globose, green with pink blush.

RANGE New Mexico, extending to just within Arizona and into southwestern corner of Colorado; separate population in White Sands region between San Andres and Sacramento mountains.

REMARKS Remarkable spines. White Sands population in unusual habitat which enables it to grow to sizes it cannot match or maintain elsewhere; grows in small clumps under cedar trees on higher, sandy hills.

Echinocereus triglochidiatus var. *octacanthus* (Muehlenpf.) Marshall
Strawberry Cactus, Claret-Cup Cactus

STEMS Branching or clustering, sometimes to 50; globular to cylindrical, bright green or pale yellow-green; plump, with shiny surfaces; varying heights, loosely clustered, 5 in. maximum height in northern range, 9–12 in. in southern part; thick, to 4½ in. diameter; 5–9 wide, shallow ribs with slight enlargements at areoles, no—or only slight—cross-furrows between areoles.

AREOLES Round, ³⁄₁₆ in. across, ³⁄₈–1¼ in. apart; much short white wool at first, later bare and entirely filled by swollen bases of spines.

SPINES ¹⁄₃₂–¹⁄₁₆ in. diameter, round, straight, very bulbous bases; yellowish when young, often with red streaks and shadings, especially toward bases; may remain yellowish or darken to gray or black when old, depending on incidence of sunlight; 3–9 radials, upper ones only slightly smaller, ½–1¼ in. long; may be 1 central standing out at right angle to stem, ⅝–1½ in. long.

FLOWERS As the species, except only 1½–2 in. tall; short, blunt petals; ovary tube has almost no wool, clusters of 2–6 slender spines to ½ in. long; 5–8 light green stigma lobes.

FRUITS Round, smooth, red, ¾–1½ in. diameter; naked when ripe.

RANGE 100-mile-wide band from central Texas west through Big Bend; northeastern limit near Lampasas, Texas; southeastern limit near Kerrville, Texas; westward past Del Rio, south to Davis Mountains; southern limit takes in all of Big Bend.

REMARKS Weak growth in northeastern region due to wetter climate; spines in western range more uniformly dark gray; more resistant to rot than most others in this genus. Includes part of Benson's *E. triglochidiatus* var. *melanacanthus*.

Echinocereus triglochidiatus var. *octacanthus*. Stems 4¼ inches tall.

Echinocereus triglochidiatus var. *hexaedrus* (Eng.) Boissevin & Davidson

STEMS Few in clump, each 4–6 in. high, 2–2½ in. diameter; 6 obtuse ribs with wide, shallow grooves between.

AREOLES ¹⁄₁₆–⅛ in. diameter, ½–⅝ in. apart; woolly when young.

SPINES Slender, with bulbous bases, distinctly angular or flattened; 5–7 (usually 6) radials, lowers ⅜–⅞ in. long, yellowish-red; uppers ⅝–1⅛ in. long, stouter, darker; central usually missing; if present ⅞–1⅜ in. long, flattened, not very thick.

FLOWERS Unknown.

FRUITS Unknown.

RANGE Mountains of New Mexico.

REMARKS May be some of Benson's *E. triglochidiatus* var. *melanacanthus* and var. *gonacanthus*.

Echinocereus coccineus Eng.
Aggregate Cactus, Bunch-Ball Cactus, Turk's Head Cactus, Heart Twister, Red-Flowered Hedgehog Cactus

STEMS Clusters of short, equal-sized stems tightly packed to form dense, hemispherical mass 1–6 ft. diameter, containing up to several hundred heads, each 2–6 in. high, to 2½ in. diameter; 8–11 ribs, either straight or composed of pronounced tubercles, areoles on tips.

AREOLES Large, circular to oval, ³⁄₁₆–½ in. apart; woolly when young, becoming bare.

SPINES Slender to medium thick, bristlelike, straight, round; white, gray-white, or straw-colored; 8–12 radials, ¼–1⅛ in. long, standing out from stem, uppers shorter; 1–4 centrals, either round, very slender to medium thick, ⅜–1¾ in. long, standing out perpendicular to stem; or main central is flattened, a little stouter, directed downward, 1–3 in. long.

FLOWERS Deep crimson to orange-red, 1½–2 in. long, 1–2 in. diameter; fuchsia stamens shorter than petals; 6–12 green stigma lobes; tube surface has white wool, 8–11 slender white spines, ¼–½ in. long in each areole.

FRUITS Red, juicy, deciduous bristles.

RANGE Wide territory from Colorado south along upper Pecos River to Santa Fe and Albuquerque, New Mexico; west into Arizona and Utah.

REMARKS Apparently dispersed into Benson's *E. triglochidiatus* var. *melanacanthus* and var. *neomexicanus*.

Echinocereus coccineus var. *coccineus*. 6½ inches tall.

Echinocereus coccineus var. *coccineus* (Eng.)

STEMS As the species, except have definite, pronounced tubercles at areoles.
AREOLES As the species, except to only ⅜ in. apart.
SPINES As the species, except all are round, centrals all slender, spreading, to only ⅞ in. long.
FLOWERS As the species, except 6–8 stigma lobes.
FRUITS As the species.
RANGE As the species.
REMARKS Typical form of the species.

Echinocereus coccineus var. *conoideus* (Eng.) Weniger
Beehive Cactus

STEMS 3–6 in. high, 2–2½ in. diameter, conical tips markedly smaller in diameter; 9–11 ribs, straight with at most modest swellings at areoles, deep furrows between.

Echinocereus coccineus var. *conoideus*. 8 inches tall.

AREOLES Large, woolly when young, later almost bare, ¼–½ in. apart.
SPINES 9–12 slender radial spines, upper 2–3, ¼–½ in. long, lowers to
1⅛ in. long; round with enlarged bases, white to straw-colored; 3–4 centrals, upper ones similar to radials, lower directed downward, somewhat
curved, definitely flattened, often quadrangular, darker in color, 1–3 in. long.
FLOWERS 2 in. diameter, 9–12 green stigma lobes.
FRUITS As the species.
RANGE Upper Pecos River in New Mexico north into southern Colorado and
west into Arizona.
REMARKS Var. *conoideus* similar to var. *coccineus*; var. *conoideus* has
longer spines and less tuberculate ribs, with more widely separated areoles;
long, flattened, and darker central spine serves to identify it quickly. Growth
habits similar to *E. coccineus*, except grows in higher mountains, on more
rocky locations; difficult to find growing wild.

Echinocereus polyacanthus var. *rosei*. 8 inches tall.

Echinocereus polyacanthus var. *rosei* (Wooton & Standley)
Red-Goblet Cactus, Pitahaya

STEMS Flat, loose clumps of unequal stems, usually 12 or fewer heads; cylindrical, tapering toward smaller, rather pointed tip; 10+ in. long, 4 in. thick at base in ideal situations; 9–11 ribs, broad with very shallow grooves between on older parts of stems; fairly prominent tubercles at areoles, deep, narrow grooves between them at tips.

AREOLES Most conspicuous areoles of group; ¼ in. across, circular, bulging outward with much white or yellowish wool covering bases of new spines when young; ⅜–1 in. apart.

SPINES Most variable in size of any in group; all straight, medium stout, always round; 7–10 radials ⅜–1 in. long, lowers usually twice as long as uppers; 3–5 centrals on mature plant; young seedlings always have only 1 central per areole; ½–2 in. long, always round, from enlarged bases, spreading at various angles; reddish, ashy gray, or dark, purplish-gray, with centrals usually darker than radials.

FLOWERS Varies from pale red to orange, often in same flower; 1½–2½ in. long, with short, rigid petals broadening and blunt at ends; fuchsia stamens; 7–10 stigma lobes; brownish or yellowish spines on ovary, ⅛–⅝ in. long, with reddish tips, plus some short wool.

Echinocereus polyacanthus var. *neo-mexicanus*. 4½ inches tall.

FRUITS ¾–1 in. long, greenish-purple when ripe, with deciduous spines.

RANGE From Mexico northward over west Texas and much of New Mexico, into southern Colorado and southeastern Arizona; northeastern limit near San Antonio, Texas, then through Guadalupe Mountains into New Mexico, along Pecos River into Colorado; western edge east of Continental Divide to Lordsburg, New Mexico, then into southeast Arizona.

REMARKS Most common red-flowered Echinocereus throughout southern New Mexico and far southwest Texas; distinguished from *E. coccineus* by never growing in compact, dome-shaped clusters, not having such slender spines; differs from *E. coccineus* var. *conoideus* by nonflattened spines; has more ribs than *E. triglochidiatus* var. *octacanthus*. Comprises some of Benson's *E. triglochidiatus* var. *neomexicanus* and var. *gurneyi*, probably is his New Mexico *E. lloydii*.

Echinocereus polyacanthus var. *neo-mexicanus* (Standley) (Not Benson: *E. triglochidiatus* var. *neomexicanus*)

STEMS As var. *rosei*, except to 3 in. thick; 11–15 ribs.

AREOLES As var. *rosei*, but closer, ⅜–⅝ in. apart.

SPINES 8–16 (usually 10–13) radials, slender, straight, round, white, straw-colored, or yellow, to ⅝ in. long; 4–6 spreading centrals on mature plants, straight, round, slender, ¾–1¼ in. long; yellowish below with outer parts or tips reddish or blackish.

FLOWERS As var. *rosei*, except smaller, burnt-orange to yellow; petals narrower.

FRUITS As var. *rosei*.

RANGE Las Cruces to Socorro in central New Mexico.

REMARKS More ribs, more numerous, lighter-colored, and more slender spines than var. *rosei*; always yellowish; cold-resistant; not tolerant of excessive moisture; requires cold during winter to bloom.

Echinocereus enneacanthus Eng.
Strawberry Cactus, Pitaya

STEMS 3–30 in. long, 1½–4 in. thick, cylindrical, tapering over last third to pointed tip; loose clusters from a few to 100; new stems multiply as side branches at or just above ground level; first growth lateral, then upward; bright green, soft wrinkled flesh; 7–10 ribs, low and broad with shallow grooves between, slight to pronounced tubercles.

AREOLES Circular, ⅛ in. diameter, much gray wool when young; ¼–1½ in. apart.

SPINES Rigid, slender to stout, rising from enlarged bases; white to straw-colored or very light brown; translucent, horny appearance with age; delicate pink spines when very young, then fading quickly; 7–12 white radial spines radiating evenly, straight or slightly curved back toward stem; uppers ¼–⅝ in. long; laterals and lowers ½–1 in. long; 1 stout central perpendicular to surface or slightly deflexed, very bulbous base, round, white when young, then darker, especially toward base, flattened when old, central to 2 in. long on mature plants; many plants with 2 extra centrals above main 1, spreading upward, remaining shorter.

FLOWERS Large and beautiful, opening widely, 2–3 in. high and wide, purple-red; 10–20 short outer petals with brownish-green centers, pinkish, crinkled edges; 12–35 inner petals in 1–3 rows; oblong, linear, or spatulate; entire or toothed edges, pointed or blunt tips; stamens much shorter than petals; greenish filaments, yellow anthers, white style; 8–12 long, slender, green stigma lobes; flower tube has white wool, white bristlelike spines to ½ in. long.

FRUITS 1 in. long, almost spherical, greenish to brownish or purplish, bristlelike spines fall off easily.

RANGE Rio Grande City north along Rio Grande to Big Bend, little more than 50 miles north of Rio Grande in any area.

REMARKS Fairly hardy; withstands below-freezing temperatures, cannot tolerate excess moisture.

Echinocereus enneacanthus var. *enneacanthus*. Clustered stems, 13 inches across.

Echinocereus enneacanthus var. *enneacanthus* (Eng.)

STEMS As the species, except to 12 in. long, 2¾ in. thick; much less flabby; slight tubercles at areoles.

AREOLES As the species, except to 1 in. apart.

SPINES As the species.

FLOWERS As the species, except 10–15 outer petals, 12–15 inner petals in 1 row, oblong or linear, entire edges, pointed tips; 8–10 stigma lobes.

FRUITS As the species.

RANGE As the species.

REMARKS Typical variety of species; tidy firm clumps of stems; var. *brevispinus* seems to be the form taken by poorly grown specimens.

Echinocereus enneacanthus var. *carnosus* (Rumpl.) Quehl.

STEMS 16–30 in. long, 3–4 in. diameter; very flabby, growing out laterally from cluster, fully prostrate on ground when large, only tips turning up-ward; 8–9 broad ribs with pronounced tubercles.

Echinocereus enneacanthus var. *carnosus*. Tallest stem 8 inches high.

AREOLES ¾−1½ in. apart.

SPINES 8−9 radials, uppers ⅜ in. long (often missing entirely); laterals ½−¾ in. long; usually 1 porrect central, ½−2 in. long; rarely 2 short upper centrals; centrals round when young, flattened when old.

FLOWERS Very large and full; 13−20 short, greenish outer petals, 20−35 inner petals in 3 rows; inner petals spatulate, crinkled and toothed edges, nonpointed tips; greenish, narrow bases, broader upper parts fuchsia or reddish-purple; short white style; 10−12 green, linear stigma lobes.

FRUITS As the species.

RANGE Near Laredo and Eagle Pass, Texas.

REMARKS Small specimens of var. *carnosus* distinguished from typical form by excessive flabbiness of stems, more distant areoles, surpassing flowers; old plants to 5 ft. diameter.

Echinocereus stramineus (Eng.) Rumpl.
Strawberry Cactus, Organo, Pitaya

STEMS 10+ in. tall, 3½ in. thick, tapering to pointed apex; 11−13 sharp ribs, deep furrows between with slight tubercles at areoles; stems cluster freely, forming large, hemispherical, compact clumps to 100+ equal stems often 2−3 feet across and high.

AREOLES Small, round, white, with much wool when young; ⅜−¾ in. apart.

SPINES White to straw-colored, translucent, slender to medium thick from

Echinocereus stramineus. Clump, 30 inches in diameter.

thickened or bulbous bases, covering plant profusely; delicate pink at tip when very young, becoming straw-colored then fading quickly to whitish; 7–14 radials, ⅜–1½ in. long, size extremes often found on same areole; all round, either straight or curved; 2–5 centrals to 3½ in. long, slender, round or slightly flattened, usually darker than radials, straight or curved; lower central usually perpendicular to stem, others spread upward at various angles, interlocking with those of other areoles.

FLOWERS Very large and beautiful, produced in large numbers; 4–5 in. tall, 3–4 in. diameter, purple-red; 10–15 pointed outer petals with green centers, pink edges; 15–20 longer inner petals with narrow bases broadening to ½+ in. wide toward tips; bases bright red then bright rose toward tips; edges of inner petals ragged and toothed, blunt ends sometimes notched; short red filaments; yellow anthers; long red style with 10–13 long green stigma lobes; very long flower tube with many white, bristlelike spines.

FRUITS Spherical, 1½–2 in. long, purplish to red when ripe, with deciduous, bristlelike spines.

RANGE From El Paso to lower Pecos River in Texas, extending deep into Mexico.

REMARKS Grows commonly on upper slopes of sandy hills east of El Paso and limestone ridges in and around Big Bend National Park; flowers among largest and most numerous of any Echinocereus; must have very dry, rocky growth conditions; seldom survives when transplanted unless planted in sandy soil and shielded from moisture.

Echinocereus dubius. Tallest stem 9 inches high. Two specimens of *Lophophora williamsii* in right foreground.

Echinocereus dubius (Eng.) Rumpl.
Strawberry Cactus, Pitaya

STEMS Cylindrical, tapering to a pointed tip; 15+ in. long, 3 in. thick, light green, very soft and flabby; 7–10 broad, rounded ribs with shallow furrows between, slight enlargements at areoles; branch and cluster at all angles to form loose, irregular clumps, partly sprawling or semiprostrate, with up to 8 heads.

AREOLES Circular, ¼ in. diameter, 1–1½ in. apart, having much white wool when young, lost with age.

SPINES All white to light brown, somewhat translucent when young, opaque when old, growing from enlarged bases; 5–9 radials, very irregular in size, almost bristlelike to medium thick, ½–1½ in. long; uppers shorter, sometimes pushed aside or eliminated entirely by large bases of centrals; 1–5 very conspicuous centrals curving or spreading in all directions from mature areoles, 1½–3 in. long, ¹⁄₁₆–⅛ in. thick; markedly flattened, sometimes ridged; centrals develop very slowly, young areoles with 1–2 shorter, round centrals, especially under poor growing conditions.

FLOWERS Magenta; not opening widely, comparatively sparse; 2–3 in. long, 2 in. across; 10 outer petals, green centers with pinkish edges; 10 inner petals with entire edges, narrow bases which broaden considerably, ending in broad tip with prolonged point at apex; bases greenish with orange area above shading into magenta on broader ends of petals; brownish filaments, yellow anthers; long white style, 8–10 green stigma lobes; ovary tube has white spines ¼–¾ in. long, little or no wool.

FRUITS Globular, 1–1½ in. long, with many deciduous spines.

RANGE Near Rio Grande from near El Paso to mouth of Devil's River, extending into Mexico.

REMARKS Very closely related to *E. stramineus*, which grows in similar situations at higher elevations. *E. dubius* has fewer branches and ribs, poorer floral development, larger spines not obscuring stems, and does not form hemispherical mounds.

Echinocereus fendleri (Eng.) Rumpl.

Fendler's Pitaya, Fendler's Hedgehog Cactus, Purple Hedgehog, Strawberry Cactus, Torch Cactus, Sitting Cactus, Pink-Flowered Echinocereus

STEMS Small, loose clump of upright stems, short, almost oval to longer and cylindrical, usually tapering, often conical; maximum of 18 (usually 12) in. tall, 4 in. thick; dark green, soft, often wrinkled; 8–16 broad, somewhat wrinkled ribs with conspicuous swellings around areoles.

AREOLES Circular, not large, with some white wool when young, then bare; to ½ in. apart.

SPINES Stout from bulbous bases; truly variegated, brown and white or black and white coloring in streaks; 5–12 slightly angled radials, variegated brown and ashy gray with white streaks; lowers stoutest, ½–1 in. long; upper laterals bristlelike, usually white, ¼–½ in. long; radial missing entirely from top of areole; usually 1 central, longer, stouter, round or very slightly flattened, ⁵⁄₁₆–3 in. long, dark brown or black fading to gray when old; 2 additional centrals possible in some varieties.

FLOWERS Large, to 3+ in. high and wide; violet-purple; broad, greenish outer petals with violet edges; inner petals long, variable in shape, violet-purple with narrow, dark purple-red bases; green filaments, light yellow anthers; whitish style only slightly longer than stamens; 9–16 dark green stigma lobes; ovary tube has some white wool and many spines; white or white with brown tips, ⅜+ in. long.

FRUITS Almost spherical, 1–1½ in. long, purplish, fleshy, covered with easily lost spines.

RANGE Extreme southwestern Texas, all of western New Mexico, into Arizona, Colorado, Mexico.

REMARKS One of more western Echinocerei; great development in Arizona.

Echinocereus fendleri var. *fendleri*. Stem 5¾ inches tall.

Echinocereus fendleri var. *rectispinus*. Tallest stem pictured, 8 inches high.

Echinocereus fendleri var. *fendleri* (Eng.)

STEMS As the species, except maximum 12 in. tall (usually 6 in.), 9–12 ribs.
AREOLES As the species.
SPINES As the species, except 5–10 radials; single central 1–2 in. long, usually curving upward.
FLOWERS As the species.
FRUITS As the species.
RANGE As the species.

Echinocereus fendleri var. *rectispinus* (Peebles) L. Benson

STEMS Forming small clumps of up to 6–8 comparatively firm, columnar stems to 8 in. tall; 8–11 ribs, narrower than typical form, not tuberculate.
AREOLES As the species.

Echinocereus kuenzleri. 5 inches tall.

SPINES 10–12 radials, usually lighter in color than typical form; 1 main central with 1–2 upper accessory centrals; main 1 stout, porrect, and straight, ½–1¼ in. long; accessory centrals ¼–¾ in. long.

FLOWERS As the species, except 10–13 stigma lobes.

FRUITS As the species.

RANGE Extreme southwestern New Mexico, extreme southeastern Arizona.

Echinocereus kuenzleri Castetter, Pierce & Schwerin

STEMS Single or branching to several, to 12 in. tall by 4 in. diameter; 9–12 soft, flabby, very tuberculate ribs.

SPINES Few, very thick, angular and often curved or twisted; 2–6 radials, stout, flattened, and often curved or twisted, white and chalky, ¼–1 in. long; central usually missing, but may rarely be 1, brown or black, to 1 in. long.

FLOWERS To 4 in., purple and delicate; outer perianth segments entire, inner broad, with erose or toothed tips.

FRUITS About 1–2 in. long, with spines and wool; turning scarlet.

RANGE Sacramento Mountains of New Mexico.

REMARKS Most attractive because of unusual spines; without flowers, often confused with *E. triglochidiatus* var. *triglochidiatus*.

Echinocereus papillosus A. Linke
Yellow-Flowered Echinocereus, Yellow-Flowered Alicoche

STEMS 2–3 (in 1 variety many more) clustering, branching, forming very loose clump; slender, soft, weak, leaning at awkward angles, seldom actually prostrate; deep green, to 10 in. long, 1–2¾ in. thick; 7–9 ribs, extremely tuberculate, formed of series of conical enlargements ⅜ in. high, with areoles on tips, enlargements separated by deep valleys which almost completely interrupt ribs.

AREOLES Small, bare, ⅜–½ in. apart.

SPINES Slender, rigid, straight, round, from bulbous bases, white to brownish or yellowish; 7–11 radials, whitish to yellowish-brown, usually brownish bases; lowers and laterals to ½ in. long; upper 2–3 very much shorter, very slender, bristlelike; 1 central, ¾ in. long, with very bulbous base, perpendicular to stem surface, brownish to bright yellow, often with dark brown base, yellow zone in middle, brown tip.

FLOWERS Large, delicately fragrant, 2½–4 in. wide and high; outer petals oblong, reddish centers to yellowish ragged edges; inner petals in 2–4 rows, long, rising from narrow, bright orange-red bases, giving center of flower striking red color; upper part of inner petal much wider, tip either somewhat pointed or blunt, yellow shading to white at edges; midline of each petal on dorsal side has unique feathery ridges and furrows extending almost to tip; reddish filaments, light yellow anthers; white style; 10–13 long, broad, green stigma lobes, with furrow running length of underside; ovary surface has reddish scales, white spines to ¼ in. long.

FRUITS Greenish, covered with short bristles.

RANGE South Texas, bounded by line from 20 miles east of Laredo northeast into McMullen County, then southeast to Alice, south to near Edinburg, back to Laredo.

REMARKS Seldom found; inconspicuous plant usually well hidden under chaparral or tall Opuntias; most difficult to grow out of natural habitat of light, sandy, limestone loam; rots easily.

Echinocereus papillosus var. *papillosus* (A. Linke) Weniger

STEMS As the species, except clump of up to 10–12 stems.

AREOLES As the species.

SPINES As the species.

FLOWERS As the species.

FRUITS As the species.

RANGE As the species.

REMARKS Typical form of plant discussed above.

Echinocereus papillosus var. *papillosus*..Sprawling stems, 2 inches high.

Echinocereus papillosus var. *angusticeps*. Tallest stem pictured, 3 inches high.

Echinocereus papillosus var. *angusticeps* (Clover) Marshall
Small Papillosus

STEMS As the species, except markedly smaller, 3–4 in. tall, 1–1¼ in. diameter, occurring in dense clusters of many stems; 1–4 dozen common; sprawling to upright.

AREOLES As the species.

SPINES As the species, except shorter, central spine to ⅜ in. long.

FLOWERS As the species, except slightly smaller with more petals, usually blunter at tips; yellow coloring more greenish, red paler.

FRUITS As the species.

RANGE Northern Hidalgo County, Texas.

REMARKS Dwarflike form growing under mesquite and thickets.

Echinocereus pentalophus (DC) Rumpl.
Alicoche, Lady-Finger Cactus

STEMS Light green, flabby, to 12 in. long (usually 4–6 in.), slender, ½–1¼ in. diameter; 4–5 low ribs on old stems, with very shallow furrows between; very low tubercles at areoles, growing tips with more pronounced tubercles, more distinct furrows between ribs; stems branch and bud off new stems at any point, at any angle, forming unorganized mass, mostly prostrate; branches root at areoles; very old plants to 15 ft. diameter.

AREOLES Less than ¹⁄₁₆ in. diameter, yellowish wool when young, then bare; ⅜–¾ in. apart.

SPINES Very short, slender, rigid, from bulbous bases; 3–6 radials, ¹⁄₁₆–½ in. long, rose-colored when growing, then brownish with dark tips, gray with dark tips when old; often no central; if present stouter than radials, darker, ⅜–½ in. long; central points upward; sometimes upper radial assumes this direction.

FLOWERS 3–4+ in. diameter, opening widely; outer petals with greenish midlines, pink edges; 18 long inner petals with narrow bases, upper part broadening to maximum ¾ in. wide toward tips, entire edges, blunt ends somewhat notched with small point at apex of midline; basal third to half white shading to yellow, upper part light cerise; greenish filaments, yellow anthers; style composed of 10–16 linear, olive-green lobes with yellow furrow on ventral side; ovary has much long white wool, many brown, bristle-like spines.

FRUITS Egg-shaped, green, ½–¾ in. long, covered with white wool, brown spines.

RANGE Northeastern Mexico, extending 15–20 miles into Texas side of lower Rio Grande Valley to Rio Grande City.

REMARKS Most common Echinocerei of deep south Texas and lower Rio Grande Valley; most slender stems of genus; among easiest of cacti to grow on sandy, well-drained soil.

Echinocereus berlandieri (Eng.) Rumpl.
Berlandier's Alicoche

STEMS Sprawling, clustering, branching plant, older parts prostrate, growing tips erect; deep green to bright green, slender, not flabby, to 6 in. long, ½–1 in. (usually ¾ in.) thick; 4–6 ribs, composed of rows of distinct, conical tubercles at areoles with rounded notches between often interrupting ribs entirely; ribs usually spiral about stem, often stop, start abruptly, upper part of stem may have more or fewer ribs than lower part.

AREOLES Round, ⅛ in. diameter, with much white wool when young, then entirely bare; ⅜–⅝ in. apart.

Echinocereus pentalophus. Stems approximately ¾ inch in diameter.

Echinocereus berlandieri. Tallest stems pictured, 4 inches high.

SPINES Slender to stout, round, from bulbous bases, very light yellow to white, translucent, with slightly brownish bases, very minutely brown-tipped when young, then all gray and opaque when old; 6–8 radials, slender, yellowish white, sometimes with brownish tips and bases; ¼–1¼ in. long, lower 3 longest, upper 3 much shorter, bristlelike, except on areoles without central, where upper radial often is longer, heavier, almost in position of upward-pushing central; usually 1 central, much stouter, longer, ½–1½ in. long, almost perpendicular to stem or turned upward; areoles low on stems with short, weak centrals or none at all; those toward tips have robust, long centrals giving plant top-heavy look.

FLOWERS 3–5 in. across, 2 in. tall, opening very widely; petals in 1 row, always very long, narrow, to ⅜ in. wide, gradually tapering, pointed tips with entire edges; bases and lower third of length are whitish with cerise-pink tips; 7–11 stigma lobes; ovary surface has very short white wool, many longer, weak, dark spines.

FRUITS Green, egg-shaped, ¾ in. long, covered with long dark bristles, having a little short wool.

RANGE Most of south Texas below line from Rio Grande northwest of Laredo to near Uvalde, then southeast to San Antonio and Corpus Christi; common along Nueces River and lower Rio Grande.

REMARKS Very close to *E. pentalophus*, except *E. berlandieri* more northern form occurring over wide area of south Texas, with larger flowers, fewer, more narrow and pointed petals, fewer stigma lobes, only short wool on ovary surface, more upright-growing plant; shorter stems, more slender, more tuberculate, less flabby, longer, more numerous spines, usually with long, robust centrals. Most common on low banks of Rio Grande delta below Brownsville.

Echinocereus blanckii Poselger ex Rumpler
Alicoche

STEMS At first erect, then sprawling; very soft, wrinkled, twisted, contorted when old, bright green fading to yellowish-red; ¾–1½ in. diameter, 14+ in. long; 5–10 ribs composed of rows of unconnected tubercles when young, then ribs continuous with tubercles, less prominent, only slight depressions between tubercles or adjacent ribs; do not usually spiral; individual ribs may stop, start at any point on stem, increasing or decreasing their number; sometimes branching above ground, but not profusely; clustering.
AREOLES To ⅛ in. diameter, ¼–½ in. apart; a little short wool when young, then bare.
SPINES 6–9 even radials, very slender and translucent, ³⁄₁₆–⅞ in. long; laterals longest, white, may have black tips when young; lower shortest, very weak, bristlelike, upper very dark brown when young, fades to gray when very old, usually with brown tip; 1 central spine, stout with bulbous base, perpendicular to stem at first, later curving downward, ½–2 in. long, translucent and variegated when young, brown and white alternating throughout its length, then fades to gray.
FLOWERS Funnel-shaped, not opening widely; 2 in. tall, 2¼–3½ in. across; ovary surface has pointed, reddish, scalelike segments, clusters of white to brown spines, some short wool; narrow, pointed outer petals have purple midlines with lavender-pink smooth, unbroken edges; 26 inner petals ⅜–½ in. across near tips, smooth margins, sharply pointed; upper four-fifths light rose, base darkens to carmine; carmine filaments, orange-yellow anthers; pink style; 8–11 long, slender, very light green stigma lobes.
FRUITS Unknown.
RANGE Northeastern Mexico and southern Texas, particularly Starr and Hidalgo counties.
REMARKS Distinguished from both *E. berlandieri* and *E. pentalophus* by thicker stems with more ribs, more numerous radial spines with lower 1 smallest and upper 1 dark; downward-turning, variegated centrals, darker flower with dark center, opening only partly; narrower petals, more pointed, more numerous. Uncommon, inconspicuous; cannot tolerate much sun.

Echinocereus blanckii. Stem pictured, 10½ inches long.

Genus *Wilcoxia* B. & R.

The genus *Wilcoxia* was erected by Britton and Rose in 1909. Some earlier writers had included its members in *Cereus* and some in *Echinocereus*. Since 1909 the species in the genus have been dealt with in various ways. Berger placed them in the genus *Peniocereus*, while Benson returned both of these genera to the genus *Cereus*, and others have considered each of these a subgenus of that large genus.

Whatever they have concluded about the genus, all recent writers have agreed that while these species seem to form a rather good grouping, the separation of the genus as such from other genera is not as clear-cut as they would like. Most say that any final word on the genus will have to await further investigation. With this word of caution about its status, I use the genus in the way most authorities are using it at the present time.

Five species in this genus are usually recognized. They are almost entirely Mexican, only one species coming into the United States at all, and that one only into southern Texas.

They are also inconspicuous cacti. In form they are very slender-stemmed, sparingly branched bushes. The stems, about ⅝ inch or less in diameter, grow very long but are weak, so the plants seldom attain much size unless they have trees or shrubs to recline upon. If growing in a thicket, they clamber over the other plants, some species then becoming up to 3 yards or more long. But the slender stems are usually well hidden among the branches of the supporting plants.

Each individual grows from a cluster of tuberous roots which provide the water storage for these cacti, whose stems are too slender to handle that function adequately.

The spines are very short, ¼ inch or less long, and are appressed to the stems. There is also more or less hair on the areoles.

The flower is large and beautiful, bell-shaped or funnel-shaped, but with a short tube. It is reddish to purplish in color and diurnal. The ovary surface is scaly, woolly, and covered with bristly or hairlike spines which remain on the fruits. The seeds are black.

By way of summarizing the differences between the genus *Wilcoxia* and those genera closest to it encountered in our area, I can list the following points: genus *Wilcoxia* differs from the genus *Echinocereus* by having much more slender stems, by its clambering habit, by never being caespitose, by having fascicled, tuberous roots, by producing its flower from within its spine areole instead of from a rupture of the stem epidermis just above the areole, and by the difference of seed form. *Wilcoxia* differs from the genus *Peniocereus* by having even more slender stems with eight ribs where that genus has only three to six ribs; by having fascicled tubers while that has a single extremely large taproot; by producing red to purple flowers with short perianth tubes, which open during the day, instead of white or very occasionally rose-colored flowers with long tubes, which open nocturnally; by having fruit with wool and bristles instead of with rigid spines; and by the difference in seed form.

Wilcoxia poselgeri (Lem.) B. & R.
(Benson: *Cereus poselgeri*)
Pencil Cactus, Dahlia Cactus, Sacasil

ROOTS Cluster of to 6+ spindle-shaped, tuberous roots, to about 4 in. long, about 1 in. diameter.

STEMS Long, very slender, round with 8 very low, inconspicuous ribs, ¼–⅝ in. thick; upper parts green, lower parts becoming brown and woody; sparingly branched to form weak bush, when supported, to 3–4 ft. tall.

AREOLES Very small, very close together; with some white wool.

SPINES 9–12 very slender radial spines about ¹⁄₁₆–³⁄₁₆ in. long; perfectly flat against surface of plant; white or gray; 1 central about ¼ in. long, turned upward against upper radials; white, whitish tipped with brown, or all dark.

FLOWERS On sides of stems, very near tips; funnel-shaped, 1½–2 in. wide by 2–2½ in. long, deep pink; outer petals narrow with greenish midribs and pink edges; inner petals broader but still linear, sharply pointed, deep pink or rose-colored shading to lighter edges; pale yellow stamens; 8 long green stigma lobes; ovary surface has reddish scales and dense covering of long wool and black-and-white hairlike bristles; open about noon and close before night, usually for 2–3 days.

FRUITS Oval, becoming nearly dry, covered with wool and bristles; black seeds.

RANGE Western Hidalgo County, Texas, along Rio Grande to Laredo, Texas, and in adjacent Mexico.

REMARKS Inconspicuous and camouflaged; rather common within its range; individuals in open rarely over 1 ft.; within thickets 2–3 ft. or more; most slender stems of any U.S. cactus except *Opuntia leptocaulis*, extending several feet; 12+ branches, the thickness of a lead pencil; produces 2–3 dozen large flowers; grows from cluster of fleshy roots; does best in sandy, loose soil; easily cultivated.

Wilcoxia poselgeri. Single, upright stem, 12 inches long. *Echinocereus papillosus* var. *papillosus* on ground.

Genus *Peniocereus* (Berger) B. & R.

This is another small genus erected by Britton and Rose. The name means something like "thread Cereus," referring to the slender stems of all the members.

Before Britton and Rose made this separation, the group had been part of the large genus *Cereus*. It is very hard to show significant characters to distinguish the genus *Peniocereus* from several other closely related genera. Perhaps its standing as a separate genus cannot be well justified, but the old genus *Cereus* has been so subdivided and reduced that it would be impossible to weigh the question of putting it together again without a restudy of many Central and South American genera, and that places the question beyond the scope of this book. It should be noted that Benson placed these small genera back into *Cereus*, but that at the same time Backeberg and others have gone on very rapidly carving new genera out of the territory formerly covered by the original genus *Cereus*. It appears to be a matter which will be decided by the turn of taxonomic philosophy.

One cannot even state the number of species in the genus *Peniocereus* definitely or give an unequivocal set of characteristics for the genus, because these will be different depending upon whose limits to the genus one elects to follow. The number of species will be from two in the case of the most restrictive authors to seven in the case of Backeberg, who places back into this genus such things as Marshall's genus *Neoevansia* and some species from the genus *Acanthocereus*.

Therefore, I can give characteristics of this genus only in a very general way here. I can say that the members of the genus all have a single extremely large, fleshy taproot, from which grow one to several slender stems which are ribbed at first but then become round. All have fragrant, nocturnal flowers with long perianth tubes, the flowers produced from within the spine areole, and all have very short spines on the stems and rigid spines on the fruits.

A comparison of this genus with the genus *Wilcoxia* was made in the discussion of that genus. The other genus in our area to which it is most closely related is *Acanthocereus*. The differences between these two genera are as follows: *Peniocereus* has a huge, fleshy taproot, stems ribbed but becoming round when old, very short spines, and more elongated fruits, while members of *Acanthocereus* have fibrous roots, stems always markedly ribbed, much longer spines, and fruits more nearly spherical.

Peniocereus greggii. Flowers 2⅞ inches in diameter.

Peniocereus greggii (Eng.) B. & R.
(Benson: *Cereus greggii* var. *greggii*)
Arizona Queen of the Night, Texas Night-Blooming Cereus, Deer-Horn Cactus, Chaparral Cactus, Sweet-Potato Cactus

ROOTS 1 huge, fleshy taproot, carrot- or turnip-shaped, in very old plants to 2 ft. diameter, to 125 lbs.

STEMS Slender, erect, sparingly branched to form weak bush; dark, dull, grayish-green, becoming reddish in too much sun; ½–1 in. thick; 3–6 very strong ribs; old stems shrink, lose areoles and ribs, become brownish, woody, and circular.

AREOLES Very tiny, closely situated on tiny tuberclelike prominences crowning ribs; much white wool at growing tips, some remaining when older; round to elliptical.

SPINES 6–9 spreading radials, 1–2 centrals per areole; blackish fading to gray; very short, $\frac{1}{32}$–$\frac{1}{8}$ in. long, stout, and rigid, from bulbous bases.

FLOWERS Strictly nocturnal, well down on branches, large, extremely fragrant; 5–8 in. long by 2–3 in. diameter; whitish; outer perianth segments tinged with brown; very long, very slender perianth tube; inner perianth segments spreading very widely, outer segments usually recurved; ovary surface has tubercles and areoles bearing short, rigid spines; outer surface of tube has scales and longer, more bristlelike spines; perianth segments lanceolate, sharply pointed; stamens erect, exserted; cream-colored anthers; slender style; white stigma.

FRUITS 2–3 in. long, ovoid, upper end attenuated, ending in persistent remains of perianth ("beak"); strongly tuberculate, each tubercle with round, black areole about $\frac{1}{8}$ in. diameter; areoles bear short, black, rigid spines; bright green until very ripe; magenta pulp; as fruits soften, surface becomes brilliant orange-red; black seeds, very broadly obovate, about $\frac{1}{8}$ in. diameter.

RANGE Trans-Pecos Texas, west through southern New Mexico, across southern Arizona, and in adjacent Mexico.

REMARKS 1 of 2 night-blooming Cereus species in our area; always growing within thicket, which provides support, light, shade, and shields stems and branches.

Genus *Acanthocereus* (Berger) B. & R.

Here is a small genus of somewhere around a dozen species carved out of the huge old genus *Cereus*. No one seems to dispute this one. Whether it is so little criticized because it is more of a natural group or because so little is certainly known about it is a question which might occur to anyone reading the numerous but remarkably incomplete and often contradictory statements about its members. From Linnaeus on we have had not a lack of, but actually too many, references to these plants. What we do lack are enough good data on which solid decisions can be based.

The members are more or less shrubby plants. The stems grow upright at first, but usually cannot support their own weight for long, and thus recline upon some support—usually other plants—or else become more or less prostrate and thicket-forming. Supported stems may grow to at least 20 feet tall and branch sparingly, but prostrate stems throw up many upright branches. Stems may be from an inch or so to 4 inches in diameter. Mature stems have three to seven conspicuous ribs. The areoles are not close and bear strong and rigid spines. The flowers are nocturnal, large, and white, with the perianth tube long and the ovary usually spiny. The fruit is round or nearly so, spiny or with the spines deciduous. The seeds are black or brown.

This is a group of tropical, lowland cacti. They are never found far from a coast and seem to thrive best on semiarid coastal plains. However, they can tolerate much more moisture than most cacti, and when given it their rate of growth is often amazing. I have had one species, when planted in an outdoor bed where it got sufficient water, produce a 6-foot stem in one summer's growing season. But they are most severely limited by cold, being among the most tender of the cacti. A frost will kill the tips of the stems, and at 32 degrees Fahrenheit the whole of the plant above the ground is killed, although the roots may sprout again.

The combination of conditions these plants need is found in various coastal areas in Central and South America. There are species of Acanthocerei native in eastern Mexico, Guatemala, and Panama and in northern, coastal regions of Colombia, Venezuela, and Bahia, Brazil. In the United States they have a precarious hold along the coast in south Texas and in Florida. Besides these locations, they have been introduced in Cuba, the islands of St. Thomas and St. Croix, and probably some other areas.

Acanthocereus pentagonus (L.) B. & R.
(Benson: *Cereus pentagonus*)
Triangle Cactus, Night-Blooming Cereus, Organo, Pitahaya

ROOTS Fibrous.

STEMS Upright, later reclining, becoming practically prostrate and rooting to form low thickets; if supported, grows to 6 ft. tall; may branch once or twice and rebranch to at least 20 ft.; thickness extremely variable: 1¼-4 in. diameter; 3, 4, or 5 high, narrow ribs; extremely small central axis; essentially a triangle, quadrangle, or pentagon with deeply concave sides; wing-like ribs about ½−2 in. high; summits somewhat tuberculate, becoming almost smooth; light to medium green.

AREOLES Round, ⅛−⅜ in. across, bulging on slight prominences on summits of ribs; spaced about ¾−2+ in. apart; very short whitish wool.

SPINES 5−7 even radial spines; 1−3 upper ones ³⁄₁₆−1 in. long; sometimes 2 upper laterals, always 2 lower laterals, each ¾−1 in. long; 1 lower radial more slender than laterals, ¼−¾ in. long; 1−4 central spines; always 1 lower central, porrect or slightly deflexed, ¾−1½ in. long; 0−2 laterally directed centrals, ¾−2 in. long, 0−1 upper central 1−2¼ in. long; medium thick to heavy, straight and round, from bulbous bases; light brown when growing, rough and gray when old.

FLOWERS Nocturnal, extremely large and showy, only slightly if at all fragrant; white, 5½−8 in. long, about 5½−6 in. wide when fully expanded; ovary hardly expanded more than long green tube, ½−¾ in. diameter; conspicuous areoles on slight prominences rather closely placed on ovary, becoming very widely spaced up tube; white wool, 1 to several rigid spines on each, very short on ovary, becoming progressively longer up tube, to about ¼ in. long on upper tube areoles; outer perianth segments greenish, inner ones white, all lanceolate and pointed; stamens shorter than perianth segments; white filaments; straw-colored anthers; white stigma, with 10−12 close-standing lobes.

FRUITS Oval to egg-shaped, about 3 in. long by 2 in. diameter, slightly tuberculate, with 1−4 spines per areole; bright red and edible when ripe; seeds obovate, about ⅛ in. (3 mm) in size, bright, shining black.

RANGE Along coast in Kenedy, Willacy, and Cameron counties, Texas; southern Florida; east coast of Mexico; coast and islands near Guatemala, Panama, Colombia, Venezuela, and Bahia, Brazil; widely introduced elsewhere, including Cuba, Virgin Islands, and southern Louisiana.

REMARKS Beautiful cactus, clearly tropical, never attaining full growth in the United States; only U.S. cactus which can outdo large Opuntias in rate of growth (5−6 ft. per growing season); tender to frost; mature stems 3-angled, hence name triangle cactus.

Acanthocereus pentagonus. Flower 6½ inches long, including ovary and tube.

Genus *Echinocactus* Link & Otto

Most of the cacti in the genus *Echinocactus* live up to the meaning of the name. Some of them present among the strongest, most rigid spines found on any cacti, and most of them are covered with as complete a spine cover as is found anywhere. Their main spines are often made especially troublesome by being hooked at the end, but, because they are never barbed along the shaft, they are actually not as vicious as the much more slender spines of the Opuntias. Although these heavy spines are a feature of most of the Echinocacti, a few of them present more slender and flexible spines, and there are even a few spineless members of the group.

These cacti are often known as the barrel cacti, and this term is a good one if it reminds us of their heavy, fleshy bodies and we do not let it limit our concept of them to something only barrel-shaped or barrel-sized. In size they may actually range from the huge, truly barrellike species usually thought of under this name and sometimes weighing hundreds of pounds to miniature forms essentially the same but, in some cases, only a few inches high when mature. In shape they are typically globular, although they may be very flattened, hemispherical, or sometimes heavily cylindrical.

The exteriors of these cacti are typically firm and solid. They are shaped into from eight to more than twenty vertical or spiraling ribs, which may be broad or narrow, high or low, smooth and even throughout their lengths or undulating, notched, or cross-furrowed, but never completely interrupted. These ribs may be thought of as partly or completely fused tubercles, but with the fusing process always clearly visible. They are never rows of completely separate tubercles. The areoles are on the summits of these ribs.

The presence of these ribs distinguishes the Echinocacti handily from the tubercled cacti, but not from the Cerei. For the characters which separate these, we have to look to the reproductive structures. All the Cerei produce the flowers on the sides of the stems, have a flower tube prolonged above the ovary, and also have a spiny ovary surface. Echinocacti, however, produce their flowers at or near the apex of the plant and have no distinct floral tube, and the ovary bears scales and sometimes wool, but not spines.

It is harder to state differences between the Echinocacti and their other relatives. Ribs versus tubercles will usually do it, giving us a handy way to tell them from any of the Mammillarias and the members of the genus *Pediocactus* or genus *Ariocarpus*, but the genus *Lophophora* has what are best thought of as low ribs. These are small, spineless forms, different from the Echinocacti in various ways, but for clearly observable differences one has to look to their ovaries and fruits, which are naked, with no appendages of any kind. Most of the Mammillarias can also be separated from the Echinocacti by having such naked fruits, but several of them may have some scales on their fruits.

The genus *Echinocactus* is used here in practically the old and original sense given it by Link and Otto. It was originally described as a large and complex grouping of ribbed cacti which produced their flowers at or near the apex of the plant, where the blossoms grew out of the upper edges of the young spine-bearing areoles, and whose ovary and fruit surfaces were to some degree scaly. Schumann organized a series of subgenera within it, and later Britton and Rose divided the old genus up into a whole array of separate small genera, leaving the original name, *Echinocactus*, to cover in their system only a few species of large barrel cacti.

The dividing process has continued until we have had at least twelve genera carved out of the old genus, among them *Echinocactus* (in the sense of Britton and Rose), *Ferocactus*, *Homalocephala*, *Hamatocactus*, *Glandulicactus*, *Astrophytum*, *Sclerocactus*, *Thelocactus*, *Ancistrocactus*, *Neolloydia*, *Echinomastus*, and *Coloradoa*.

Due to the large influence of Britton and Rose's publications these are no doubt the names that most cactus fanciers are familiar with today. Most people probably think of them as distinct and definite groupings, even though almost all would be hard-pressed if they had to try to tell the differences between them.

Actually, these genera were erected upon very small differences and these differences are used to divide them so arbitrarily that, for instance, the presence or absence of wool on the ovary is taken to be important enough to divide the woolly *Echinocactus* (*sensu* B. & R.) from the nonwoolly *Ferocactus*, while the equally woolly ovary of *Homalocephala* is considered of no significance and the single species placed in this latter genus is linked in this system no more closely to *Echinocactus* than to *Ferocactus*. Another example: *Glandulicactus* is a genus recently erected almost entirely, as the name implies, because of the presence of glands on the plants, even though other plants left in three other genera of the group may have equally obvious glands.

These small genera erected upon this sort of extreme use of the dividing rather than the synthesizing method are so poorly defined that their actual history is one of continual shifting of species from one to another and continual disagreement among the authorities who have tried honestly to define them. *Echinocactus uncinatus*, for instance, was placed during the first fifty years after the move to break up the original genus into five different genera, Britton and Rose placing it in *Ferocactus*, Knuth putting it in *Echinomastus*, Marshall in *Thelocactus*, Buxbaum in *Hamatocactus*, and finally Backeberg making the new genus *Glandulicactus* for it. Various other species have been shifted from genus to genus and the genera themselves have been both combined and redivided from time to time. The result is that the index of any recent book on cacti is used only with difficulty because it either lists many of these forms under different genera from the book last consulted or else is rendered overly long by listing each species repeatedly under the various genera each has been placed into by one authority or another.

This situation looks, on the face of it, like the dividing process gone to excess, and this attitude toward the problem was taken by one contemporary authority. Lyman Benson, in his book *Arizona Cacti*, ignored these newer genera and placed them all back into the old genus *Echinocactus*.

Over thirty years have passed since Benson's welcome recombination of these genera into something we could count on. It would seem that we should have gotten rid of the confusion by now. But it has only compounded. Backeberg published his large work with the genus divisions at their extreme, and in his long-awaited *Cacti of the United States and Canada* Benson has not only reversed himself and gone back to most of the microgenera but rearranged them yet again. For instance, he now places *Echinocactus uncinatus* in the genus *Ancistrocactus*. This is the sixth of these genera to which some leading authority has assigned it. Doesn't this tell us something about the doubtfulness of the distinguishing characters used to try to divide these supposed genera?

On most of the features used to divide the old genus *Echinocactus* into the many microgenera proposed, much has been written, but there is little new evidence. Some good authority could be quoted for each distinguishing character proposed, and other equally eminent students on reasons why the particular feature is of doubtful value. The result is that almost every new publication reshuffles these supposed genera again.

The last word is clearly not in, so it seems undesirable to perpetuate in this book genus names which have so little meaning now and such unpredictable futures. Nor do I care to try to weigh one authority against another and pick which of the six genera the unfortunate *uncinata*, for instance, should be in. For these reasons, as I did in the original edition of this work, I am returning them all to the old genus *Echinocactus*. However, for the convenience of those concerned with the stricter genera, I am also including the name for each used by Benson in his latest major work.

The Echinocacti, understood in this way, are especially interesting to cactus fanciers because of their heavy bodies and conspicuous, often beautiful spine covers. They include all of the huge barrel cacti, except the huge saguaro, growing within the United States, which inspire such feelings of awe in us. Because they are such favorites, collectors especially like to grow them.

But fanciers must always remember that these are the real old desert rats. If one were to rate the cacti on their adaptation for survival in extreme desert situations, the finest and most beautiful of these Echinocacti would be among the most specialized for the extremes of heat and drought. And one should always remember that this makes the big, tough-looking specimens one most admires among the least capable of surviving in our cool, moist gardens and patios. It is a sad sight to see a venerable old desert barrel turning to mush in an overwatered situation. We feel sorry for anyone who has to watch a desert planting of these cacti going to pieces in the yard, but there are unscrupulous nurserymen who will extract large prices for selling and installing fine old plants in places where they cannot possibly live. Many growers have shown that all of these can be raised almost anywhere if they are protected and cared for properly, in which case their beauty is well worth the trouble they take, but anyone wishing to grow them must go to the trouble of learning their requirements and providing for them properly.

Key to the Echinocacti

1a. Plants spiny—2.
  2a. Central spines never more than 1—3.
    3a. Central spine hooked if present, or else absent—4.
      4a. Radial spines 7 or 8 in number, ¾ to 2 inches long, the upper 4 or 5 of them straight and flattened, the lower 3 round and hooked; central spine 2 inches or more long; flower red-brown
          —*E. uncinatus* var. *wrightii.*
      4b. Radial spines 8 or more, ⅜ to 1¼ inches long, all round and straight; central spines absent or less than 1¾ inches long; flower cream or yellow in color—5.
        5a. Radials 10 to 19; central spine always present and ¼ to 1¾ inches long; flower large and yellow with red throat—6.
          6a. Stem becoming to 5 inches in diameter; radial spines 10 to 13 in number; flowers 2 to 3 inches tall
            —*E. setispinus* var. *hamatus.*
          6b. Stems becoming to only 3 inches in diameter; radial spines 12 to 19; flowers 1¾ to 2 inches tall
            —*E. setispinus* var. *setaceus.*
        5b. Radials 8 to 11; central usually absent and when present (in rare cases) only ½ inch or less long; flower cream-colored to pale yellowish without red coloring   —*E. mesae-verdae* (in part).
    3b. Central spine present and straight—7.
      7a. Mature plants large, 6 to 12 inches in diameter; spines very heavy and cross-ridged; radials 5 to 8 in number; central deflexed—8.
        8a. Ribs 5 to 13; areoles ½ to ⅞ inch apart; stigma lobes 6 to 10; fruits embedded in much long wool, soon-drying, and not bright-colored—9.
          9a. Spines extremely heavy, very flattened and very severely recurving against the plant; stems remaining at most pyramid-shaped instead of cylindrical, with the ribs noticeably tuberculate   —*E. horizonthalonius* var. *curvispina.*
          9b. Spines not so heavy, only somewhat flattened and not recurving against the plant; stems becoming columnar, with the ribs hardly tuberculate —*E. horizonthalonius* var. *moelleri.*

8b. Ribs 13 to 27; areoles 1 to 1¼ inches apart; stigma lobes 10 to 17; fruits standing exposed beyond the wool, very slow drying, and bright red in color   —*E. texensis.*

7b. Mature plants not so large, 1½ to 4 inches in diameter; spines rigid but not extremely heavy or cross-ridged; radials 8 to 16 in number; central porrect or turned upward—10.

10a. Central usually present on only some areoles and ½ inch or less long; radials 8 to 11 in number and ½ inch or less long
                      —*E. mesae-verdae* (in part).

10b. Central always present, ⅝ to ⅞ inch long; radials 10 to 16 in number and to ⅞ inch long   —*E. warnockii.*

2b. Central spines more than 1 on mature plants—11.

11a. Lowermost central spine hooked; upper ones straight—12.

12a. Mature plants massive in size; radial spines 12 to 20, all but the lower 3 of them slender, flexible, bristlelike, and white; central spines very heavy and cross-ringed   —*E. wislizeni.*

12b. Mature plants small to large, but not massive, radial spines all rigid; centrals various but not cross-ringed—13.

13a. Mature plants large, 7 to 12 inches thick; largest central spines 2 to 6 inches long—14.

14a. Ribs very high and broad and composed of massive, rounded tubercles 1½ to 2 inches tall and in diameter at their bases; central spines 4 to 8 in number, all round or nearly so and smooth   —*E. hamatacanthus.*

14b. Ribs high but acute, composed of indistinct tubercles only about ⅜ inch across; central spines 4, all flat and pubescent
                      —*E. sinuatus.*

13b. Mature plants small, not over 6 inches and usually 4 inches or less thick; largest central spines 2 inches or less long—15.

15a. Radials brown, yellowish, or tan, fading to gray; upper centrals conspicuous for forming an erect V of straight, diverging spines; flowers greenish or yellowish—16.

16a. Radials 12 or more, ribs 13; flowers greenish and not opening widely—17.

17a. Roots fibrous; radials 12 to 14; flowers green suffused with rose color   —*E. brevihamatus.*

17b. Roots composed of a long, fleshy, white taproot; radials 13 to 28; flowers plain green   —*E. scheeri.*

16b. Radials 7 to 12; ribs 8; flowers yellow and opening widely
                      —*E. tobuschii.*

15b. Radials: all but the lower 1 on each side of the areole white, these 2 lower radials brownish; upper centrals not forming an erect V but having 1 long, erect, whitish, and somewhat flattened upper central; flower rose, pink, or whitish—18.

18a. Plants to 12 inches tall, uppermost central ⅛ inch or less wide, flower's perianth segments ¼ to ¾ inch wide, filaments greenish, stigma lobes 5–6 and pink or rose
—*E. whipplei* var. *intermedius*.

18b. Plants to only about 7 inches tall, uppermost central ⅛ to ³⁄₁₆ inch wide, flower's perianth segments ⅜ inch or less wide, filaments red, stigma lobes 4–6 and pink or yellowish
—*E. whipplei* var. *heilii*.

11b. All central spines straight—19.

19a. Radial spines predominantly white—20.

20a. Radials 25 to 36; plant small, 3½ inches or less tall
—*E. mariposensis*.

20b. Radials 7 to 16; plants becoming larger than 3½ inches tall
—*E. conoideus*.

19b. Radial spines with various strong colors besides white—21.

21a. Ribs 8 in mature plants
—*E. bicolor* var. *schottii*.

21b. Ribs 12 to 14—22.

22a. Spines with bright red zones and some of them flattened and 1 inch or more long on mature plants; flowers large and very bright rose-pink
—*E. flavidispinus*.

22b. Spines gray or yellowish to dull purplish or reddish, but not bright red; all spines round and none over ⅜ inch long; flowers small and pale pinkish—23.

23a. Lowermost porrect central only ⅛ to ³⁄₁₆ inch long; ribs ¾ to 1 inch wide—*E. intertextus* var. *intertextus*.

23b. Lowermost porrect central ¼ to ⅝ inch long; ribs narrower, only ⅝ to ¾ inch apart
—*E. intertextus* var. *dasyacanthus*.

1b. Plants spineless —*E. asterias*.

Echinocactus horizonthalonius Lem.
Turk's Head, Devil's Head, Eagle Claws, Bisnagre, Bisnaga de Dulce, Bisnaga Meloncillo

STEMS At first depressed hemisphere, later elongates to pyramid or short cylinder; to about 8 in. tall, 8 in. diameter; almost always single, rarely 2 or very rarely 3; almost always 8 ribs; 5–13 reported; ribs very broad and rounded, with shallow grooves between; with shallow cross-furrows when old; vertical or spiraling; dull gray-green; young plants with very little short wool at apex, old plants have tuft of long wool filling apex.

AREOLES Spherical or nearly so, ½–⅞ in. apart; much long wool when young, nearly bare when old.

SPINES ¾–1½ in. long, heavy to very heavy from enlarged bases, almost round to distinctly flattened; surfaces rough, more or less cross-ridged; brownish or reddish fading to grayish or almost black; 5–8 even radial spines; no lower radial present; in one form radials strongly recurved against plant, those of adjacent areoles interlocking extensively; 1 central spine on mature plants, more or less strongly deflected and curved downward on other spines.

FLOWERS Very brilliant rose-red; 2–3 in. wide and long; ovary covered with small scales and dense white or pink wool; outer segments short, narrow, sharply pointed, sometimes ending in blackish spine; inner petals longer, somewhat lance-shaped, with notched, toothed, or ragged edges, usually ending in spinelike point; very many short yellow stamens; pink style; 6–10 long stigma lobes, reddish or pink on lower side, upper or inner sides salmon to somewhat orange or olive.

FRUITS Oblong, to 1¼ in. long by about ½ in. thick; some scales on surface and enclosed in long wool at apex; drying from tip downward; upper, dry part usually breaking off, leaving base and many seeds embedded in long wool; seeds about ⅛ in. long, somewhat irregular and angular, with large, depressed hila; rough, dark brown surface.

RANGE Trans-Pecos Texas, southern New Mexico into Arizona and Mexico.

REMARKS Small barrel cactus; surface hard, spines strong, rigid, and spreading, hence name eagle claws; grows on arid, rocky hilltops and slopes with no brush, little grass to shade it; once used for making cactus candy; strictly a desert plant.

Echinocactus horizonthalonius var. *curvispina* SD

STEMS As the species, except old specimens short and pyramid-shaped instead of cylindrical, with very flat ribs interrupted by distinct cross-furrows.

AREOLES As the species.

SPINES As the species, except very heavy, very flat, and very severely re-

Echinocactus horizonthalonius var. *curvispina*. 6 inches in diameter.

curved against plant; no spines projecting outward.

FLOWERS As the species.

FRUITS As the species.

RANGE West Texas, lower Pecos River to Davis and Guadalupe mountains.

REMARKS Most Texas specimens are of this form, the eastern form of the species, with extremely heavy, recurved spines on squat, pyramid-shaped barrel; spines symmetrical, appressed against surface.

Echinocactus horizonthalonius var. *moelleri* Haage Jr. (Benson: *E. horizonthalonius* var. *nicholii*)

STEMS As the species, except with age more columnar than pyramid-shaped and taller but not so large in diameter; ribs high, with very shallow cross-grooves.

AREOLES As the species.

SPINES As the species, except not so heavy, only somewhat flattened, straighter; not recurving against plant, but standing out at angles from surface.

FLOWERS As the species.

FRUITS As the species.

RANGE Franklin and Guadalupe mountains west into Arizona.

REMARKS Western form of the species, smaller diameter but taller and more columnar, with sharper, higher, less interrupted ribs; spines chaotic, interlacing, much less heavy or flattened.

Echinocactus texensis Hopff.
Devil's Head, Horse Crippler, Candy Cactus, Manco Caballo, Viznaga

STEMS Very broad, greatly flattened to dome-shaped; plant up to 12 in. across, 2–8 in. high; usually single, occasionally 2–3; when injured may produce cluster of small heads on top of old one; dark green; ribs prominent and acute, normally 13 or 14, 20 or 21, or 27; apex filled with long white wool.

AREOLES Triangular to inverted heart-shaped, 1/4–3/8 in. diameter, covered with white or gray wool; about 1–1 1/4 in. apart.

SPINES Reddish or brownish-gray, becoming whitish when old; only a little flattened, ringed by regular ridges; very heavy and rigid; 6–7 radial spines 3/8–2 in. long, 2 diverging upper radials, comparatively small and short, 2 lateral radials, very heavy and long—often the longest, 2 smaller lower diverging radials; may be 1 additional radial, also comparatively small and di-

Echinocactus horizonthalonius var. *moelleri*. 7 inches in diameter.

rected straight upward; radials straight and spreading to strongly recurved; 1 stout central spine ⅛+ in. thick at base, ¾−2¾ in. long, deflexed, straight to recurved or slightly hooked.

FLOWERS Bell-shaped, 1−2¼ in. diameter and length, slightly fragrant and very beautiful, each displaying range of shades; ovary densely covered with long white wool and many short, sharp-pointed, soft, blackish scales which lengthen upward, while wool thins; outer perianth segments short, narrow, sharp-pointed; midribs fleshy, greenish or brownish, ending in brownish point; edges greenish to whitish, fringed, more or less covered with web of wool; inner perianth segments narrowly lanceolate from narrow red bases; pale rose midline up petal, darkening near apex, ending in pronounced purplish or brownish mucro; expanded part of petal pale lavender, salmon, pink, or almost white; petal edges fringed to tips, feathery; reddish to pinkish filaments, pale yellow anthers; yellowish or pinkish style; 10−17 rather long yellowish or pinkish stigma lobes, often with red stripe on lower side.

FRUITS Spherical to oval, ¾ to about 1½ in. long; fleshy, brilliant red; after long time on plant usually splitting open vertically; dried, hardened, bristlelike ovary scales on surface, each with tuft of white wool in axil; on top dried remains of perianth; seeds black, kidney-shaped, slightly less than ⅛ in. long.

RANGE West of line from mouth of Colorado River to Fort Worth and Wichita Falls, except Texas Panhandle and Texas west of Guadalupe Mountains; extreme southwestern Oklahoma and southeastern New Mexico; deep into adjacent Mexico.

REMARKS One of widest ranges of any cactus in Texas; low, flat, inconspicuous; 2−5 in. high; surface hard and unyielding, covered with loose system of robust and rigid spines; can stand more moisture and cold than most other barrel cacti; better adapted to cultivation.

Echinocactus asterias Zucc.
Sea-Urchin Cactus

STEMS Extremely flat, depressed, disc-shaped to low dome-shaped; mature plants 2−6 in. diameter by less than 1−2½ in. tall; simple body divided by very narrow but distinct vertical grooves into 8 broad, almost flat ribs, forming triangular sections with no cross-grooves; line of areoles up center of each section; dull green, with tiny, less than pinhead-sized clusters of very short whitish wool.

AREOLES Circular, a little less than ⅛−¼ in. across, filled with dense wool, first straw-colored, then gray; about ¼−⅜ in. apart.

SPINES None.

FLOWERS Yellow with orange throats, 2−3½ in. across, about 2 in. tall, opening widely; ovary densely covered with scales with blackish, bristlelike

Echinocactus texensis. 6 inches in diameter.

Echinocactus asterias. 2½ inches in diameter.

points at summits; much cobwebby wool in axils; outer perianth segments
short, narrow, pointed, greenish; covered with short fuzz on outer surfaces;
inner segments long, slightly spatulate, from narrow orange bases; upper
parts clear yellow, edges entire, tips entire and slightly pointed to erose and
irregular; filaments orange at bases, yellow above; yellow anthers; yellowish style; 10–12 yellow stigma lobes.

FRUITS Oval, about ½ in. long, densely covered with spines and wool, becoming dry and finally breaking off at or near base; seeds black or nearly so,
shiny, about ¹⁄₁₆ in. long.

RANGE Lower Rio Grande Valley, Starr and Hidalgo counties, Texas.

REMARKS Diminutive barrel cactus; dwarfed relative of large, columnar barrels found in Mexico, closely related to biggest barrels; small, inconspicuous, with no typical covering of spines; body said to be suffused with chemical compounds distasteful to enemies; clusters of short white wool on
surface, said to substitute for lack of shade from spines; unique and beautiful form, projecting very short distance above ground even when water-
filled; shrinks to flat disc almost covered by sand; common name comes
from resemblance to sea urchin without spines; precarious foothold north
of Rio Grande.

Echinocactus wislizeni. 14 inches in diameter.

Echinocactus wislizeni Eng.
(Benson: *Ferocactus wislizeni*)

Barrel Cactus, Fishhook Barrel, Candy Barrel, Visnaga, Biznaga, Biznaga de Agua

STEMS Spherical, then ovate or conical, finally cylindrical; plant massive, up to 4+ ft. tall, about 2 ft. diameter; 13–25 sharp ribs, about 1¼ in. high, somewhat undulate because of slight bulging of areoles; dark green.

AREOLES ⅝–1 in. long, ¾–1¼ in. apart; elliptical to linear; before producing flowers upper end prolonged as narrow groove; after blooming upper part permanently broadened and connected to lower, spinous part by narrower neck; short brownish wool, fading to gray, mostly lost when old; some glands.

SPINES 12–20+ slender radial spines; upper and lateral ones flexible, bristlelike, whitish, about 1–2 in. long; lower 3 a little shorter and rigid, approaching character of centrals; 4 very strong centrals 1½–3 in. long, yellowish to red or purplish-red, ringed by conspicuous annular ridges; upper 3 straight, spreading upward, round to somewhat flattened; lower 1 porrect or slightly deflexed, usually hooked downward at end (rarely nearly straight), much heavier than other centrals, somewhat to greatly flattened.

FLOWERS Yellow, gold, orange, or red; about 2 in. long by 2–3 in. across; ovary covered with green scales, edged in white; outer perianth segments short, triangular to ovate, with pointed apexes; midlines greenish to reddish or yellowish, edges entire and lighter; inner segments linear and sharply pointed, edges slightly irregular or erose; most commonly orange-red on midlines shading to conch-shell pink on edges but may be all yellow or all red; extremely numerous yellow or red filaments; very small yellow anthers; 18–26+ long, pointed, erect stigma lobes, yellow or reddish below, yellowish above.

FRUITS Oblong, 1¼–2¼ in. long, practically covered with white-edged scales; yellowish and fleshy at first, becoming dried and hard; seeds nearly ⅛ in. long, black, rough but not tuberculate.

RANGE Arizona east through southern New Mexico into El Paso County, Texas; also in adjacent Mexico.

REMARKS Largest cactus in our area, truly barrellike; once used for food and in making candy, hence the common name candy barrel; now very rare in Texas.

Echinocactus uncinatus var. *wrightii* Eng.
(Benson: *Ancistrocactus uncinatus* var. *wrightii*)
Turk's Head, Cat-Claw Cactus, Brown-Flowered Hedgehog, Texas Hedgehog

STEMS Oval, to 8 in. tall, 4½ in. thick, usually much smaller; almost always single, occasionally 1–2 branches at or near base; bluish-green with gray glaucescence; formed into 9–13 fairly high and conspicuous ribs, separated by broad grooves, consisting of rather distinct but fused tubercles; areole on upper slope of tubercle, which is prolonged below or ventral to areole into chinlike swelling more or less overhanging upper end of areole on next tubercle; sharp cross-indentation of ribs when old.

AREOLES Elongated oval, about ⅝ in. long, upper end prolonged into narrow extension, sometimes called a groove; spines all grow from broader lower portion of areole; flower produced from narrower upper end; several yellowish glands in narrow neck of areole joining these 2 regions; with gray or slightly yellowish wool.

SPINES Very heavy; at first red, later reddish-brown, straw-colored, or grayish, with darker points; 7–10 even radial spines; upper and lateral 4–5 straight, flattened, ¾–2 in. long; lower 3, ¾–1¼ in. long, round, more or less curved, hooked at tips; 1 central spine 2–4+ in. long, porrect or turned upward; very heavy, angled, usually twisted, hooked at tip.

FLOWERS Maroon to garnet; funnel-shaped, not opening widely; ¾–1¼ in. long, about 1 in. across; narrow ovary covered with short, broad scales with

Echinocactus uncinatus var. *wrightii*. 8 inches tall.

brown centers and broad white, membranous edges; outer perianth segments triangular to long triangular with bluntly pointed tips and white, entire, but often crinkled edges; maroon to garnet inner segments linear, edges sometimes lighter, often irregular or toothed above; apex slightly pointed, irregular, or squared off; brown or maroon filaments; cream-colored anthers; brown style; stigma has 10–14 broad, fat lobes, cream-colored above, maroon below.

FRUITS Oblong to egg-shaped, ⅝–1 in. long; pale reddish between whitish scales, becoming dry and colorless, remaining on plant a long time; seeds about ¹⁄₁₆ in. long, curved, compressed, with basal hila; seeds finely tuberculate.

RANGE Southern New Mexico, south Texas, and adjacent Mexico.

REMARKS Small barrel cactus; U.S. form not typical of species, *E. uncinatus* Galeotti, which has 3–4 central spines and different seed form, restricted to Mexico; rare; tough, desert-loving, not easy to cultivate; rots quickly from too much moisture.

Echinocactus whipplei Eng. & Big. var. *intermedius* (Peebles) Benson
(Benson: *Sclerocactus parviflorus* var. *intermedius*)
Devil's Claw Barrel

STEMS Usually single but occasionally small clusters of 2–3; practically spherical to cylindrical, to about 12 in. tall, with 13–15 ribs composed of conspicuous tubercles ¼–⅜ in. high.

AREOLES Circular at first, but growth of flower produces narrow extension upward, leaving areole elliptical or practically so, about ³⁄₁₆–¼ in. long, with much white wool.

SPINES 7–11 straight, even radial spines ½–1 in. long, all but 1 lower lateral on each side white, these 2 lower laterals gray or brownish; 4 centrals on mature specimens, lowermost 1 porrect to slightly deflexed, strong, round to somewhat flattened, hooked at end, 1–2 in. long, gray or tan to reddish-purple, usually streaked with white; 2 lateral centrals similar but straight; uppermost central whitish, more flattened, straight or nearly so, ⅛ in. or less wide.

FLOWERS Beautiful, more or less funnel-shaped, mostly fuchsia but sometimes purplish, pink, or whitish, about 1–2 in. diameter and length; ovary has a few short, greenish, triangular scales with membranous, crinkled edges and short hairs in axils; outer perianth segments greenish in midline, edges whitish, membranous, crinkled, to about ½ in. wide; inner perianth segments fuchsia, pink, or whitish, lanceolate, edges entire or nearly so; green or yellowish filaments; orange anthers; pinkish or rose style and stigma with 5–6 lobes.

Echinocactus whipplei var. *intermedius*.

FRUITS Oblong, to about ½–1 in. long, green to pinkish and fleshy at first, surface with several scales, when ripe becoming dry and opening by splitting.

REMARKS Beautiful though diminutive barrel cactus. It is inconspicuous, adapted to extremely arid conditions and extra-sensitive to moisture. There seems to be general agreement that typical *E. whipplei* does not grow in New Mexico. The New Mexico plants formerly considered this have been placed by Benson in a new species, *Sclerocactus parviflorus* Clover & Jotter, and then made a variety of that new species. This species was erected on the characteristic of having longer flower buds which open in less intense light than those of *E. whipplei*. If the species concept is to mean anything it must be based on more than this, so I do not choose to follow Benson here. I therefore leave the New Mexico plants in the original species. In this conservative view it seems they should be considered varieties of that species. I cannot find any way to consistently separate var. *reevesii* described by Castetter, Pierce, and Schwerin from this form and so leave it as a synonym.

Echinocactus whipplei var. *heilii* (Castetter, Pierce & Schwerin)

STEMS As the previous variety, except to only about 7 in. long.

Echinocactus whipplei var. *heilii.*

AREOLES As the previous variety.

SPINES As the previous variety, except uppermost central white or straw-colored, more flattened, and ⅛–³⁄₁₆ in. wide.

FLOWERS As the previous variety, except to only about 1½ in. long; outer perianth segments to less than ⅜ in. wide; red filaments, 4–6 pink or yellowish stigmas.

FRUITS As the previous variety, except a little smaller.

REMARKS Form found in very small area of San Juan County, northwest New Mexico; precise relationship to relatives yet to be determined. If future studies show it is distinct, it must be regarded as one of the very rare cacti of that region.

Echinocactus mesae-verdae. 1¾ inches in diameter.

Echinocactus mesae-verdae (Boissevain) L. Benson
(Benson: *Sclerocactus mesae-verdae*)
Mesa Verde Cactus

STEMS Depressed-globose to short-cylindrical; mature plants mostly 1½– 3 in. tall and wide but said to reach 7 in.; 13–17 ribs, tuberculate on young plants, on older plants tubercles become confluent, with deep grooves between ribs; pale grayish-green.

AREOLES Ovate, ⅛–¼ in. long, containing much wool, at first yellowish, fading to gray.

SPINES 8–11 irregular radial spines; straight or slightly curved, round or nearly so, tan or straw-colored, about ⅜–½ in. long, rigid; central spines usually missing, very rarely 1 per areole, ½ in. or less long; gray with dark tip, porrect to ascending, straight or hooked.

FLOWERS Cream to whitish, funnel-shaped, ¾–1¼ in. wide and tall; ovary and tube have a few broadly triangular scales placed high; no wool; outer perianth segments triangular to oblanceolate, brownish with yellowish, entire margins; inner perianth segments cream-colored or whitish from greenish bases, oblanceolate, entire or somewhat erose at tips; green or yellowish-green filaments; yellow anthers; 6–8 light green stigma lobes; fragrant.

FRUITS Very small, about ³⁄₁₆ in. long, cylindrical; greenish at first, becoming brownish and dry, finally splitting near middle; black seeds, ⅛+ in. long.

RANGE Extreme southwestern Colorado and extreme northwestern New Mexico.

REMARKS One of rarest of our cacti; adapted to drought and extremely alkaline soil.

Echinocactus brevihamatus Eng.
Fishhook Cactus

ROOTS Fibrous.

STEMS Globose, egg-shaped, or, when older, columnar; about 5 in. high by 3½ in. diameter; not clustering; very dark, dull green; 13 straight or slightly spiraling ribs made up of rows of tubercles separated by deep notches; about ½ in. tall from bases nearly as broad, compressed to leave groove between ribs.

AREOLES Almost linear; lower end slightly expanded, containing spine cluster; above is a narrow groovelike portion with 1 to several glands; flower produced at upper end, which remains expanded after flowering; mature areole ¼–½ in. long, running three-fourths to all the way to base; at first filled with white wool, mostly lost when old.

SPINES 12–14 rather heavy, slightly spreading radial spines; ⅜–1 in. long, upper ones longest; opaque, tan with dark brown tips at first, then turning gray; typically 4 centrals, occasionally 1–2 more; uppermost 1 erect in front of upper radials, slender, straight, upper surface flat, lower side rounded; ¾–1¼ in. long; on either side 2+ similar centrals diverging upward, to 1¾ in. long, colored like radials except flattened upper sides may be rust; lowermost central perpendicular to plant, heavier, distinctly flattened, hooked, ¾–1 in. long, yellowish-brown, rust, or dark brown on flat upper side, lighter below, hook dark brown.

FLOWERS Green, suffused with rose; 1–1⅝ in. long, ½–¾ in. wide, spines restricting opening; ovary has up to 12 small scalelike segments with fringed edges; about 8 outer perianth segments, oblong with bluntly pointed ends; 12+ inner segments almost linear, about ⅝ in. long, pointed; dark green with faint rose midline on outer side, dull rose fading to green edges on inner surfaces; bright rose filaments; yellow anthers; short style; 10–11 rose-pink stigma lobes.

FRUITS Egg-shaped, green, becoming faintly pinkish when very ripe; ⅝–1 in. long; scales on surface remain somewhat fleshy until disintegration; dark brown to blackish seeds.

Echinocactus brevihamatus. 4 inches tall.

RANGE Along Rio Grande from mouth of Pecos River to Eagle Pass, northeast to Uvalde and Brackettville, Texas.

REMARKS Benson's "mature" *Ancistrocactus scheeri*, which he says includes this form, is really mixture of this plant and certain *E. scheeri* specimens most approaching it. True *E. brevihamatus* not as large, never branches, has different roots and flowers, fewer radial spines; I still have not seen a specimen of it from within the other's range.

Echinocactus scheeri SD
Fishhook Cactus, Root Cactus

ROOTS Long, fleshy, white taproot ¼–½ in. diameter, a few in. to 3 ft. long; occasionally branching.

STEMS Globular at first, becoming columnar or club-shaped; upper end often twice diameter of lower; 7+ in. tall, 3 in. diameter; single until very old, then may branch from base to form clumps of 6–8; medium to dark green; 13 straight or spiral ribs composed of slightly connected, almost perfectly conical or slightly compressed tubercles to ½ in. tall, same width at bases on large specimens.

AREOLES Broadly ovate on unflowering tubercles; on flowered tubercles prolonged by short groovelike extension with several glands and flower at upper end; typically extends from spinous part at summit of tubercle about halfway down upper side of tubercle; no groove in immature plants; short in young flowering plants; often extends three-fourths of the way to axil on old plants; ⅛–⅜ in. long; much white wool at first.

SPINES 13–28 very slender radial spines, tending to recurve toward plant; ¼–½ in. long; to 1⅛ in. long on very old specimens; very light, translucent yellow with red-brown tips; 3–4 centrals: 2 straight upper diverge to form V, ¾–2 in. long, distinctly flattened, upper side brown to dark mahogany, lower or outer side tan to whitish; may be 1 more upper central bisecting V formed by first 2, this shorter and more slender; lowermost central perpendicular to stem, stout, flattened above or almost round, almost always hooked; ½–1½ in. long; variegated, mostly dark brown or black above, light brown or whitish below.

FLOWERS Green or yellow-green; about 1 in. long, ½–¾ in. wide, spines restricting opening; about 12 fringed scales on ovary; about 8 outer perianth segments, linear with blunt ends, deep green with yellowish edges; about 13 inner segments, about 1 in. long, almost ¼ in. wide, with pointed ends; bright green or yellowish; green, yellowish, pink, or reddish filaments; yellow or pale orange anthers; style somewhat longer than stamens; 5–10 stigma lobes, ³⁄₁₆–¼ in. long, green to yellowish, cream-colored, or brown.

FRUITS ¾–1⅜ in. long, not including old perianth; club-shaped; 12–24 scales widely spaced; green in summer, yellowish tinged with pink when

Echinocactus scheeri. 2½ inches tall.

very ripe, until disintegration or splitting; seeds about ¹⁄₁₆ in. long, very dark mahogany; dull due to extremely fine pitting; globular, compressed, with large, deeply concave hila.

RANGE In Texas south of line from Eagle Pass to Pleasanton to Kingsville; also deep into Mexico.

REMARKS Much confusion because Engelmann's early description was of immature specimen; my description includes mature, clustering individuals larger than any related forms, with own root form, spine characters and numbers, and flower characteristics; not found within range of their relatives.

Echinocactus tobuschii (Marshall) Weniger (Benson: *Ancistrocactus tobuschii*)

ROOTS Short, turnip-shaped, tapering brown taproot.

STEMS Low, flattened hemispheres, up to 3½ in. diameter and height; single or to 8–10 heads; dark green; 8 broad, flat ribs made up of pyramidal tubercles to almost ½ in. tall from greatly flattened, quadrangular bases to ⅝ in. wide.

AREOLES Linear or nearly so, extending inward and upward from spine cluster as narrow groove half to three-fourths length of tubercle to floral part; some white wool when young, later lost; 1–2 glands in groove.

SPINES 7–12 slender radial spines, ⅝–¾ in. long, equal in length on 1 areole; yellowish, becoming gray with age, tips a little darker; 3–5 centrals; upper 2 diverge to form erect V in front of upper radials, 1½ in. long, flattened, ridged; may be 1 other upper central bisecting V formed by first 2, this more slender, to ⅞ in. long, recurving somewhat back toward plant; very rarely 2 erect centrals in V; always 1 lower central perpendicular to plant or directed upward; stout, hooked, angled, and ridged, to 1 in. long; translucent yellowish to gray.

FLOWERS 1–1½ in. long and wide, opening almost completely; ovary and tube have many scalelike segments which are greenish, triangular, with yellowish, entire edges, intergrading to almost linear outer perianth segments, with blunt tips; midlines greenish tinged with brown; edges yellow and entire; 20–25 inner segments, clear citron or golden-yellow, no variation at midline or edges; shorter than outer segments, almost spatulate, coming to pointed tips, often with very small, soft spine at apex; yellowish filaments; pale orange anthers; green style, to ¼ in. longer than stamens; 5–9 yellow or whitish stigma lobes, small at first, over ⅛ in. long when expanded.

FRUITS Elongated egg-shaped, about 1 in. long; greenish, flushing pinkish when very ripe; with numerous small scales; seed almost spherical, very dark brown and shiny, with large hilum.

RANGE Very small area in Hill Country from near Vanderpool and Medina to Ingram and Mountain Home, Texas.

Echinocactus tobuschii. 2⅝ inches in diameter.

REMARKS One of rarest forms in Southwest and on endangered species list; might be mistaken for small specimens of *E. brevihamatus* with fewer ribs made up of broader tubercles and fewer radial spines; but bright yellow, broadly opening flowers with entire edges on outer perianth segments and greenish-yellow filaments, long styles, and 5–9 stigma lobes on *E. tobuschii* differ from green suffused with rose, hardly open flowers of other form, with rose-pink filaments, short styles, and 10–11 rose-pink stigma lobes.

Echinocactus setispinus Eng.
(Benson: *Ferocactus setispinus*)
Fishhook Cactus, Hedgehog Cactus, Twisted-Rib Cactus

STEMS Hemispherical at first, later ovate, finally columnar; single or branching around base to form clusters of up to 7–8 heads; great variation in size, 3–12 in. tall, 3–5 in. diameter; light or dark green; 13 sharp, spiraling or straight and vertical ribs about ⅜ in. high, undulating, with shallow cross-furrows between areoles.

AREOLES At first elliptical or ovate, about ³⁄₁₆ in. long, elongating to nearly twice that length and becoming obovate as floral part develops; after flower and fruit are gone, floral part remains, with several glands, then contracts to narrow groove running about ⅛ in. inward and upward from spine-bearing part; much yellowish wool when young, most lost with age.

SPINES 10–19 round, slender, bristlelike to somewhat rigid radial spines straight or recurved toward plant, these ³⁄₁₆–1¼ in. long, upper ones longest; dark mahogany, yellow, or whitish; 1 central spine perpendicular to plant, round, weak, hooked, ¼–1⅜ in. long; translucent yellow fading to gray or opaque brown.

FLOWERS Ivory or cream-colored with red centers, extremely fragrant and 1¾–3 in. tall, 2¼–3 in. wide; ovary cylindrical with a few scales; outer perianth tube with many green, brownish, or reddish-green triangular scales, with white or yellowish, fringed edges; outer perianth segments triangular to oblong with blunt ends or with upper parts much broader than bases, flaring into earlike projections just below blunt tip; greenish midlines with yellowish, fringed edges; inner segments spatulate, ivory or cream-colored with red bases, edges somewhat ragged and often toothed, tips pointed; filaments reddish, weak, and swirled; cream-colored or pale yellow anthers; style long, thick, greenish-yellow, 5–11 (usually 9–10) yellow or pale orange stigma lobes, to ¼ in. long, rough, blunt, usually curving in all directions.

FRUITS Spherical or nearly so, ⅜–¾ in. across, bright scarlet with smooth, shiny skin, almost no scales, remaining on plants a long time, then splitting to release seeds, which are about ¹⁄₁₆ in. long, black, finely pitted, somewhat irregular in shape with large hilum surrounded by broad lip with unpitted, shining surface at or near end of seed.

RANGE Central and south Texas and on into Mexico; as far north as San Saba, Lampasas, and Georgetown, then south along Colorado River; limit of northwestern range near mouth of Devil's River.

REMARKS One of most common cacti in south Texas and one of most colorful: blooms all summer. One of most easily grown because resistant to rotting; recommended for amateur grower. Readily distinguished from *E. sinuatus*, which has broader, not so sharply edged ribs, fewer radial spines, and 4 central spines which are always flattened.

Echinocactus setispinus var. *hamatus*. 7 inches tall.

Echinocactus setispinus var. *hamatus* Eng.
Twisted-Rib Cactus, Fishhook Cactus, Hedgehog Cactus

STEMS Hemispherical when young, becoming columnar; usually single, occasionally branching at base to form clump; to 12 in. tall, 5 in. diameter; dark, dull green; 13 very sharp ribs, undulating but not interrupted by cross-grooves, about ⅜ in. high, usually spiral.
AREOLES As the species.
SPINES 10–13 very slender, bristlelike, straight and flexible radial spines, translucent yellow at first, when mature, lower 3, ⅜–¾ in. long, dark mahogany or honey-yellow; lateral 2 or 3, ⅝–1 in. long, white; only tips sometimes honey-yellow; 3–5 uppermost ⅜–1¼ in. long, dark mahogany or variegated brown; 1 central spine perpendicular to stem, hooked, 1–1¾ in. long, round, very slender, easily flexible; brown, often very dark.
FLOWERS As the species, except 2–3 in. tall, 2½–3 in. wide; inner perianth segments almost linear, to about ¼ in. wide; edges crinkled but not toothed or fringed; tips pointed.
FRUITS As the species.
RANGE Northern and eastern part of species range.
REMARKS Species contains well-marked and constant variations with 2 distinct and separable varieties. *E. setispinus* var. *hamatus* is larger, occurs over greater range, a bulky plant up to 1 ft. high, dark green, with very slender, flexible spines; blooms April–October with several large, extremely fragrant, yellow and red flowers at a time; ribs very sharp, not interrupted between areoles, almost always spiral, hence name twisted-rib cactus; grows in much of south-central Texas; common from mouth of Devil's River through Hill Country and along lower Texas coast. In gap along Rio Grande where this variety does not grow is found the other distinct variety, *setaceus*, a much smaller form with much more slender stems, straight ribs, and heavier, more rigid, more numerous spines.

Echinocactus setispinus var. *setaceus* Eng.
Fishhook Cactus, Hedgehog Cactus

STEMS Hemispherical when very young, becoming ovoid and finally columnar when very old; single or may branch to form clusters of up to 7–8 heads; clustering plants to 3 in. tall, single plants to 12 in.; to 3 in. diameter; light green with 13 sharp ribs which are straight, vertical, shallow, less than ¼ in. deep, interrupted by cross-furrows between areoles.
AREOLES As the species.
SPINES 12–19 round, rigid radial spines, straight or recurved toward plant; lower 3–4, ³⁄₁₆ to about ½ in. long, translucent honey-yellow, bases sometimes reddish-brown; lateral 3–5 on each side ⅜–¾ in. long, whitish with

Echinocactus setispinus var. *setaceus*. 10 inches tall.

translucent yellow tips; upper 3–5 radial spines ⅝–1⅛ in. long, translucent honey-yellow, often with dark red-brown bases; 1 central spine approximately perpendicular to stem, round, hooked, weak but rigid, ¼–1½ in. long; translucent honey-yellow becoming gray with age or partly or all dark red-brown.

FLOWERS As the species, except 1¾–2 in. tall by 2¼–3 in. wide; inner segments spatulate.

FRUITS As the species.

RANGE Starr and Hidalgo counties, Texas, and into Mexico.

REMARKS Readily recognized by straight, shallow ribs, shiny, pale green color, more numerous and more rigid radial spines, and slender stems never over 3 in. diameter. Found in great numbers in very restricted area of south Texas. Shows 2 obvious growth forms: one a single stem, when old a very slender column to 12 in. tall, 2–3 in. thick with upper radials and hooked centrals variegated with brown or wholly dark brown and ½–1½ in. long; other form branches around bases when about 2½ in. tall, producing 7–8 egg-shaped stems, to 3 in. tall, with spines shorter and honey-yellow, becoming gray when old and never brown, with hooked centrals ¼–⅜ in. long and heavier than on other form; not as massive and spectacular as previous variety, not as well adapted for amateur growing, much less tolerant of moisture and shade; flesh firmer and lighter in color, flowers somewhat shorter, deeper yellow.

Echinocactus sinuatus Dietrich
(Benson: *Ferocactus hamatacanthus* var. *sinuatus*)
Lower Rio Grande Valley Barrel

STEMS Spherical, becoming conical and finally elongated ovate with pointed tip, to at least 12 in. tall, 8 in. thick; usually single; may have 1–2 branches at base; very dark, dull green or blue-green; 13 deep but compressed ribs, 1–1¼ in. deep, undulating, acute and sharp between areoles with somewhat rounded, indistinct tubercles, about ⅜ in. across at areoles.

AREOLES Round or slightly oval, about ¼–⅜ in. long at first; flower comes out of upper end, leaving short groovelike extension which broadens and remains; with some wool and several large, elongated glands; about 1 in. apart.

SPINES 8–12 spreading radial spines; lowermost ⅜–1⅛ in. long, round or slightly flattened, sometimes slightly hooked, red or purplish with translucent yellow tip; spines on each side similar color but ⅝–1¾ in. long, slightly flattened, sometimes slightly hooked; 2 lateral radials on each side flat, straight, 1–2¼ in. long, yellowish, often slightly banded, becoming gray and rough with age; upper 1–3 radial spines round, 1¼–2⅛ in. long, straight, slender, reddish with yellow zones or all yellow, becoming gray with age; 4

Echinocactus sinuatus. 5 inches in diameter.

flat and pubescent centrals; upper 3 spread upward in front of upper radials; 1¼–2½ in. long, straight, yellowish with reddish zones, becoming gray with age; lowermost approximately perpendicular to stem, hooked, very flat and wide, 2–3½ in. long, up to ⅛ in. wide, reddish, becoming purplish-gray with age.

FLOWERS 2–3 in. long and wide, clear lemon- or greenish-yellow without red centers; hardly fragrant; ovary has a few rounded, fringed scales; outer petals short, greenish with reddish-brown midlines and greenish-yellow, fringed edges; tips pointed, otherwise wide and irregular; inner petals long, with entire edges, sharply pointed, all clear lemon-yellow with narrow yellow bases; yellow filaments and anthers; yellow style; stigma has 8–10 rough lemon-yellow lobes about ⅜ in. long.

FRUITS Green; oval or egg-shaped; about 1 in. long, ⅜ in. wide at widest part with about 6–12 small scales; old flower parts persist; fruits remain on plant for months, then rot and split open; seeds about ¹⁄₂₅ in. long, almost globular except compressed and prolonged beaklike at one end surrounding small, sunken hilum; slightly shiny, with small but comparatively widely spaced pits all over.

RANGE From Brownsville in lower Rio Grande Valley along river to Eagle Pass, Texas, then northeast to Montell and Camp Wood, Texas, and west to mouth of Devil's River.

REMARKS Beautiful barrel growing from just back of south Texas beach all along Rio Grande Valley to mouth of Devil's River and into edge of Hill Country, becoming rare in lower range. Much confused with its relatives; may be told from *E. setispinus* by flattened spines, flowers and fruits without red, and smaller seeds with small hila; from *E. hamatacanthus* by flattened radials, much more flattened and markedly pubescent centrals, fewer stigma lobes, fruits remaining strictly green, and seeds much smaller and with small hila.

Echinocactus hamatacanthus Muehlenpf.
(Benson: *Ferocactus hamatacanthus*)
Turk's Head, Visnaga, Biznaga Costillona, Biznaga es Pinosa, Biznaga Ganchuda, Biznaga Limilla, Biznaga de Tuna

STEMS Large and heavy, hemispherical or almost spherical, becoming columnar; to at least 2 ft. tall, 1 ft. diameter; usually single but occasionally double or triple by branching; when injured may form larger clusters; dull green or gray-green; usually 13, occasionally up to 17 massive, broad ribs 1½–2 in. high and wide, divided between areoles into very distinct, rounded tubercles 1½–2 in. tall and wide at bases; rounded tops of tubercles about ¾ in. wide on mature plants, with areoles on tops.

Echinocactus hamatacanthus. 12 inches in diameter.

AREOLES About 1–1½ in. apart, oval to oblong, about ⅜–½ in. long; very wide, felted grooves running inward and upward about ⅜ in. from spinous parts on mature plants; with very large, elongated glands; flower comes from upper end of groove.

SPINES 8–14 radial spines (usually 10 or more); lowermost ¾–2 in. long, variegated reddish, turning gray-brown with age; 3 laterals on each side 1–3 in. long, same color or whitish; all round or nearly so and straight; 3–5 upper radials do not radiate but spread upward, ¾–3¼ in. long, round, slender, straight, reddish or gray, often variegated; 4–8 round or somewhat flattened, smooth central spines per areole; 1 extremely large lower central approximately perpendicular to stem, usually curving and twisting, hooked at end, entirely round or round below and flattened on upper surface, 2–6 in. long, heavy but somewhat flexible, yellow mottled with red or all dull red at first, often indistinctly annulate, becoming gray-brown with age; 3 more upper centrals spreading upward; straight, round, relatively slender, reddish often mottled with yellow, later gray-brown, 1–3½ in. long; 2–3 upper centrals added with age, shorter and more slender, erect just behind previous upper centrals.

FLOWERS Straw to yellow, with or without red centers, 2¼–4 in. tall, 2¾–3 in. wide; very fragrant; ovary and tube have many small triangular scales whose centers are reddish or brownish, and whose edges are greenish-yellow, crinkled, often with a few twisted cilia; 55–80 outer perianth segments, short, scalelike to oblong, with reddish midlines; outer parts greenish, edges yellowish; about 30 long, wide, pointed inner petals; edges entire or often toothed irregularly; inner petals all yellow or with red bases; yellow or reddish filaments; yellow anthers; yellow style, longer than stamens; 11–14 stigma lobes, about ¼ in. long, yellow, rough, usually much curved and twisted.

FRUITS Egg-shaped to oblong, 1–2 in. long, not including persisting perianth; 30–40 small scales on each; remaining green all summer and fall, ripening in winter, then becoming brownish-red; seeds practically round, about 1/16 in. long, black, pitted, with large hila.

RANGE Along Rio Grande from mouth of Devil's River to El Paso, Texas; very rarely west about 50 miles in southern New Mexico; abundant in Mexico.

REMARKS Second largest of this genus in United States. Often called *E. longihamatus*. Distinguished from relatives by great rounded ribs composed of massive tubercles swelling around each areole; both *E. setispinus* and *E. sinuatus* have sharp ribs without large rounded tubercles; also thus distinguished from *E. wislizeni*, which has very large but uninterrupted, sharp ribs. Liable to rot if given much water and not as resistant to freezing as other west Texas cacti.

Echinocactus bicolor var. *schottii*. 4 inches in diameter.

Echinocactus bicolor var. *schottii* Eng.
(Benson: *Thelocactus bicolor* var. *schottii*)
Glory of Texas

STEMS Egg-shaped or conical to almost columnar, sometimes to 10 in. tall, 5 in. diameter, usually smaller; usually single, but very old plants may form small clusters of 3–4 heads by branching from base; 8 broad, flat ribs composed of wartlike tubercles about ½ in. high from almost perfectly square bases to ¾ in. wide.

AREOLES Oval or nearly round with yellow wool at first, later egg-shaped on immature plants; on adult tubercles floral part forms short groove about ⅛–³⁄₁₆ in. long, often so wide as to make areole obovate; in old plants glands often visible.

SPINES 12–18 radial spines per areole; upper 1–4 are erect, straight, flattened, ¾–2¼ in. long; yellow when young, becoming gray with age; lateral and lower radial spines round, ½–1¼ in. long, varicolored with bases gray, middle zones dark red, ends yellowish; lower radials often recurving a little back toward plant; 3–4 straight central spines; uppermost erect just in front of upper radials, 1–3½ in. long, very flat and broad, often ⅛ in. wide, flexible; erect beside this 1–2 other centrals, flat or round, not quite so long; yellow at first, becoming gray; lower central perpendicular to plant or turned downward, perfectly round or oval, stout and rigid, ¾–2¾ in. long, gray, red, yellow like lower radials at first, becoming all gray when very old.

FLOWERS 2–3 in. long, 3–4 in. across, opening widely with petals usually recurving backward; brilliant fuchsia with scarlet throats and shining, satiny surface; varying sepals from short, rounded scales on ovary wall to more elongated, oblong sepals above, with greenish midlines and whitish, fringed edges; inner petals oblong from narrow bases, about ⅜ in. wide at widest point, margins entire but crinkled, tips pointed and recurving; bases bright scarlet, upper three-fourths bright, satiny fuchsia; bright scarlet filaments, matching petal bases; yellow anthers; style pink, a little longer than stamens; 8–11 rough, blunt stigma lobes, light rose to brownish-pink.

FRUITS About ⅜–½ in. long, becoming dry and splitting open; seeds about ¹⁄₁₆ in. long, almost globular, with very large hila.

RANGE Starr and Brewster counties, Texas.

REMARKS Primarily Mexican species occurring in two widely separated areas in Texas. Has bright-colored, variegated spines and the brightest and most exotic flowers of any cactus in our area.

Echinocactus flavidispinus (Backbg.) Weniger
(Benson: *Thelocactus bicolor* var. *flavidispinus*)

STEMS Hemispherical at first, becoming columnar and sometimes branching at base or if injured; to only 4+ in. tall, 3 in. diameter; 13 ribs composed of rows of conical tubercles to about ⅜ in. high; distinct in young specimens, somewhat confluent on older plants; light green or yellowish-green.

AREOLES Oval at first, ovate after flowering, upper part prolonged into short groove containing glands.

SPINES 14–20 radial spines recurved against plant; yellow or streaked with red at first; lower and lateral ones remaining round, ¼–¾ in. long, bright red in middle zones with yellow tips; uppermost becoming flattened, cream-colored to gray, to at least 1 in. long; juvenile plants have only round radials

Echinocactus flavidispinus. 2 inches in diameter.

at first; then add 1 strong, round central perpendicular to stem or turned downward; pubescent, yellow or yellow at base and tip with bright red in middle, ⅜–⅞ in. long; mature plants add 3 more centrals turned upward; 2 like radials; uppermost 1–1½ in. long, flattened, more or less curved toward plant; yellow, fading to gray with age.

FLOWERS About 1½ in. tall, 3–4 in. diameter when fully open; scales on ovary and outer perianth segments have brownish-green midlines shading to whitish, entire edges and scarlet bases; inner segments have very narrow scarlet bases widening to bright rose-pink or fuchsia upper parts with entire edges, very sharp-pointed, do not recurve; yellow filaments and anthers; yellow or pink style; 11 stigma lobes, scarlet at bases fading to yellowish at tips.

FRUITS Not seen.

RANGE Near Marathon, Texas.

REMARKS Easily distinguished from *E. bicolor* var. *schottii* or typical *E. bicolor*, neither of which grows near limited range of this form. Much less robust than its relatives in any feature of body or flower.

Echinocactus intertextus Eng.
(Benson: *Neolloydia intertexta*)
Early Bloomer, White-Flowered Visnagita

STEMS Individual, spherical at first, becoming egg-shaped or conical; short, thick columns when very old; to 6 in. tall, 3½−4 in. diameter; almost always 13 ribs, distinct and broad but low, ⅝−1 in. wide, ¼−⅜ in. deep; tubercles distinct, almost entirely separated by deep cross-grooves; conical at first, square bases on older sides of stem; summits of tubercles prolonged below areole into sharply peaked, chinlike ridge almost overhanging next lower tubercle; at cross-groove between them ridge terminates suddenly with straight drop into pitlike depression for axil.

AREOLES Rather large, slightly oval, very woolly, becoming bare when old; when mature, elongated by woolly groovelike extension running inward and upward from spinous portion to base of tubercle, where it meets cross-groove between tubercles; flower produced from end of extended areole in axil of tubercle; usually a tuft of longer, yellowish-white wool remains in depressed axil after flowering and fruiting.

SPINES Round with slightly enlarged bases, dull gray or yellowish at bases, upper half darkening into purplish or reddish-brown tips; 16−27 even radial spines which recurve slightly and lie tightly against plant or spread outward; upper ones weakest, almost bristlelike, ³⁄₁₆−⅝ in. long; lateral radials heavier and longer, to ⅞ in. long; 3−5 centrals similar to radials, but a little heavier and slightly darker; 2−4 erect in front of and against upper radials or spreading upward; ½−⅞ in. long; lowermost central standing straight out from center of areole; heavy but very short, ⅛−³⁄₁₆ in. long in one form; not so heavy; ¼−⅝ in. long in another; juvenile plants have 16−18 strictly radiating radial spines, no centrals.

FLOWERS Salmon to white, ¾−1+ in. long, ½−1+ in. diameter; with minimum of water, spines prevent petals from opening fully; when well watered, opening widely, appear very different (see photos); about 6 small scales on ovary; outer perianth segments very short to about ¾ in. long and ³⁄₁₆ in. wide; pink midlines with very pale pink edges; pointed, with edges entire or sometimes somewhat toothed and ragged; inner petals about ¾ in. long, about ⅛−³⁄₁₆ in. wide, whitish at bases, with very pale pink midline shading to white edges; pointed, often with tiny, soft spine at apex; edges usually irregular; greenish filaments; yellowish anthers; greenish style; 6−12 bright pink to brilliant purple-red stigma lobes.

FRUITS Small, ⅜−½ in. diameter, globular to somewhat oblong; old perianth persists, becoming dry and brown, then splitting to release seeds; has a few scales on surface; seeds about ¹⁄₁₆+ in., black and shining, rough; nearly kidney-shaped, with large hila.

RANGE From Big Bend and lower Davis Mountains west to El Paso and Franklin Mountains, Texas; west through New Mexico into southeastern

Echinocactus intertextus var. *intertextus*. When collected, 2¾ inches in diameter.

Arizona and adjacent Mexico.

REMARKS Deepest penetration into United States about 100 miles north of Rio Grande; fairly common in past, now much rarer. First cactus in locale to bloom each year, as early as February 13; stringent growing requirements: must be kept dry at all times or rots; full sun and heat.

Echinocactus intertextus var. *intertextus* (Eng.)
(Benson: *Neolloydia intertexta* var. *intertexta*)

STEMS As the species, except ribs broader, ¾–1 in. wide.
AREOLES As the species.
SPINES As the species, except radial spines even, recurving, lying tightly against plant; upper radials to ½ in. long; lateral radials to ¾ in. long; lower radials to ⅜ in.; upper centrals erect in front of and against upper radials; lower, porrect central very heavy and only ⅛–³⁄₁₆ in. long.
FLOWERS As the species.
FRUITS As the species.
RANGE From Big Bend and lower Davis Mountains west past El Paso, Texas, along border into Arizona.
REMARKS Typical form of the species, occurring over wide range; variety appears as single small hemisphere or short column made of distinct ribs composed of curiously shaped tubercles; areoles close together, plant encased in purplish-red spines, flat against surface, except for 1 very short and stout lower central, standing straight out, almost unnoticeable; spines meet and interlock over top of plant and completely enclose growing tip, very woolly when active; flowers come out of woolly summit, restricted by interlocking spines.

Echinocactus intertextus var. *dasyacanthus* Eng.
(Benson: *Neolloydia intertexta* var. *dasyacantha*)

STEMS As the species, except to 6 in. tall; ribs somewhat narrower, ⅝–¾ in. wide.
AREOLES As the species.
SPINES As the species, except longer and more spreading than on typical variety; upper radials ½–⅝ in. long, very slender; lateral radials ⅝–⅞ in. long, heavier; lower ones ½–⅝ in. long, rather heavy; upper centrals spreading upward instead of lying appressed against radials as in other form, ¾–⅞ in. long; lower central practically perpendicular to stem, as in other form, but no heavier than upper centrals and ¼–⅝ in. long.
FLOWERS As the species.
FRUITS As the species.

Echinocactus intertextus var. *intertextus*. Same plant after 1 year of cultivation. 2⅞ inches in diameter.

Echinocactus intertextus var. *dasyacanthus*. 2¾ inches in diameter.

RANGE Near Lake Valley and Rincon, New Mexico, south to El Paso, Texas, and probably into Mexico; most common in Franklin and Organ mountains.
REMARKS Var. *dasyacanthus* differs from var. *intertextus* in maximum stem size and spine character, most obviously in length and character of lowermost, porrect central spine and in spreading instead of appressed character of all spines; juvenile individuals show this latter difference much more strongly than mature plants.

Echinocactus warnockii (L. Benson)

STEMS Single until very old, then occasionally producing several short branches just above ground; globose at first, becoming oblong or short columnar; to 6 in. tall, 4 in. diameter when old; 13 spiraling ribs when young, increasing by branching of ribs to 21+ on large stems; ribs to ⅝ in. deep, composed of definite tubercles, varying greatly in shape; some compressed, ¼ in. wide; others to ½ in. wide at bases; tubercle prolonged as short, sloping ridge running downward from areole, often rising a little to form second, shorter, chinlike projection behind main tubercle; then ending abruptly by falling to definite though narrow cross-furrow between tubercles.
AREOLES Elongated and very woolly at first, becoming nearly round and almost bare, except for woolly groove extending inward and upward from spinous portion to floral portion in axil, often almost overhung by chin of next higher tubercle.
SPINES Very light straw-colored with pale brown tips when young, becoming darker with tips sometimes dark purplish-brown on old plants; 10–16 round, rigid radial spines spreading out at angle from plant; 5–6 upper radials spreading erect are longest of plant, ¾–⅞ in. long; in front of these at very tip of areole or occasionally scattered as much as halfway down groove to axil often 1–3 additional very tiny spines, 1/16 in. long; lateral radials spreading outward, about ¾ in. long; lower 2–4 radials almost perpendicular to plant, ⅜–¾ in. long; 1 central spine turned upward to stand in front of upper radials, round and a little heavier than radials, with bulbous base, ⅝–⅞ in. long.
FLOWERS 1–1½ in. wide and tall, white; a few whitish scales on ovary; perianth segments on lower tube small and scalelike with arrowhead-shaped edges, gradually lengthening up tube, becoming oblong, blunt-tipped segments about 3/16 in. wide; greenish-brown midlines and whitish, entire edges; inner petals cream-colored or pure white, ⅛ in. wide, pointed, with entire edges; green or whitish filaments; yellow anthers; 6–10 slender, light green stigma lobes.
FRUITS Spherical, about ¼ in. diameter; light green, sometimes with pinkish areas when ripening, becoming dry and papery when ripe; perianth persists; a few whitish scales on fruits; splits when mature; seeds black, finely tuberculate, about 1/10 in. long, with very large, concave hilum.

Echinocactus warnockii. 2½ inches in diameter.

RANGE Lower Big Bend, Texas.

REMARKS Very close to Arizona cactus *E. erectocentrus* Coult.; stem and spines almost alike, with only quantitative differences; *E. erectocentrus* grows to 8 in. tall; *E. warnockii* to 6 in.; radials of former appressed rather tightly against plant; radials more spreading in Texas plant; centrals the same, except to 1 in. on Arizona plant, to ⅞ in. on Texas plant; flowers and fruits more definitely different: *E. erectocentrus* has pink flowers with 8–10 pink to deep purple stigma lobes; Texas cactus has pale cream or pure white flowers, with 6–10 light green stigma lobes; fruits differ in shape, those of *E. erectocentrus* cylindrical, ½–⅝ in. long by ¼ in. wide; Texas form perfectly or nearly spherical, ¼ in. across; both split to release seeds.

Echinocactus mariposensis. Green-flowered. 1⅝ inches in diameter.

Echinocactus mariposensis (Hester)
(Benson: *Neolloydia mariposensis*)

STEMS Single, practically globose, egg-shaped, or short oblong; to about 3½ in. tall by 2 in. diameter, but usually smaller; 13 ribs, increasing to 21 as mature; usually twisted and wrinkled into more or less distinct but small tubercles.

AREOLES At first practically spherical, about ⅛ in. across, with much short brownish wool; when mature, extending forward as narrow groove on upper side of tubercle; flower produced at end of groove in axil of tubercle, accompanied by long wool and tuft of persistent white bristles in axil.

SPINES 25–36+ even radial spines, rigid, ³⁄₁₆–³⁄₈ in. long; pure, shining white to gray, sometimes tipped with light brown; 4–7 centrals; upper 3–6 spreading upward or somewhat appressed against upper radials, comparatively heavy, ½–¾ in. long; lower central porrect or curving downward, heavy, ³⁄₁₆–½ in. long; centrals whitish, gray, or pale yellow below, distal sections usually light brown or bluish-gray.

FLOWERS About ¾–1¼ in. diameter and length, opening funnel-shaped or wider; ovary and tube have about 12 whitish scales; outer perianth segments have somewhat erose edges; inner segments somewhat spatulate, tips bluntly pointed, sometimes notched or toothed; 2 distinct colors: outer perianth segments with green midribs and white edges, inner segments with light green midlines and white edges; or outer segments with brown midlines and pink edges, inner petals pink fading to whitish at edges; cream-colored stamens, sometimes with pinkish filaments; long greenish or brownish style; 5–8 green stigma lobes.

FRUITS Globose or oblong, to ³⁄₈ in. long; yellowish-green at first, becoming dry, then splitting; a few scales; seeds slightly over ¹⁄₁₆ in. long, ovate, black.

RANGE Extreme southwest Brewster County, Texas.

REMARKS Smallest of barrel cacti in our area—usually little larger than golfball; very limited range in very rough country. Tough, desert species; grows in open in thin layer of soil overlying hot, exposed limestone ridges; in cultivation must be kept drier and in brighter sun than most other small species of area.

Echinocactus conoideus (DC) Poselgr.
(Benson: *Neolloydia conoidea*)

STEMS Globular to egg-shaped at first, becoming conical or cylindrical; 4+ in. tall, 2¾ in. thick; simple or sprouting near base or higher on sides to produce 2–3 branches; dull gray-green, shaped into 8 or 13 indistinct ribs composed of spiral rows of almost completely separate tubercles, about ½ in. long, conical, from bases broad but somewhat compressed horizontally by crowded, almost overlapping position.

AREOLES Circular, about ¹⁄₁₆ in. diameter, with white wool when new; becoming enlarged by formation of narrow groovelike extension forward from spinous part; when mature, groove extends to axil of tubercle, broadening into larger felted area from which flower comes; after blooming, original circular part remains as spine-bearing portion, usually losing wool; felted groove running upward and inward.

SPINES 10–16 even radial spines per areole, straight, rigid, white fading to gray, ¼ to about ½ in. long; also 1–4 spreading central spines ³⁄₈–1+ in. long, straight, rigid, blackish when young, fading to gray; lowest is longest and heaviest.

Echinocactus mariposensis. Pink-flowered. 1⅞ inches in diameter.

Echinocactus conoideus. 3 inches tall.

FLOWERS Beautiful violet or violet-pink, 1–2 in. diameter, about 1 in. tall, opening rather widely; ovary surface and tube usually naked of scales but occasionally have 1–2 small, rounded, white-edged scales; outer perianth segments have pink centers with whitish, entire edges; inner segments violet or pinkish-violet, lanceolate, with pointed tips and entire edges; bright orange stamens; 5–7 long white or yellowish stigma lobes.

FRUITS Spherical, yellowish or reddish at first, drying and becoming brown; most naked but sometimes having 1–2 tiny scales; seeds about 1/16 in. diameter, black, tuberculate, with large basal hila.

RANGE Central Mexico, into Texas about 30 miles along Rio Grande from near Del Rio west to Boquillas.

REMARKS Texas plants do not form a variety distinct from Mexican population; this species and its close relatives stand at opposite end of Echinocacti from huge barrels, with ribs indistinct and ovaries having very few scales. It is never very common in Texas, growing on rocky hillsides, more or less in the open. It is fairly easy to grow, not as badly affected by moisture as most other members of group.

Genus *Lophophora* Coult.

We come here to one of several cactus genera which seem to lie between the Echinocacti and the Mammillarias. Although there have been attempts in the past to submerge them in first one and then the other of these larger groups, they seem to defy either combination. The reasons for this may seem rather technical to the nonspecialist, but they are the stuff out of which cactus taxonomy is constructed.

Although some of its members were first described by Lemaire as Echinocacti, the significant points which seem to rule the Lophophoras out of the genus *Echinocactus* are the facts that the ovary and fruit on them are entirely naked and that the fruit remains always fleshy. These characters would put them in agreement with the Mammillarias, but they are even more clearly set apart from that genus by the facts that their stems are ribbed and that their monomorphic areoles produce the flowers from the apexes of young tubercles rather than from the axils. So this small genus is left by all recent students to stand alone.

There are only a very few species in this genus, and as yet little agreement exists as to exactly how many they number. Most authors list two and some three or four, but there is no standardization of species and varietal arrangement, so no definite figure can be given.

The members of *Lophophora* are small, globose, or depressed globose cacti growing from comparatively large, carrot-shaped taproots. Usually the stem of the plant is to about 3 inches in diameter, and although one form sometimes reaches to about 5 inches, they stand no more than 2 inches above the ground. The stems of an individual may be single or may sometimes branch from the base to form large clusters.

The surfaces of these cacti are blue-green, usually with much gray glaucescence. There are no spines at all after the early seedling stage. The very broad and flat ribs are composed of some of the broadest, flattest, most confluent tubercles seen anywhere. The areoles are small and round, with long white to yellowish wool which tends to persist. The flowers are small, bell-shaped, and pink, pale rose, white, or rarely pale yellowish. The fruits are club-shaped and rose-pink or reddish.

The insignificant little members of this genus have been famous out of all proportion to their size and appearance as far back as we can trace them. They are the sacred plants of the Indians best known by the ancient Indian name, *peyotl*, which has become the peyote of common usage. This is all because these plants contain in their flesh a group of alkaloids which, when taken into the human body, have remarkable effects upon the nervous system. From ancient times to the present, Indians of Mexico and the U.S. Southwest have eaten these cacti specifically for the effects they have on their senses.

Lophophora williamsii (Lem. in SD) Coult.
Peyote, Mescal Button, Whisky Cactus, Dry Whisky

ROOTS Large carrot-shaped taproot, same diameter at top as stem, tapering slowly below, usually 3–5 in. long.

STEMS At first single, often clustering to form up to 50 in 1 variety; hemispherical or usually depressed-globular; to about 5 in. diameter and about 2 in. tall; flesh soft and flabby; blue-green, usually with gray glaucescence; 5–13 very broad, very low ribs separated by narrow grooves, straight or sinuous, each rib more or less divided into tubercles; at apex tubercles fairly distinct; lower, only very slight projections or almost entirely obliterated; may have small wrinkles.

AREOLES Round, or nearly so; small, about ⅛ in. diameter, ¼–1¼ in. apart on summits of tubercles; at first filled with much long white or yellowish wool; with age, wool usually turns gray and may be worn off; flowers produced from within areoles at summits of young tubercles.

SPINES Spineless after very young seedling stage.

FLOWERS Small, usually pale pink or whitish, rarely rose or pale yellowish; bell-shaped, ½–1 in. diameter; small, naked ovary; outermost perianth segments greenish with entire edges; inner segments almost linear, pale pink to rose, white, or yellowish; whitish filaments; yellow anthers 3–7 reddish or yellowish stigma lobes.

FRUITS Club-shaped, ⅜–¾ in. long, pale pink or very pale rose when ripe, remaining fleshy and indehiscent; seeds about ¹⁄₁₆ in. long, with basal hila.

RANGE From Mexico across Rio Grande a short distance into south and southwest Texas, in Hidalgo, Starr, and Zapata counties and a few locations in Brewster County.

REMARKS The famous peyote; individual stems often called mescal buttons. Some plants remain single until very large, others sprout new heads or buttons all around almost from beginning; much variation in rib shape, number, and size, some in flower features.

Lophophora williamsii var. *williamsii* (Lem. in SD)

ROOTS As the species.

STEMS As the species, except to only 3 in. diameter; tubercles less distinct than in other form, smaller, about ⅝–¾ in. across bases; clustering extensively.

AREOLES As the species, about ¼–⅝ in. apart.

SPINES As the species.

FLOWERS As the species, except sepals and petals each in fewer than 3 series; 3–5 stigma lobes.

FRUITS As the species.

Lophophora williamsii var. *williamsii*. Largest stem 3 inches in diameter.

RANGE Central Mexico to south Texas, in Hidalgo, in Starr, and in Zapata counties.

REMARKS Typical form of the species; the form growing in south Texas, with smaller stems forming large clusters when old; more tender form, growing under partial shade, rather easily damaged by frost.

Lophophora williamsii var. *echinata* (Croiz.) Bravo

ROOTS As the species.

STEMS As the species, except remaining single or forming 2–3 heads in very old specimens; larger than in typical form, to at least 5 in. diameter; tubercles more conical and larger, bases ¾–1¼ in. across.

AREOLES A little larger than typical form, with more wool.

SPINES As the species.

FLOWERS As the species, except sepals and petals more numerous, usually in 3 series each.

RANGE Northern Mexico, from Chihuahua and Coahuila into Texas Big Bend, in lower Brewster County.

REMARKS Larger, tougher form of the species; little difference in structure, except that stems of this form are heavier and larger, although not clustering much; grows on dry, exposed hillsides; can survive greater heat and cold; seems to have more alkaloids than the typical variety.

Lophophora williamsii var. *echinata*. Largest stem 2½ inches in diameter.

Genus *Ariocarpus* Scheidweiler

This is a small genus containing about half a dozen very strange cacti, one of which is found in Texas, the rest in Mexico.

The body of an Ariocarpus consists of one or occasionally a cluster of low, flattened stems from only about 2 inches in diameter and not projecting above the soil level at all in some forms to as much as 10 inches across and 5 inches tall in one form. This stem sits on top of a large, carrotlike taproot.

The surface of the stem does not have ribs but is divided into very distinct, usually imbricated but noncoalescent tubercles. These are very firm, often have a horny, rough epidermis, and are of peculiar shapes, usually more or less triangular and flattened above. There are no spines after the first seedling growth.

The members of this genus are unusual among cacti of our area because they flower in the fall of the year, usually from September to December. The flowers come from the woolly axils of the young tubercles at the center of the plant. They open widely, are diurnal, and are white, yellowish, or purplish in color. The ovary and fruit are both naked; the fruit is fleshy at first, becoming dry at maturity and disintegrating, leaving the seeds in the wool at the center of the plant.

This genus was described and named *Ariocarpus* by Scheidweiler in 1838. The next year Lemaire redescribed it, calling it *Anhalonium*, and many students, including Engelmann and Coulter, thought that Lemaire's name had precedence, so for many years there was confusion over these names.

This is another genus which falls into the gap between the Echinocacti and the Mammillarias or, rather, which has some characters typical of each of these major groups but will not rest easily in either.

The members have fruits which become dry, as do those of the Echinocacti, and some of them have monomorphic areoles also, but they have never been considered Echinocacti. This is partly because they have no ribs and because they have naked ovaries.

They actually seem to be closer to the Mammillarias. In fact, for most of his life Engelmann persisted in including them in the genus *Mammillaria*. This is because they have a tuberculate surface and naked ovaries, and some species have dimorphic areoles with the nonproducing spinous portion of the areole at the tip of the tubercle and the floral portion separated from it at the base. However, the tubercle characters are very different; the flowers come from the apex of the stem instead of from older tubercles away from the apex; the fruits become dry and open; and there are differences of seed structure, all of which seems to separate these plants from the Mammillarias as well. Coulter remarked with obvious relish in 1896 that Engelmann had "finally come" to the opinion that these must be kept distinct from *Mammillaria*.

The confusion over this sort of thing had no more than subsided when in 1925 Berger noted an obvious difference between certain members of the genus. Most have no groove on the upper surface of the tubercle, but two have a woolly groove on it. Berger seized upon this difference and proposed that those with grooves should be removed from the genus *Ariocarpus* and put into a new genus, *Roseocactus*.

Since that time there has been a history of disagreement over Berger's proposal. In brief, Marshall did not think that the difference was fundamental enough to warrant completely separating the plants into different genera and proposed that *Roseocactus* be put back into *Ariocarpus* as a subgenus. Buxbaum seemed to agree with Marshall. The main recent champion of Berger's view was Backeberg, who backed it vociferously in his large work on cacti.

Only very recently was detailed study of the mode of development of the tubercles and areoles carried out and the information acquired, together with other factors, applied to the problems. However, it seems already to have brought some welcome clarification, as well as results of significance to the classification of some other cactus groups. Edward F. Anderson made these studies and reported on them in a series of articles beginning in 1961.

He found that in all of this group there is a single original growing point for the areole development which is located near the base of the tubercle instead of at its tip. From this single point develop all areolar structures, including the spinous portion (if represented), groove (if present), and floral portion. But there are differences in the species in the way these develop from the original growing point. In *Ariocarpus* (*Roseocactus*) *fissuratus*, the floral development is at the base, with elongation of the tubercle occurring beneath the vestigial spinous part of the areole and thus drawing that part of the areole out into the already mentioned groove. In *Ariocarpus retusus*, the type species of the genus *Ariocarpus*, the rudimentary spinous part of the areole soon separates from the floral part and elongation between them then leaves the floral part in its basal position, while it pushes the spinous part to near the tip of the tubercle, where it persists as a woolly spot. In *Ariocarpus trigonus* the elongation occurs ahead of the spinous portion and never allows it to separate from the floral part at the base at all.

The usual interpretation of these events requires us to call the elongated, groovelike areoles of *A. fissuratus* and also the short, basal areoles of *A. trigonus*, whose meristems do not divide, monomorphic. At the same time the areoles of *A. retusus*, where the floral and spinous parts separate, are entirely dimorphic.

Essentially this same difference has, since Britton and Rose, been made the reason for separating the Coryphanthas out of the genus *Mammillaria*, and if it is so fundamental a difference as some have thought, it should also make mandatory the division of the genus *Ariocarpus* as well. But Anderson carried on many other investigations of seedling development, seed structure, other aspects of stem anatomy, fruit composition, and hybrid re-actions and concluded from these that they should all make up one genus, *Roseocactus* being at most a subgenus. The lack of importance of those details of areole structure which have been used so much in separating cacti is further indicated by Anderson's report of *A. fissuratus* individuals without the groove and *A. retusus* individuals which have no spinous portion of the areole at all. This means that in at least *A. retusus* both the monomorphic and the dimorphic areoles occur in the same species, a situation which Dr. Boke has also found in certain Coryphanthas. This study has far-reaching implications for the taxonomy of other groups, where, it seems, too much emphasis has been put on grooves or their absence.

The members of *Ariocarpus* are retiring species, often not rising above the ground level at all, with usually horny and discolored surfaces which make them almost invisible. They are very difficult to find in their native haunts, but this is the point of their method of growth. They have no spines, and they depend instead upon being so insignificant as to be overlooked, upon camouflage, and upon some unpalatable alkaloids in their flesh for their survival. They are so unusual in their appearance that most people find it hard to believe they are cacti at all.

Ariocarpus fissuratus (Eng.) K. Schumann
Living Rock, Star Cactus, Star Rock, Sunami, Chautle, Peyote Cimarron

ROOTS Carrotlike taproot.

STEMS Entirely flat to somewhat rounded and depressed-globose, usually level with ground or only 1 in. above it; covered with very crowded and over-lapping tubercles with broad, flattened bases, upper surfaces flattened, tri-angular in shape, ½ to about ¾ in. long; upper surfaces crossed by many small fissures, with warty appearance; epidermis very firm, gray-green when young or well watered, yellowish or brownish in older plants or in desert; hard, horny, dead-appearing; apex has long wool, often almost covering younger tubercles; usually single, occasionally branching to form cluster of up to 12.

AREOLES At first circular, at or near base of young tubercle, filled with dense mass of woolly hairs; later easily visible on elongated tubercle, stretching into woolly groove from axial floral part to tip of tubercle on upper surface; indistinct and linear when old; ⅜ to about ⅝ in. long; very rarely not elongating and remaining in axil of tubercle.

FLOWERS From axils of young tubercles at or near center of stem, arising out of long wool; 1–2 in. across, opening rather widely; almost white to pink or magenta; naked, short ovary; outer perianth segments almost linear with pointed tips, brownish or greenish with whitish, entire edges; inner seg-

Ariocarpus fissuratus. 3⅝ inches in diameter.

ments pinkish or purple with whitish edges, rather oblong from narrow bases; tips with small, hairlike points at apex; white filaments; bright orange anthers; white style and stigma, with 5–10 lobes.

FRUITS Oval, about ¼–⅝ in. long, pale green or whitish at first, becoming dry and disintegrating; seeds about ¹⁄₁₆ in. long, black, rough.

RANGE Northern Mexico into Texas, along Rio Grande from mouth of Pecos River to Presidio; in Big Bend north almost to Alpine.

REMARKS Grows on barren, rocky slopes, surviving by hardly projecting above ground and by having thick, horny, brownish epidermis; water storage in thick taproot, with stem a flattened cap; root shrinks during dry seasons, pulling stem down into ground: uncactuslike appearance; blooms with fine flower when most other cacti are through blooming; one of most extreme of desert-adapted; cannot tolerate much moisture or shade. *A. fissuratus* var. *lloydii* (Rose) Marshall has higher stems, more rounded and larger in size; tubercles more rounded, with less distinct fissures, apparently found only in Mexico; difficult to find east of Big Bend, where it is fairly common.

Genus *Pediocactus* B. & R.

The genus *Pediocactus* can be characterized as follows: the stems are either single or branching sparingly; flattened, spherical, or cylindrical; usually very small but in one form up to 6 inches in diameter and height. The surface of the stem is covered with small but prominent, noncoalescent tubercles, spirally arranged. Areoles are small and entirely on the tips of the tubercles, sometimes with glands present. The spines are variable. The flowers are bell- or funnel-shaped. The ovary is naked or with two or three small scales, these sometimes having a few hairs or bristles in their axils. The outer perianth segments are fringed to entire. The fruits are green at first, often changing to tan or yellowish, and then becoming dry. They are naked or have several small scales. In shape they vary from nearly spherical to almost club-shaped. The fruits are dehiscent, opening by a ring around the apex, by a lateral slit on the upper side, or sometimes rather irregularly by both of these. Seeds are black or gray, the surfaces rough or shiny but always textured when seen under the microscope.

The members of this genus are once again cacti which fall between the major groups, the Echinocacti and the Mammillarias, overlapping each to some extent. Most technical discussions of these cacti have become involved with trying to balance the characters in which they coincide with the one group against the characters in which they agree with the other. This began even with Engelmann, who had the type species of this genus as an Echinocactus, but who said that this species, with some others, "forms a small section of Echinocacti with the appearance of Mammillarias named by Prince Salm *Theloidei*." Although he insisted that they were still "true" Echinocacti, he repeated that they "constitute the closest and most imperceptible transition to *Mammillaria* subgenus *Coryphantha*."

To show the reasons for the divergent opinions over these cacti in the past and the way they overlap both adjacent major cactus groups while actually falling outside of either one, I will mention here the most significant of the characters involved. They share with the Echinocacti the following points: the areoles are monomorphic with the flower coming at or near the tips of the tubercles; the flowers are similar to those of the Echinocacti, the ovary often with two or three tiny scales, and occasionally these have a few bristles in their axils; the fruit becomes dry and splits open—but they differ from the Echinocacti by having no ribs and by having mucilage cells, which are not found in any recognized Echinocactus. On the other hand, they share with the Mammillarias the following characters: the stems are tubercled instead of ribbed; the ovary is sometimes naked or has only two or three scales—while differing from them by producing the flowers from a monomorphic areole at the tip of the tubercle and by having dry, dehiscent fruits. In possessing mucilage cells, as Dr. Boke has pointed out, they look

toward the Echinocerei. The result of all this is that this genus is left standing with those few others which are somewhat alone, outside of any of the
major groups. Buxbaum has considered it significant, because of its peculiar
combination of characters, as an ancestor of other groups, but other scholars
have disputed his theories on this.

The members of this genus can be as exasperating to the ordinary cactophile as to the taxonomist. If it is difficult to view them in the proper sys-
tematic niche, it is even harder to view them in their native habitat. They
are all extremely retiring cacti. They are usually so well camouflaged in
their natural environment that there are places where it is more rewarding
to hunt for them by feel than by sight. And it is not easy to find their locations. With the exception of one species, they all occupy very small ranges,
several only a few miles in extent, and some are noted more for their rarity
than for anything else. Each is restricted to a particular soil type or geologic
formation, and some are associated with one other specific plant. The one
species which is more widespread is usually a high mountain inhabitant,
where only hardy collectors will come across it.

So these are especially challenging little cacti not seen by many people
and perhaps fully appreciated by only the specialist. However, they are part
of the huge group known as cacti and they contribute to its amazing diversity.

Pediocactus simpsonii var. *simpsonii* (Eng.) L. Benson
Mountain Cactus

STEMS Globose or sometimes a little elongated in growing season, usually
depressed, often almost flat in winter; to 5 in. diameter, 1–6 in. tall; almost
always single; surface covered with spirally arranged tubercles, conical or
somewhat pyramidal and ¼–⅝ in. long; light green.

AREOLES Situated on tips of tubercles, circular or nearly so; when young, at
apex of plant, large, to ³⁄₁₆ in. diameter, with much long white wool; when
older, shrink to ⅛ in. and lose most or all of wool.

SPINES 15–35 radial spines, white or whitish, rigid and straight, very slender, radiating, ¼–½ in. long, shortest and most slender at top of areole; 5–
11 widely spreading centrals on mature plants, heavier than radials, rigid,
straight or nearly so, ⅜–¾ in. long; whitish, cream-colored, or pale yellow
below, outer half darkening to brown or red-brown.

FLOWERS Bell-shaped, opening rather widely; ⅝–1 in. diameter and length;
pale pink, pale purplish, whitish, or yellowish; ovary has several small
scales near top; outer perianth segments broadly rounded, greenish with
pink to whitish, somewhat fringed, ragged, or notched edges; inner segments pink, pale, purple, whitish, or yellowish, almost linear, with pointed
tips and entire edges; yellow stamens; 5–7 yellowish stigma lobes.

FRUITS ¼–⅜ in. long; almost spherical to short-cylindrical; green, some-

Pediocactus simpsonii var. *simpsonii*. 3 inches in diameter.

times suffused with reddish, later becoming dry; when ripe, split open;
seeds gray or black, rough, ¹⁄₁₆–¹⁄₈ in. long.

RANGE Idaho, Montana, Wyoming, Nevada, Utah, and Colorado, entering
northern mountains of Arizona and New Mexico.

REMARKS Found in mountains of northern New Mexico, seldom if ever below 6,000 ft. altitude and ranging to 10,000 ft. in high Rockies; one of most
hardy forms for cold climates, but not adapted to desert conditions. Small
specimens are set apart by many under the name var. *minor*, but I have
found no consistently distinguishing character except size.

Pediocactus knowltonii. 1 inch in diameter.

Pediocactus knowltonii L. Benson
Knowlton Cactus

STEMS Very small, ½–1 in. diameter; depressed-globular or globular; less than 1½ in. tall; usually single, may form small clusters; covered by small tubercles ¹⁄₁₆–¹⁄₁₀ in. long.

AREOLES Almost circular at first, becoming elongated oval; very small, about ¹⁄₂₄ in. long; much white wool at first, shorter with age but persistent.

SPINES 18–24 radial spines, pectinate or recurving somewhat; ¹⁄₂₄–¹⁄₁₆ in. long; somewhat flattened; magnification reveals fine hairs; white, pinkish, or reddish-tan.

FLOWERS Opening widely to about ¾ in. across by about ³⁄₈ in. long; pinkish; ovary naked; outer perianth segments entire and blunt, inner segments somewhat pointed; yellow stamens; 4–5 rose-purple stigmas.

FRUITS Egg-shaped or somewhat club-shaped, about ³⁄₈ in. long, becoming tan, dry, and dehiscent; black seeds about ¹⁄₁₆ in. long.

RANGE Near Los Pinos River in northwestern New Mexico.

REMARKS Very small, very inconspicuous species; clearly a Pediocactus; no outstanding features; very rare.

Pediocactus papyracanthus (Eng.) L. Benson
Paper-Spined Cactus, Grama-Grass Cactus, Toumeya

STEMS Ovate or nearly so when young, becoming cylindrical; usually single, old plants sometimes branching; surface covered by dark green tubercles ⅛–³⁄₁₆ in. long when mature.

AREOLES Round or nearly so, very small on immature stems, to ³⁄₁₆ in. long on robust stems; with yellowish wool at first, becoming gray and short, persisting; may have 1 to several pinkish glands on upper edge.

SPINES 6–9 even radial spines, straight, rigid, flattened; less than ⅛–¼ in. long; lowermost heavier, wider, longer than others; white or gray, often snowy; 1–4 centrals, lowermost almost always present after very early stage, greatly flattened, to ¹⁄₁₀ in. wide at base, flexible, papery, twisted and curved; when young, tends to stand somewhat upward, lower down on stem may be aimed in any direction; ¾–1¼ in. long, usually mottled brown, fading to pale gray or whitish.

FLOWERS Bell-shaped, not opening very widely, whitish; ¾–1 in. long and wide; ovary usually has a few small, toothed scales, may be bare; outer perianth segments triangular, edges entire or ragged, but not fringed; midlines dark brownish, edges whitish; inner perianth segments practically white; cream-colored stamens; cream-colored style and stigma with 4–5 lobes.

FRUITS Almost spherical, ³⁄₁₆–¾ in. long, becoming tan and dry, then splitting; may have a few scales; black, shiny seeds, with fine texture under magnification; to about ⅛ in. long.

RANGE Scattered locations in western half of New Mexico and eastern Arizona.

REMARKS Among the rarest in our area; excellent camouflage; grows in open grasslands, almost always associated with grama grasses, hence common name grama-grass cactus.

Pediocactus papyracanthus. 2 inches tall.

Genus *Epithelantha* (Weber) B. & R.

Although it is developed into a number of forms in Mexico, there seems to be but one distinct species of this genus in the United States. It is a very small but unique cactus.

The whole stem of this cactus is covered with very many, very tiny tubercles—apparently the smallest tubercles of any U.S. cactus. Hiding these almost entirely from view are very many tiny spines. The growing tip of the stem is in the form of a rather distinct depression which is filled with a great deal of hairlike wool and covered over by the converging, later deciduous tips of the longer spines. This makes it very difficult to observe the formation of the tubercles, areoles, and flowers, but the way these are formed has assumed much importance and has been studied very closely. This is because taxonomically almost everything hinges upon them.

Originally Engelmann described this cactus as *Mammillaria micromeris*. In most of its characters it is a perfectly good Mammillaria. Later, however, something unusual was noticed about the cactus. It produces its flower not in the axil of the tubercle but at the top of it. Mammillarias otherwise produce their flowers from halfway down the dorsal side of the tubercles to deep in the axils.

When this was noticed, it was assumed that the flower was produced from within a single, unlengthening, monomorphic areole on the tip of the tubercle. This is the situation in the Echinocacti. Because of this difference, Weber seemed unable to come to a real conclusion about this cactus, listing it once as a Mammillaria, once as *Echinocactus micromeris*, but also coining a new name, *Epithelantha*, for it. He apparently did not officially describe this latter as the name of a new genus, however. Britton and Rose then took the name *Epithelantha* and applied it to a new and separate genus. This genus, because of the supposed production of the flower from within the spine areole, has usually been placed in the subtribe Echinocactanae, although its other features, such as the naked fruits and lack of ribs, seem to point more toward the Mammillarias.

Recently Dr. Norman H. Boke has done most thorough studies of cactus anatomy and development, and examined this species very carefully. In the course of his studies he has discovered that this cactus does not produce its flower from within a monomorphic spine areole after all. The blossom is, in fact, produced after a division of the meristem into a determinate spinous portion and a separate, indeterminate floral or vegetative meristem. This gives essentially a dimorphic areole, very different from those of the Echinocacti. It is actually more removed from the Echinocactus arrangement than is that of the many Mammillarias often set apart as Coryphanthas because they usually have monomorphic areoles elongating toward the axils instead of dimorphic areoles. The situation in this cactus can be interpreted as good dimorphic Mammillarian areoles in which the floral meristems merely remain at the tops of the tubercles. Boke notes Moran's remark that for many years no one has linked *Epithelantha* to *Mammillaria*, but Boke's conclusion is that a strong case for doing just this can be built.

This possibility is very attractive, since the cactus is in so many ways a better Mammillaria than many of the Mammillarias themselves. It does seem that the work of Boke has made it impossible to classify it any longer with the Echinocacti and that it points it toward the Mammillarias. Yet the fact remains that its flower is produced at the top of the tubercle, which is a trait not found in other members of that genus, and this difference in itself may be justification for keeping the cactus separate from the genus *Mammillaria*.

As a separate genus based upon this cactus, *Epithelantha* seems, like *Lophophora* and *Ariocarpus*, to fall somewhere between the two major genera, *Echinocactus* and *Mammillaria*. It is worth noting in this connection that the Epithelanthas possess alkaloids similar to those of *Lophophora* and *Ariocarpus*, which seems to link them in some way.

I, therefore, leave this genus in this difficult middle area. Buxbaum has made elaborate schemes in attempting to relate these plants phylogenetically, but others have pointed out that entirely different schemes could be devised which would appear just as logical as his, if different assumptions were made to start with. I am not primarily interested here in such phylogenetic schemes, so I merely list this as a small genus because it seems in some way a separate entity among the cacti.

Epithelantha micromeris (Eng.) Weber
Button Cactus, Mulato

STEMS Spherical or spheroid, usually with depressed top; usually ½–1 in. diameter, sometimes to 1¾ in.; usually single, occasionally forming small clusters; covered with tiny wartlike or somewhat conical tubercles about ¹⁄₂₀ in. long.

AREOLES Dimorphic; small spinous areole at tip of tubercle; much long hair, later lost; flower comes from separate, adjacent floral areole, also at top of tubercle.

SPINES About 20–40 slender, rigid, more or less hairy spines per areole; 1 series on immature plants, several series when mature; outermost stronger, upper ones often ¼–⁵⁄₁₆ in. long when first produced; outer half somewhat club-shaped, with acute tips, forming incurving tuft of long spines over shorter spines and hairs of new growth in more or less depressed top of mature plant; enlarged outer sections break off, shed hairs, leaving only short spines about ¹⁄₁₆–⅛ in. long; white, sometimes with faintly gray tips.

FLOWERS Very small, about ³⁄₁₆–¼ in. long, ⅛–³⁄₁₆ in. wide, only partly ris-

Epithelantha micromeris. 1½ inches in diameter.

ing above long wool and spines in top of plant, only partly opening; pale, whitish-pink; ovary rather clavate, greenish-yellow, naked; 3–5 outer perianth segments with greenish-brown or pinkish midlines and pinkish-white, somewhat notched or eroded edges, sometimes bearing a few short cilia; 5 inner petals whitish-pink with entire edges; greenish-white stamens; greenish-white style and stigma, with 3–4 lobes.

FRUITS Club-shaped, ⅜–¾ in. long by ⅛–³⁄₁₆ in. diameter, red, fleshy, naked, with perianth remains persisting; black seeds, about ¹⁄₁₆ in. (1½ mm) long.

RANGE Great arc west from Medina County, Texas, past mouths of Devil's and Pecos rivers, into Brewster and Pecos counties in Big Bend, then northwest into mountains of southern New Mexico.

REMARKS Tiny, tidy buttons, almost perfectly round; growing on exposed ridges and hillsides and in riverbeds with extensive root systems to anchor against water. A separate form, var. *greggii*, is larger, densely clustering, with clumps of 10–20 heads and beautiful, larger rose-colored flowers, probably found only in Mexico. Some have separated out the most robust Texas individuals as *E. bokei* L. Benson, but they intergrade, and I cannot see this as justified.

Genus *Mammillaria* Haw.

The members of this genus are for the most part comparatively small or sometimes extremely tiny cacti. The plant stems vary in different species from depressed and almost flat to globular or sometimes even columnar in shape and are often referred to as heads. In some species these remain single, while in many others they multiply from the base to become caespitose, one individual thus sometimes forming a large clump of these heads. In a few species the stems may branch sparingly from higher up on the stem.

Each stem is entirely covered by a system of nipplelike projections called tubercles. These are usually arranged in spiral rows but in a few cases are more loosely organized. These tubercles are usually cylindrical or conical but sometimes may have more or less quadrangular bases and sometimes are mildly keeled below.

Very early the knowledge of cacti progressed to the point where it became obvious that the huge assortment of forms they present could not be left in the one catchall genus *Cactus* L. By the middle of the eighteenth century Miller felt it necessary to divide the lot. By using the four old names of Turnefort, he separated out many cacti into *Pereskia*, *Opuntia*, and *Cereus*, leaving the rest in the genus *Cactus*. By 1812 even this narrowed genus *Cactus* was too broad, and Haworth abandoned it entirely, erecting five new genera out of it, one of which was *Mammillaria*, including all of the unjointed, tubercled cacti.

Discoveries of new species continued, and as even this genus came to include a myriad of forms, the process of subdivision began all over again. Engelmann proposed two sections of the genus *Mammillaria*. He had section *Coryphantha*, which he characterized as having grooved tubercles, green fruits, and yellow or brown seeds, and section *Eumammillaria* with grooveless tubercles, scarlet fruits, and black or blackish seeds. Lemaire very soon elevated the section *Coryphantha* to a separate genus. Many concurred—although not all, as for instance Berger, who left this group as a subdivision which he rechristened *Eu-coryphantha*.

This was the situation, rather uneasy and not wholly satisfactory to anybody, when Britton and Rose presented their major study, and they swept it all away by dividing the old genus *Mammillaria* into a whole spectrum of new and much smaller genera. Their names are in constant use and are most familiar to us today. The old section *Coryphantha* became the genera *Coryphantha*, *Escobaria*, *Neobesseya*, and others, and the old genus *Mammillaria* was eliminated as the rest of its forms were separated out into new genera such as *Dolichothele* and *Neomammillaria*. It seemed that the process of subdivision had been carried to its logical conclusion by this courageous leap of Britton and Rose, and almost the whole cactophile world adopted their array of new genera with surprising speed and many sighs of relief.

But the genera of Britton and Rose were not to go unchallenged for long. They were assaulted from two directions. As early as 1931 Fosberg questioned the basis for separating *Escobaria* from *Coryphantha* and concluded that the two should be recombined. This was an early expression of a desire for simplification by recombination. Many people had already found the genera of Britton and Rose so hard to tell from one another that it was often more difficult to determine the genus of a specimen directly than it was to determine its species first; and some had noted that the distinguishing characteristics of these genera were not always consistently present.

But at the same time the trend to still more subdivision was continued by various students. J. Pinkney Hester conducted very detailed studies of the seeds of cacti and concluded that their variations did not well uphold the alignment of Britton and Rose's genera but actually, if regarded as diagnostic characters, would require a new realignment. As a result, in 1941, he shifted some species from one to another of these genera and erected such new genera as *Escobesseya*.

Backeberg had already started subdividing further with his subgenera *Subgymnocarpae* and *Neocoryphantha*. Buxbaum conducted large studies of the cacti and proposed his own new subgenera, such as *Pseudocoryphantha*. He also proposed major theoretical schemes of cactus evolution which would appear to indicate radical new alignments of the species in this group. Thousands of words have been written concerning Buxbaum's phylogenetic theories, but we do not need to study them here, because no one has yet actually followed his lead and there has been no essentially new scheme for classifying this group since Britton and Rose.

What we do have at the present time are two opposing philosophies of classification giving two different concepts of this group, just as they do of the Echinocacti. One considers very small differences in plants to be adequate bases for establishing genera, resulting in lists of very slightly varying microgenera. This attitude is well expressed in Backeberg's major work, where all of Britton and Rose's genera are perpetuated and even some new ones added. The other attitude is the more conservative one that a genus should be a major group based upon some rather obvious and very fundamental differences. This attitude regards the newer genera based on very small differences as no more than sections or subgenera or, at most, microgenera of an entirely different level from such larger plant genera as, for instance, *Euphorbia*. This approach had expression in Benson's *Arizona Cacti*, where all of these proposed genera were recombined once again into the original genus *Mammillaria*. But Benson has reversed himself completely in his latest work and set out a whole array of microgenera once again.

Every serious cactus student is faced today with the battle between these opposing views, and even the amateur is affected by it, since, in order to be conversant, he or she often has to remember two or even more names for each cactus.

It cannot be said that either view is established at this time. The present study does not presume to answer a major taxonomic question such as this. It is not even addressed to such a purpose. I would have preferred to avoid the issue entirely, but under the circumstances even to list a series of species is to take sides.

Since a decision was thrust upon me, I wished to make it as intelligently as possible, so I have studied the arguments for each view and then applied to the problem the most recent evidence to come to my attention. After the most exhaustive study of which I am capable, I feel constrained to follow here the recombination of these cacti under the genus *Mammillaria* and to consider this genus in the older and larger sense. The result of research reported since the publication of the last major work on these cacti has figured largely in my decision, so it may be of value to mention that newer evidence here.

Most significantly, the old distinction between those plants with grooved tubercles and those with grooveless tubercles which prompted Engelmann to make the first division of the group into two sections, and which is still so much emphasized that all artificial keys use it, seems to have failed us. Dr. Norman H. Boke, in a series of very detailed studies of cactus shoot form and development, has recently shown that both *Coryphantha erecta* and *C. clava*, two common Mexican species, may have grooved and grooveless tubercles on the same mature heads at the same time or may change the form of their growth back and forth from the one to the other. This would appear to make it impossible to classify these particular species in either the proposed genus *Coryphantha* or *Neomammillaria* and to make it possible for a given specimen to fulfill the characteristics of both of these genera at once, which would seem to cast real doubt upon the divisions themselves.

In terms more technical but more meaningful to the botanist, the grooved group has areoles monomorphic, which means producing from a single meristem not only both vegetative structures (leaf primordia and spines) but also the later reproductive structures (flowers and branches), while the grooveless forms have areoles dimorphic, with two separate meristems, one producing only vegetative structures at the summit of the tubercle and the other producing only reproductive structures, usually at the axil of the tubercle. This distinction appeared at first to be an essential one, dividing the whole group handily, but here again Boke was able to show that in the two species mentioned above, the areoles may be either monomorphic or dimorphic on the same adult head of the same specimen.

Since these distinctions have broken down, there apparently remains no character by which the large group formerly known as genus *Mammillaria* can be divided into two major subdivisions. Such things as sepals fringed versus sepals entire, fruit green at maturity versus fruit red at maturity, fruit with a few scales versus fruit naked, and details of seed form all show exceptions on one side or the other in all major subdivisions which have been proposed.

But what about the status of the array of small genera erected within this large group of tubercled cacti? As already mentioned, the division into *Coryphantha* and *Escobaria* was challenged almost immediately by Fosberg. The distinguishing character usually given of green fruit on the one hand and red fruit on the other obviously does not work, because the fruits of some Coryphanthas become brownish or reddish when very ripe and those of several Escobarias remain green barely flushed with apricot on the sunny side. Nor is seed color always reliable to separate these two proposed groups. One searches in vain for a valid reason why Fosberg has not been followed and why these two groups have been allowed to stand so long in most of the literature.

To make a long story short, all other distinguishing characters proposed for these microgenera have proved as uncertain. We have, therefore, been left with only such quantitative characters as long tubercles versus short tubercles, tubercles grooved all the way versus tubercles grooved more or less of the way, flowers predominantly yellow versus flowers brownish through pink to purple, and so on, which hardly seem adequate to distinguish genera—and there are exceptions to all of them anyway. Attempts to separate on this sort of basis have resulted in a constant shifting of species from one to the other genus and finally in the proposal of *Escobaria* subgenus *Pseudocoryphantha* Buxbaum and subgenus *Neocoryphantha* Backbg., as well as of genus *Lepidocoryphantha* Backbg., for those which burst out of the closely drawn genera.

The other genera which Britton and Rose proposed for this group fare little better. We have seen that monomorphic versus dimorphic areoles and grooved versus ungrooved tubercles will not divide them. Neither will flower color, since we have the whole range of colors in the proposed genus *Coryphantha*, in *Neobesseya*, and in Britton and Rose's strictly drawn *Neomammillaria*. Fringed versus nonfringed sepals and even various degrees of fringing in the same species are found in both *Coryphantha* and *Neomammillaria*. Seed form fails also, with both *Escobaria* and *Neomammillaria* showing the whole range of seed coats, shapes, and hilum positions so completely that Buxbaum has to theorize parallel evolution within each of these groups because of it.

It seems that there are no characters left strong enough upon which to erect genera and that the whole group is best considered one genus, as originally conceived. Boke's judgment after his research would seem justified:

> In any event, it is my opinion that the discovery of a combination of areole monomorphism and areole dimorphism in *Coryphantha clava* and *C. erecta* weakens one of the principal distinctions between the Mammillarias (sensu lato) and other tubercled cacti. I think that it also indicates a cautious, conservative approach in delimiting genera in these cacti.

Those who can take the larger view will find in the genus *Mammillaria* a rich and diverse group of cacti presenting almost every sort of interesting variation on the theme of the small, tubercled cactus body. As a group they present all of the challenges in collecting, classifying, and culturing cacti which the most ardent cactophile can desire.

For those who are fascinated by the Britton and Rose type of genus divisions and who want to concern themselves with this sort of thing, as well as for those who may be familiar with only those plant names, I have added for each form described here the name which Benson uses in his microgenus system.

Key to the Mammillarias

1a. Diameter of stems on mature plants 2 inches or more and the length of the tubercles ¼ inch or more—2.

2a. Stems on mature plants hemispherical to flattened, always as broad as they are tall on normal specimens and usually much greater in diameter than in height—3.

3a. Areoles always dimorphic, with the spinous portion at the tip of the tubercle and the floral portion in the axil of the tubercle and having no groove connecting them—4.

4a. Central spines 1 or 2 per areole, short and always straight; outer perianth segments entire—5.

5a. Color of the plant surface deep green or blue-green; tubercles firm and their bases quadrangular and more or less keeled; flowers whitish, rose, or pinkish—6.

6a. Radial spines 5 to 9; tubercles strongly keeled and to ⅞ inch long; plant to 12 inches in diameter   —*M. meiacantha.*

6b. Radial spines 9 to 26; tubercles with bases quandrangular but not so strongly keeled; plants to about 5 inches in diameter— 7.

7a. Radial spines 20 to 26   —*M. heyderi* var. *heyderi.*

7b. Radial spines 9 to 20—8.

8a. Radial spines 14 to 20   —*M. heyderi* var. *applanata.*

8b. Radial spines 9 to 13   —*M. heyderi* var. *hemisphaerica.*

5b. Color of plant surface light yellowish-green; tubercles flabby and egg-shaped to cylindrical; flowers brightly yellow

—*M. sphaerica.*

4b. Central spines 1 to 4 and at least some of them hooked; outer perianth segments fringed—9.

9a. Radial spines 8 to 15; flowers bright purple with about 20 inner perianth segments and 11 yellow stigma lobes   —*M. wrightii.*

9b. Radial spines 14 to 22; flowers paler pinkish-purple with about 40 inner perianth segments and 5 to 9 green stigma lobes

—*M. wilcoxii.*

3b. Areoles normally and predominantly monomorphic and prolonged into a groove extending halfway or more toward the axil of the tubercle on mature stems, with the flower produced in the end of this groove—10.

10a. Tubercles equal in size or nearly so on a given stem and arranged regularly; central spines 0 or 1 per areole and ¼ to ⅝ inch long; flowers greenish-yellow, brownish, or pink; fruits scarlet when ripe—11.

11a. Flowers greenish, greenish-yellow, or brownish, sometimes streaked with pink; the outer perianth segments fringed
—*M. similis*.

11b. Flowers pure pink without stripes or zones of various colors; the outer perianth segments not fringed but entire
—*M. roseiflora*.

10b. Tubercles unequal in size and shape on a given stem and arranged irregularly; centrals 1 to 4 per areole and ¾ to 2 inches long; flowers purplish or rose-pink; fruits remaining greenish when ripe   —*M. runyonii*.

2b. Stems on mature plants spherical to columnar, usually taller than they are broad and often markedly so—12.

12a. Having at least 1 and often several hooked central spines; areoles dimorphic with the spinous portion at the tip of the tubercle and the floral portion in the axil of the tubercle, the two never connected by a groove   —*M. microcarpa*.

12b. Without hooked centrals; areoles mostly or entirely monomorphic, the flower always produced at the end of the undivided areole which is prolonged into a groove running at least part of the way down the tubercle—13.

13a. Having fleshy taproots and 2 to 8 central spines to 2¼ inches long; flowers purplish   —*M. macromeris*.

13b. Having no fleshy taproots and having central spines not over 1⅝ inches long—14.

14a. Having 1 brownish gland in the groove formed by the elongated areole   —*M. bella*.

14b. Without glands—15.

15a. Centrals 0 to 4 on mature plants—16.

16a. Centrals present—17.

17a. Centrals not hooked—18.

18a. Flowers yellow, orange-yellow, or yellow with red centers—19.

19a. Stems single or very sparingly branched; flowers yellow or orange-yellow, sometimes reddish when fading, but not yellow with red centers; radials and centrals to at least ¾ inch long—20.

20a. Plants large and robust, to at least 6 inches tall
and 4 inches or more in diameter when old; tubercles ½ to 1 inch long—21.
21a. Radials 6 to 16; outer perianth segments lacerated and more or less fringed
—*M. scheeri* (in part).
21b. Radials 14 to 28; outer perianth segments entire and smooth　　　　—*M. scolymoides.*
20b. Plants small, to a maximum of 3 inches tall or
wide; tubercles ⅜ to ½ inch long
—*M. echinus* (in part).
19b. Stems greatly branching by new heads arising from
the grooves in old tubercles all around their bases
to form large masses of often dozens of stems;
flowers yellow with red centers
—*M. sulcata* (in part).
18b. Flowers pale pink to deep rose-purple
—*M. ramillosa.*
17b. 1 central hooked　　　　—*M. scheeri* (in part).
16b. Centrals absent—22.
22a. Tubercles over ½ inch long; radials ⅜ to ⅝ inch long;
flowers yellow with red centers
—*M. sulcata* (stunted or atypical plant).
22b. Tubercles ½ inch or less long; flowers not yellow with
red centers—23.
23a. Radials ⅜ to 1 inch long; flowers yellow
—*M. echinus* (stunted or atypical plant).
23b. Radials only ⅛ to ½ inch long; flowers light purple
—*M. hesteri.*
15b. Centrals 4 to 17 on mature plants—24.
24a. Fruits green or greenish when ripe, sometimes becoming
brownish or apricot on part of the surface when very ripe,
but never bright red—25.
25a. Radial spines 12 to 20—26.
26a. Flowers rose-purple to deep purple and 1 inch or more
long and wide; stigma lobes 7 to 12; at least some of
the spines over ½ inch long—27.
27a. Tubercles ⅜ to 1 inch long; centrals pale mottled,
and brown-tipped, but never blackish over half or
more of their lengths; flowers 1½ to 2½ inches
across when fully opened; seeds 1½ to 1¾ millimeters long with ventral hila—28.
28a. Radials to only ⅝ inch or so long; stigma lobes 7
or 8 in number and rose-purple in color; seeds

about 1½ millimeters long, dark brown, with the
hila small   —*M. vivipara* var. *vivipara*.

28b. Radials to around 1 inch long; stigma lobes 8 to
10 in number and white in color; seeds about 1¾
millimeters long, light brown in color, with the
hila large   —*M. vivipara* var. *arizonica*.

27b. Tubercles ½ inch or less long; centrals very dark
brown or purplish-black over one-half to all of their
lengths; flowers 1 to 1½ inches across when fully
opened; seeds 2 millimeters long with subbasal
hila   —*M. vivipara* var. *borealis*.

26b. Flowers white, pink, or very pale rose in color and
about ¾ inch long; stigma lobes 5 or 6; all spines
½ inch or less long   —*M. varicolor*.

25b. Radial spines 20 to at least 60—29.

29a. Spines strong and somewhat flexible; seeds 1 to 2½
millimeters long—30.

30a. Flowers pink to brilliantly purple or else reddish-
purple; radial spines white or white-tipped light
brown—31.

31a. Flowers 2 inches or more long and broad; radials
20 to 30; seeds very dark brown—32.

32a. Tubercles about ¾ inch long; centrals 4 to 7
and straw-colored or whitish; flowers deep
purple with 7 to 9 rose-colored, blunt stigma
lobes; seeds oval, brown, 2 to 2½ millimeters
long, with the surfaces very finely pitted
                              —*M. vivipara* var. *radiosa*.

32b. Tubercles about ½ inch long; centrals 6 to 12
and purple-black or dark brown; flowers
reddish-purple with 6 to 10 pure white or
slightly pinkish, somewhat pointed stigma
lobes; seeds 2½ to 3 millimeters long, markedly reniform and much flattened, with their
surfaces shiny smooth and unpitted
                              —*M. fragrans*.

31b. Flowers to only 1 inch or only slightly more in
width and length; radials 20 to at least 60; seeds
lighter brown —*M. vivipara* var. *neo-mexicana*.

30b. Flowers yellowish suffused with purple; radial
spines straw-colored with reddish tips
                              —*M. vivipara* var. *deserti*.

29b. Spines heavy but very brittle and glassy, breaking at

slight pressure; seeds 1 millimeter long
      —*M. albicolumnaria.*
24b. Fruits bright red or scarlet when ripe—33.
   33a. Stems hardly over 2 inches in diameter; length of radial
      spines ⅛ to ⅜ inch; 4 to 7 centrals with 1 conspicuous,
      heavy central standing porrect or turned downward a
      little; flowers over 1 inch in diameter, opening widely,
      lavender-white or very pale purplish in color, with 5 or 6
      white stigma lobes   —*M. tuberculosa* (in part).
   33b. Stems to 2¾ inches in diameter; radials ½ to 1 inch
      long; 7 to 17 centrals without a conspicuous, heavy,
      porrect one; flowers ¾ inch or less in diameter and not
      opening widely, pinkish in color streaked with brown
      and with 4 or 5 very green stigma lobes
            —*M. dasyacantha.*
1b. Diameter of stems on mature plants less than 2 inches and length of tubercles ¼ inch or less—34.
34a. Radial spines 13 to 18; spines club-shaped, thick almost their whole
length and coming to a point very suddenly   —*M. nellieae.*
34b. Radial spines 20 or more; spines not club-shaped, but awl-
shaped, bristlelike or hairlike—35.
  35a. Centrals present—36.
   36a. All spines rigid—37.
    37a. Having a fleshy taproot—38.
     38a. Single or sparingly clustering; radials 24 to 36 in number; tu-
       bercles grooved all of the way from the tips to the axils by the
       greatly elongated, monomorphic areoles; stigma lobes bright
       yellow   —*M. duncanii.*
     38b. Densely clustering with dozens of heads in a typical plant;
       radials 40 to 85 in number; tubercles either ungrooved or
       grooved to around one-half of their lengths; stigma lobes pure
       white   —*M. leei* (in part).
    37b. Roots all fibrous—39.
     39a. Stems single to sparingly branching; 1 to 2 inches thick and
       standing well over 3 inches tall when old—40.
      40a. Centrals from very bulbous bases; flowers coming from the
        sides of the stems, ½ inch or less in diameter and dark red in
        color; tubercles not grooved   —*M. pottsii.*
      40b. Centrals not conspicuously bulbous; flowers produced at
        the summit of the stem, 1 inch or more in diameter and
        clear lavender or very pale purplish in color without darker
        midlines   —*M. tuberculosa* (in part).
     39b. Stems branching greatly into large masses, but each stem no

more than 1¼ inches thick or 3 inches tall—41.

41a. Radial spines 20 to 30, gray or straw-colored tipped with brown; centrals 5 to 10, ⅜ to ⅝ inch long and dark brown, red-brown, or black for most of their lengths; stigma lobes green —*M. roberti.*

41b. Radial spines 24 to 85 and all white in color; centrals 6 to 22, ⅜ inch or less in length; stigma lobe⌐ white—42.

    42a. Radials 24 to 45 —*M. sneedii.*

    42b. Radials 40 to 85 —*M. leei* (in part).

36b. Radial spines soft, flexible, and hairlike —*M. multiceps.*

35b. Centrals absent; radials 40 to 80 in number, slender and bristlelike but rigid—43.

43a. Spines pubescent under magnification

    —*M. lasiacantha* var. *lasiacantha.*

43b. Spines smooth and naked under magnification

    —*M. lasiacantha* var. *denudata.*

Mammillaria scheeri Muehlenpf.
(Benson: *Coryphantha scheeri*)
Long-Tubercled Coryphantha, Needle "Mulee"

STEMS Spherical, becoming egg-shaped or somewhat conical when old; to 9 in. tall by 5½ in. diameter; usually single, sometimes a few branches at base; bright green or yellowish-green with large, rather soft, spreading tubercles, arising from broad bases often ¾ in. or more across, becoming cylindrical above, ¾–1½ in. long.

AREOLES Monomorphic; when young very woolly; consisting of roundish spinous portion at tip of tubercle and long, narrow, deep, groovelike portion running part or all of the way down upper side of tubercle when mature; often 1 or more brownish glands in groove.

SPINES 8–16 stout to very stout radial spines, radiating or slightly spreading outward; ½ to about 1¼ in. long, lower ones heaviest and longest; round, from slightly bulbous bases; 1–5 centrals, ¾–1½ in. long, stouter than radials; 1 very stout, porrect, straight, curved downward slightly, or with hooked tip; other centrals more like radials, spreading upward in front of them; when growing, reddish or brownish with blackish tips; remain yellowish or become ashy gray.

FLOWERS About 2 in. long and wide; orange, bronze, or bronzy-yellow, darkening to reddish as wilt; outer perianth segments lacerated, edges may approach true ciliated fringe; 20 or so inner segments, narrow below, broadest near tips, often somewhat pointed and toothed; orange stamens; short style; 6–10 yellowish or flesh-colored stigma lobes.

FRUITS Egg-shaped to almost club-shaped, 1–1½ in. long with smooth greenish surface; shiny, smooth, dark red-brown seeds; about ⅛ in. long, flattened ovate.

RANGE Pecos River west into Arizona and Chihuahua, Mexico.

REMARKS Largest in bulk of Mammillarias in our area; gives impression of a barrel cactus; nowhere common; adapted to dry, sunny conditions; beautiful flowers of unusual color. Closely related to *M. robustispina* Schott., which has stouter and fewer spines, but which I have only seen in Mexico and Arizona.

Mammillaria scolymoides Scheidweiler

STEMS Single, spherical to conical, 6+ in. tall, 4 in. diameter; deep bluish-green, some grayish glaucescence; tubercles to 1 in. long, bases as wide as long, firm, overlapping upward.

AREOLES When mature, prolonged beyond spinous part into deep grooves extending to bases of tubercles; bare except for tuft of wool at base in axil of tubercle.

Mammillaria scheeri. 6 inches in diameter.

SPINES 14–28 even radial spines, ¾–1⅛ in. long with smallest ones bunched into bundle at top of areole; 1–4 heavy centrals to about 1 in. long; usually 3 turned upward and lower 1 curving downward; all yellowish and hornlike when young, then gray with dark tips.

FLOWERS About 2 in. long; clear yellow, later darkening to reddish; no red center; about 20 outer petals, short, pointed, with entire edges; about 35 inner petals, similar but longer, wider; pinkish filaments; pale orange-yellow anthers; 9 rough, yellowish stigma lobes about ¼ in. long.

FRUITS Not seen.

RANGE Higher elevations of Big Bend, most common in Glass Mountains near Alpine, Texas.

REMARKS Small specimens almost indistinguishable from *M. echinus* except for longer and heavier spines and tubercles; *M. scolymoides* grows at least twice as large as *M. echinus*, as tall as *M. scheeri* but a little smaller in diameter. It is close to the Mexican species, *M. cornifera* DC.

Mammillaria scolymoides. 3¼ inches in diameter.

Mammillaria echinus Eng.
(Benson: *Coryphantha cornifera* var. *echinus*)

STEMS Usually spherical, sometimes egg-shaped or conical when old; almost always single but may branch at base when old to form small clumps; 2–3 in. tall when mature; covered with very firm, conical tubercles about ⅜–½ in. long, turning upward and somewhat overlapping those above.

AREOLES At first nearly round; when mature, normally elongated by groovelike extension part way or all the way to base of tubercle; flower produced from end of groove; white or brownish wool in grooves at tip of plant; on sides grooves are bare except for tuft of wool at base.

SPINES 16–30 even radial spines around edge of each areole; ⅜–1 in. long; more numerous and bunched at upper edge; flat against plant or curving back a little, interlocking with spines of neighboring areoles; slender, very rigid, round or sometimes slightly flattened; when young, yellowish and partly translucent, usually with black or dark brown tips; gray when old; 3–4 much thicker centrals from center of typical adult areole, with enlarged bases, round, about ½–¾ in. long, usually gray with black tips; occasionally black almost to bases; 2–3 centrals turned upward, lying directly on upper radials; lowest central always straight out from center of areole; thick and conspicuous, usually perfectly straight, sometimes curved downward; when immature or in poor growing conditions may lack centrals.

FLOWERS At least 3 in. across, to 2 in. tall; very clear sulphur-yellow; outer petals narrow, brownish-green, with yellowish, smooth edges; 20–30 clear yellow inner petals about ⅜–⅝ in. wide, pointed, edges slightly ragged toward tips; rose-pink filaments; bright orange anthers; style about length of stamens; 10–12 rough, cream-colored stigma lobes about ³⁄₁₆–¼ in. long.

FRUITS Oval or egg-shaped, to nearly 1 in. long; light green; flower remains persist; dark brown seeds, smooth, kidney-shaped, about 1½ mm long.

RANGE Mouth of Pecos River to level of Fort Stockton, then southwest into mountains of lower Big Bend, Texas.

REMARKS Very common in rather limited area of west Texas; small sphere or cone 2–3 in. high; completely covered and enclosed by spines; 1 heavy central to 1 in. long, straight out on each areole, perpendicular to surface of plant; resembles sea urchin, hence the name. *M. pectinata* Eng. was an atypical growth form without centrals, which is occasionally seen.

Mammillaria sulcata Eng.
(Benson: *Coryphantha sulcata*)
Nipple Cactus, Finger Cactus, Pineapple Cactus

STEMS Rapidly and densely clustering, new stems growing from grooves on old tubercles around base of plant; old plants often several feet across, with

Mammillaria echinus. Stem 2¼ inches in diameter.

dozens of heads; stems spherical, usually with somewhat flattened tops, often wider than tall; to 3 in. across and about 1½–3 in. tall; dark green and soft, divided into tubercles to about ¾ in. long, nearly cylindrical, with bases somewhat broadened when old; curving upward to overlap slightly or standing out from each other; very soft, often sagging from lack of water.

AREOLES Practically round, very woolly; when mature, elongated by formation of groovelike extensions reaching axils of tubercles, filled with much white or yellowish wool; almost bare when old.

SPINES 8–15 even radial spines ⅜–⅝ in. long; round and rather heavy; yellowish and partly translucent, then gray with black or dark red-brown tips; 0–3 centrals per areole; if 1, perpendicular to stem; if 2, 1 perpendicular or downward, the other turned upward; if 3, 1 perpendicular or down-turning, other 2 spreading upward, sometimes almost against upper radials; centrals same length as radials but heavier; usually same color, occasionally streaked with black almost to bases on upper sides.

FLOWERS 2–3 in. across, 1–2 in. tall; greenish-yellow to dark golden-yellow; centers usually very bright red, rarely paler brownish-red or greenish; 20–30 outer petals, short and greenish with yellowish, smooth edges; about 25 inner petals, long and rather narrow from narrow red bases, upper part golden, same width as outer petals, tapering gradually to definite point; upper margins entire or sparingly ragged and toothed; bright red filaments, except greenish in rare flowers without red; yellow anthers; style equal in length to stamens or somewhat longer, greenish, ending in 7–10 yellow, greenish-yellow, or cream-colored lobes.

FRUITS Oblong, green, about ¾ in. long; light brown, pitted seeds, about ¹⁄₁₆ in. (1½ mm) long.

RANGE South-central Texas, within triangle drawn from Houston to Fort Worth to mouth of Pecos River.

REMARKS Not striking in growth form; found under junipers, oaks, and brush plants of limestone hills at edge of Edwards Plateau; large flowers, usually of satiny golden color with red centers and sheaves of red filaments; very rarely greenish-yellow flower with red center almost completely lacking; apparently the basis for *M. wissmannii* Hild. ex K. Schum and *M. similis* var. *robustior* Eng. Not strictly a desert species so can be cultivated easily; can tolerate more water and humidity; does well in limestone soil.

Mammillaria ramillosa (Cutak) Weniger
(Benson: *Coryphantha ramillosa*)

ROOTS Entirely fibrous.

STEMS Single or very sparingly clustering; to 3½ in. diameter; spherical or nearly so; tubercles about ¾ in. long, tapering from very flattened bases, wider than tubercles are tall; tubercles firm, regularly arranged, overlap upward very much; dark green.

Mammillaria sulcata. 4⅛ inches in diameter.

Mammillaria ramillosa. 3¼ inches in diameter.

AREOLES Monomorphic, becoming linear and extending as grooves to axils of tubercles; woolly at first, bare when mature except for small tuft of wool at end of each groove in axil of tubercle.

SPINES 14–20 slender, even radial spines ⅜ to about 1 in. long; flattened, usually curving and twisted; gray, often with darker tips; 4 centrals, also slender, but round, 1–1⅝ in. long, gray mottled with brown, spreading and curving in all directions; radials pinkish when growing; centrals wine-colored.

FLOWERS Pale pink to deep rose-purple; about 2½ in. long and 2 in. wide; spines prevent full opening; outer petals from small, green scales on flower tube to greenish-purple, linear, unfringed segments; inner petals about 1 in. long, to 3/16 in. wide; lower half white, upper half pink to rose-purple; white filaments; pale orange anthers; style about length of stamens; 6–7 stigma lobes ⅛–¼ in. long.

FRUITS ¾–1 in. long; oval or egg-shaped; green, covered with minute white or silvery, hairlike scales, giving silvery sheen; old flower parts persist; brown seeds, less than ¹⁄₁₆ in. (1 mm) long; very broad above with flattened sides below, long, narrow point of attachment toward end of ventral side.

RANGE Southeastern corner of Brewster County, Texas, and downstream from Mariscal Canyon along Rio Grande in Big Bend.

REMARKS Vegetative characters like Coryphanthas, but purple flower similar to *M. macromeris*; distinguished from *M. macromeris* by firm, compact, spherical, squatty stems; *M. macromeris* more cylindrical, with longer, looser, flabbier tubercles; *M. ramillosa* has more slender spines, especially round centrals; small fibrous roots, instead of large taproot, never forms large carpets of plants; single or may cluster sparingly; significance of minute hairs on fruit surface unknown; grows on limestone hills. This species is on federal endangered species list.

Mammillaria macromeris Eng.
(Benson: *Coryphantha macromeris*)
Long Mamma

ROOTS Long, fleshy taproots.

STEMS Usually short columns to about 4 in. tall, sometimes to 8 in.; to about 3 in. thick; usually clustering by formation of new stems from grooves on lower tubercles, forming flat mats or occasionally hemispherical mounds; to several feet across; very soft, flabby, long tubercles standing upright at top of stem but usually flattened, curving upward or standing at angles on sides of stems; tubercles ¾–1½ in. long; cylindrical; dark green.

AREOLES Deep groove usually runs about halfway down length of tubercle and sometimes all the way to axil; groove is linear extension of areole forward from spinous portion; flowers or new shoots arise within groove.

SPINES 10–18 slender radial spines ⅝–2 in. long, the upper ones usually longest; gray, sometimes mottled with pale brown; flattened and ridged, usually twisted and curved; 2–8 heavier centrals on mature plants, 1–2¼ in. long, spreading in all directions from center of areole; mottled brown, dark brown, purplish, or black; angled and often ridged, straight or twisted, bulbous bases.

FLOWERS Light purple or pinkish; 2 in. tall and wide; prevented from opening wider by long spines; green ovary has several white-edged, fringed scales; 20–30 outer petals short, narrow, greenish-brown with pink, fringed edges; 20–25 inner petals about 1¼ in. long, ³⁄₁₆ in. wide; midlines deep pink, edges almost white; edges rough and often fringed; ends pointed, toothed, and notched; rose-colored filaments; pale orange anthers; style a little longer

Mammillaria macromeris. Young plant, not yet clustered. 3 inches tall.

than stamens; 7–10 rough, white stigma lobes about ³⁄₁₆ in. long, slender, each with smooth, pinkish point like soft spine on end.

FRUITS Almost round or broadly egg-shaped, ⅝–1 in. long; greenish; seeds practically spherical, light brown, smooth.

RANGE Southern New Mexico into Mexico and southeast along Rio Grande to Rio Grande City, Texas.

REMARKS Very common around Las Cruces, New Mexico, easily found near Presidio, Texas; sporadic occurrence elsewhere. Grows on stony crests and sides of low hills, under light shade of shrubs and trees; may form large mats. Remarkable for long, soft, loosely standing tubercles; buds new stems from middle of grooves of old tubercles; very variable; smaller in eastern part of range; with few centrals. Grows very well with perfect drainage and enough heat and sunlight; needs room to develop long taproot.

Mammillaria runyonii. 4 inches in diameter.

Mammillaria runyonii (B. & R.)
(Benson: *Coryphantha macromeris* var. *runyonii*)
Runyon's Coryphantha, Dumpling Cactus

ROOTS Large, succulent, carrot-shaped taproot.

STEMS Highly caespitose by producing many irregular stems from top of taproot, forming mass to 18+ in. across; irregular heads to about 2 in. tall, 1½ in. thick; tubercles, at any angle, about ⅜–¾ in. long; very soft, tapering from very broad bases, often wider than tubercle is long.

AREOLES Spinous portion small and practically circular; when mature, prolonged in form of groove running about halfway down tubercle but never to axil; flower produced from end of short groove.

SPINES 3–11 even radial spines, usually ¼–½ in. long, occasionally to 1 in.;

straight and round; yellowish, turning gray; 1–4 straight, round centrals, ¾–2 in. long, spreading in all directions from center of areole; gray mottled with brown.

FLOWERS Purplish or rose-pink, 1¾ in. tall, 2 in. diameter, opening widely; petals sometimes recurving; outer petals greenish or purplish, covered and fringed with white hairs; inner petals about ³⁄₁₆ in. wide, long and pointed; edges smooth except somewhat toothed toward tips; pinkish filaments; pale orange anthers; style a little longer than stamens, pale pink; 6–10 white stigma lobes, ⅛–³⁄₁₆ in. long, fairly thick, not pointed.

FRUITS Green, ½–¾ in. long, oval; brown seeds.

RANGE Lower Rio Grande Valley from Roma, Texas, to Brownsville and into adjacent Mexico.

REMARKS Most untidy growth of our cacti; branching occurs very quickly, forming ill-organized masses not over 2–3 in. high but quite broad. Grows on gravelly hillsides overlooking Rio Grande; prefers partial shade.

Mammillaria similis Eng.
(Benson: *Coryphantha missouriensis* var. *caespitosa*)
Nipple Cactus

ROOTS Fibrous.

STEMS Occasionally individual, usually clustering, often in large, irregular masses to 1+ ft. across; stems spherical, usually wider than tall, to 4 in. diameter but averaging 2–3 in.; covered by tubercles to ⅞ in. long on large plants; cylindrical on upper part, on sides of stem somewhat flattened.

AREOLES On immature plants round or oval; when mature, each tubercle deeply grooved along upper side, an extension of areole into or nearly to axil; filled with white wool, later bare except for tuft at base of groove in axil.

SPINES 10–17 slender radial spines, ⅛–½ in. long; fairly equal on any single areole, but uppermost 1–2 usually much more slender than others; sometimes no central; sometimes 1, very slightly longer and heavier than radials; gray to white, sometimes with brown tips; when young, covered with tiny white hairs or scales, visible under magnifying glass, soon worn off, then smooth, yellowish, hornlike.

FLOWERS 1–2 in. tall and wide with very narrow, linear, sharply pointed petals which are greenish, bronze, gold, gold streaked with pink, or pale, almost clear yellow, commonly mixed in same flower; 15–20 outer petals, greenish with fringed, yellowish or whitish edges; 20–25 inner petals, even narrower than outer, about ⅛ in. wide near bases, tapering very gradually to sharp point; clear yellow, gold, chartreuse, or bronze, often with pinkish midlines, with unfringed, smooth edges; white, light green, or yellow filaments; yellow or pale orange anthers; style very much longer than stamens,

Mammillaria similis. Typical small plant. 3 inches in diameter.

green or yellowish; 4–6 green or yellowish stigma lobes, ⅛–¼ in. long.

FRUITS Spherical to oval, ⅜–¾ in. long; remaining green below spines between tubercles for nearly a year, then turning bright scarlet, shriveling, and hardening; black seeds approximately 1/16 in. (1½–2 mm) across, almost spherical, pitted.

RANGE Kansas and eastern Colorado south through Oklahoma and north Texas to San Antonio and Columbus.

REMARKS Small, irregular clump of spherical stems producing flowers with narrow, sharp-pointed petals, a curious greenish-yellow, often striped with browns and pinks. Grows where few other cacti are found, shaded by prairie grass and shrubs and brush in loamy places on central plains or on calcareous hilltops; shrinks and even dies in full sun. Much more tolerant of moisture than most, but rots quickly in poorly drained, heavy soil. Rather common near Austin, Texas; occasionally found in a band about 100 miles wide, including Waco, Fort Worth, and Dallas; not common north through central Oklahoma; rather common between Ponca City and Tulsa; rare in Kansas. Better suited to cultivation than most; able to withstand ordinary winter temperature; probably best cactus for amateur grower.

Mammillaria similis. Old plant in full bloom. 12 inches in diameter.

Mammillaria roseiflora (Lahman) Weniger

STEMS Identical to *M. similis* except to about 2¾ in. across; clusters more sparingly to form only small clumps.

SPINES 13–16 equal radial spines to ⁵⁄₁₆ in. long; 2 uppermost very short and slender, almost bristlelike; gray with brown tips, with minute white hairs when young; 1 central, about ¼ in. long, turned upward.

FLOWERS About 1½ in. across and tall; pure pink, without stripes and zones; outer petals narrow, thick and fleshy, not fringed; inner petals almost thread-like; very weak and limp, spreading and bending in all directions; deep pink filaments; yellow anthers; 4–6 white stigma lobes.

FRUITS Round to egg-shaped, crimson, ⅜ in. long; seeds almost spherical, black, pitted, less than ¹⁄₁₆ in. (1½ mm) long.

RANGE Tulsa to Ponca City, Oklahoma.

REMARKS Very rare but occasionally reported by Oklahoma cactophiles; apparently not the same as the pink-striped *M. similis*. Needs study to determine its validity.

Mammillaria vivipara (Nutt.) Haw.
(Benson: *Coryphantha vivipara*)
Spiny Star, Ball Cactus, Pincushion

STEMS Spherical to columnar, single to greatly clustering by offset heads from around base; about 2–5+ in. tall and wide; deep green; divided into many cylindrical or tapering tubercles spreading or slightly overlapping upward.

AREOLES Round or nearly so on immature plants, upper part elongated on mature plants into narrow groove from spinous portion at tip of tubercle to reproductive part in axil of tubercle; when young, filled with much white or yellowish wool; when old, usually bare.

SPINES 12–60+ rather even radial spines; slender, straight, firm; ⅜ to about 1 in. long; white, white-tipped dark, or grayish with brown tips; 3–12 centrals, straight, spreading, rather slender to medium thick; ¼–1¼ in. long; whitish or yellowish with dark tips through mottled brown to partly or completely dark brown or purplish-black.

FLOWERS Purple, violet, or rose, usually very bright; pale purplish in one form; about 1–2¼ in. long and wide; perianth segments lance-shaped to linear; outer ones greenish and fringed; inner ones purple and entire; 5–10 white to rose-purple stigma lobes, obtuse, pointed, or mucronate.

FRUITS Oval, ½–1 in. long, not including dried persisting perianth, green or brownish when very ripe; seeds approximately ⅟₁₆ in. (1–2½ mm) long; almost spherical to oval or curved ovate; light or dark brown.

RANGE Canada through western United States, including Oklahoma, north and west Texas, and New Mexico, and deep into Mexico.

REMARKS Large and varied species; one of most common little cacti. Not to be equated with *Cactus viviparus* Nutt., which became *Coryphantha vivipara* (Nutt.) B. & R., a strictly delimited northern form of the species.

Mammillaria vivipara var. *vivipara* (Nutt.) Weniger
(Benson: *Coryphantha vivipara* var. *vivipara*)

STEMS As the species, except practically globular or depressed-globular, never columnar, to about 2½ in. diameter.

AREOLES As the species.

SPINES 12–21 radial spines on each areole; slender, ⅜–⅝ in. long; very white, sometimes with brown tips; 1–8 centrals, usually ½–¾ in. long, only slightly heavier than radials; 1–3 centrals directed outward and downward; others upright at top of areole, spreading fanwise in front of upper radials, varying in thickness, some as fine as radials; light brown or honey-colored, often mottled with whitish, often with darker tips or other darker zones, never blackish.

FLOWERS Deep magenta or purple, not opening widely, 1⅛–1¾ in. tall, 1½–2 in. across, with very narrow petals; outer petals greenish or brownish with pink edges fringed part or all the way to tips by long, pink cilia; about ⅛ in. wide near base, tapering gradually to sharp point; inner petals ¾ in. long, 1/16–⅛ in. wide; edges smooth or very finely toothed, tapering to sharp point; 30+ outer petals, about 17–20 elongated, others short, almost like fringed scales; about 30–47 inner petals; filaments green at bases, upper parts pink; bright orange anthers; style same length as stamens or slightly longer; 7–10 dark rose-purple stigma lobes, slender, about 3/16 in. long; somewhat pointed; may have spinelike mucros on ends.

FRUITS Oval, ½–¾ in. long; light green, brownish when old; light brown, finely pitted seeds; approximately 1/16 in. (1–1½ mm) long, very thick, almost round, except for concave hila.

RANGE Canada south through Montana, Dakotas, Nebraska, and Kansas across northwestern Oklahoma into extreme northwestern Texas, across eastern Colorado into northern New Mexico.

REMARKS Small northern cactus found in parts of Canada and northern plains where few others grow; immune to freeze damage; easily rotted by continued dampness in nonalkaline soil; in our area of study limited to northwest; cannot survive severe heat; grows on sandy hills and plains; not a mountain species. Often confused with close relatives; sometimes has fewer radial spines than most other forms, but this not a reliable character; when blooming, var. *vivipara* distinguished by 7–10 stigma lobes, long, slender, pointed, sometimes to spinelike tips; dark carmine to pink, never white; seeds most certain distinguishing character; var. *vivipara* has medium brown seeds, egg-shaped to almost round except for concave, oval hila, roughly pitted; approximately 1/16 in. (1–1½ mm) long. Small, inconspicuous; hardy; seldom common.

Mammillaria vivipara var. *radiosa* Eng.
(Not Benson: *Coryphantha vivipara* var. *radiosa*)

STEMS As the species, except ovate to columnar when mature, very rarely and sparingly clustering; to 5 in. tall, about 3 in. diameter; tubercles cylindrical, to about ¾ in. long.

AREOLES As the species.

SPINES As the species, except 17–30 radial spines, white, sometimes tipped with brown, very slender, to ½ in. long; 4–7 centrals, spreading from center of areole in no set pattern; most commonly 1–2 rather heavy down-turning centrals, others erect almost against upper radials; honey- or straw-colored, often with large zones of white.

FLOWERS About 2 in. across, 2¼ in. tall; very deep violet; petals 1–1¼ in. long, very narrow, about ⅛ in. across; 40–50 outer ones, about 17 elongated;

Mammillaria vivipara var. *vivipara.* 2¼ inches in diameter.

greenish, fringed; 30–40 inner ones, violet with entire edges; deep violet filaments; deep orange anthers; pink style ³⁄₁₆+ in. longer than stamens; 7–9 rose-colored stigma lobes, ³⁄₁₆–¼ in. long, fairly slender, not pointed.

FRUITS About ¾ in. long, oval, green; rather dark brown seeds, finely striated; more than ¹⁄₁₆ in. (2–2½ mm) long, oval, ventral surfaces convex; hila linear.

RANGE Triangle with 3 points near Springer, Oklahoma, and Austin and Sonora, Texas.

REMARKS Usually passes for *M. vivipara* var. *vivipara*, but var. *vivipara* has globose stems, 12–21 radials; stems of var. *radiosa* elongated and columnar; 17–30 radials and flowers larger—largest, most deeply colored of various forms of the species in our area; stigma lobes of var. *radiosa* never pointed; seeds of var. *radiosa* almost twice as large in each direction as those of var. *vivipara*; full and convex on all surfaces, darker brown, very finely pitted; seeds of var. *vivipara* small, flattened, concave, light brown, with more coarse pitting. Not a synonym of *M. vivipara*, but a definite Texas and Oklahoma form synonymous only with subvariety *texana* Eng.; one of largest localized forms of the species, with large, loose-standing tubercles, extremely fine flowers.

Mammillaria vivipara var. *neo-mexicana* Eng.
Spiny Star, Pincushion, New Mexico Coryphantha, Estria del Tarde

STEMS As the species, sometimes single, usually forming small clusters; spherical, short columns when old; to 3½–4 in. tall, 2½ in. thick; tubercles to ½ in. long, cylindrical or somewhat flattened from top to bottom, crowded close together.

AREOLES As the species.

SPINES 20–40 slender radial spines, to ⅜ in. long; white, sometimes with brown or purplish tips, fringing each areole, interlocking with neighboring clusters to hide flesh; 5–15 centrals on each areole of adult plant; white or yellowish with purplish to light brown tips, to ¾ in. long, spreading in all directions and at all angles.

FLOWERS About 1 in. tall and broad; pink to violet, sometimes shading to deep rose at center; outer petals narrow, pointed, fringed; inner petals very slender, sharp-pointed, with smooth edges; filaments green at bases, pink above; orange anthers; style as short as stamens, reddish; 3–10 stigma lobes, pure white to yellowish, short, fat, not pointed.

FRUITS Green, oval, ⅝–1⅝ in. long; medium brown seeds to ¹⁄₁₆ in. (1–2 mm) long, ovate or almost reniform, with bodies curved around ventral, concave, linear hila, pitted.

RANGE Mountain areas of central Colorado and New Mexico, south into Mexico, west into Arizona and east into Texas from El Paso and Guadalupe

Mammillaria vivipara var. *radiosa*. 2 inches in diameter.

Mammillaria vivipara var. *neo-mexicana*. Large stem 2¼ inches in diameter.

Mountains to Fort Stockton; very rarely if ever found in Texas south or east of Marfa.

REMARKS Comparatively distinct member of closely knit group; fairly easily distinguished from relatives by more numerous spines, more closely crowded and smaller tubercles, and smaller flowers with short, heavy, white stigma lobes only about ⅛ in. long; seeds also distinctive; mountain member of species. New Mexico specialists have erected several new taxa here: *Coryphantha bisbeeana* Orcutt, *Coryphantha orcuttii* D. Zimmerman, *Escobaria villardii* Castetter et al., *Escobaria orcuttii* var. *macraxina* Castetter et al., and *Escobaria orcuttii* var. *koenigii* Castetter et al.; all seem to me to fall within this variety, but group is still far from finalized.

Mammillaria vivipara var. *neo-mexicana*. Young plants, showing juvenile spination on sides of stem and mature spines at the tips. Larger plant 2 inches in diameter.

Mammillaria vivipara var. *borealis* Eng.
Sour Cactus

STEMS As the species, but usually single, rarely in small clusters; usually spherical, more or less egg-shaped when old; to about 3 in. tall by 2 in. diameter; tubercles to about ½ in. long, closely crowded, overlap upward.
AREOLES As the species.
SPINES 12–22 white, slender, short radial spines; 3–6 centrals, arranged much like those of typical variety *vivipara*, 1 usually turned downward, other 3–5 spreading upward just in front of upper radials; centrals or upper halves wholly purplish-black or maroon.
FLOWERS Small, about 1–1½ in. tall and wide; petals ¾ in. or less long, ⅛+ in. wide; about 20 outer petals, brownish and fringed; inner ones lavender, deep pink, or pale violet, entire; all sharply pointed; pink filaments; pale orange anthers; style about same length as stamens; 8–12 rather long, blunt, slender, pale pink stigma lobes.
FRUITS Egg-shaped, to about ¾ in. long; greenish, often brownish or faintly flushed with brownish-red when very ripe; very light brown or straw-colored seeds, approximately 1/16 in. (about 2 mm) long, oval, finely pitted; hilum near end, round or nearly so.
RANGE New Mexico from northwest of Santa Fe past Zuni northwest into Colorado, Arizona, and Utah.
REMARKS Small cactus limited to western side of Continental Divide; nearest western relative of typical northeastern form, var. *vivipara*, as var. *radiosa* is nearest southerly relative of that variety; much further removed from var. *neo-mexicana* by several characters; closer to var. *radiosa* than to any southern or western varieties, but much smaller, with smaller tubercles, fewer radials, darker centrals, smallest flowers of group; var. *radiosa* has largest; seeds about the same; relationship to other western forms more difficult. Widespread; small, usually single-stemmed spiny star with few and very weak radials and few but very dark centrals; small flowers, paler than most relatives; very light brown seeds; inconspicuous; most northern form of species other than typical var. *vivipara*.

Mammillaria vivipara var. *arizonica* (Eng.) Weniger
(Not Benson: *Coryphantha vivipara* var. *arizonica*)
Sour Cactus, Arizona Coryphantha

STEMS Simple, occasionally clustering sparingly to form 3–4 stems; spherical to ovate or conical and robust, to 4 in. diameter, 5 in. tall; tubercles cylindrical, rather loose-standing, to 1 in. long.
AREOLES As the species.
SPINES 13–20 radial spines, slender, but rigid and long, about ⅝–¾ in., said

Mammillaria vivipara var. *borealis*. 2 inches in diameter.

to reach 1¼ in. long; whitish, but not pure white, usually with brown tips; 3–6 centrals, spreading, rather stout, about ⅝–⅞ in. long; yellow or gray below with deep brown or purplish-brown above.

FLOWERS Large and showy, about 2 in. diameter and length, rose-pink to rose-purple; 30–40 outer segments slender and fringed; greenish-brown; 40 or so inner segments linear, entire, sharply pointed; 7–10 white, blunt stigma lobes.

FRUITS Oval and green; light brown, pitted seeds, approximately ¹⁄₁₆ in. (about 1¾ mm) long, broadly egg-shaped, curved, beaked around short, oval, greatly concave, ventral hila.

RANGE Far West, east from northern Arizona into extreme northwestern corner of New Mexico.

REMARKS Robust form of species in stem size, spination, and flowers; clusters only sparingly, stems large and strong, with long tubercles; spines not numerous as in some forms, stouter; open growing, well protected. Contrasts with smaller, more delicate, inconspicuous var. *borealis* and var. *vivipara*; more resembles var. *radiosa* of Texas, but has more rigid and darker spines; flowers more pinkish than deep violet flowers of var. *radiosa*; seeds of var. *arizonica* closest in size and shape to those of var. *vivipara*, but much lighter.

Mammillaria vivipara var. *deserti* (Eng.) Weniger
non L. Benson
(Not Benson: *Coryphantha vivipara* var. *deserti*)

STEMS As the species, but always simple and unbranched; at first globose, then oval or egg-shaped; to about 4 in. tall, 3½ in. thick; short, cylindrical tubercles to about ½ in. long, close-standing and compact, not overlapping.

AREOLES As the species.

SPINES 22–35 radial spines, ⅜–¾ in. long, spreading almost pectinate, interlocking with those of adjacent tubercles; upper and lower radials rather slender, laterals stout and rigid; all gray, larger usually tipped with brown; 5–10 centrals, lower 3–5 porrect or spreading outward, heavy, awl-shaped, ¼–⅜ in. long; upper 2–5 spreading upward, more slender, ½–⅝ in. long; centrals straw- or honey-colored below with red-brown tips.

FLOWERS Small, about 1 in. long and wide; pale pinkish suffused with cream color or tan; outer segments brownish and fringed; inner ones entire, straw-colored with pinkish tips; 5–6 whitish stigma lobes.

FRUITS Short, oval, about ½ in. long; green, sometimes suffused with brown or faint maroon when very ripe; seeds ¹⁄₁₆ in. (1½–2 mm) long, dark brown, pitted, obovate, somewhat curved around round or oval, convex or flat, ventral hila.

RANGE Southern Arizona into New Mexico west and south of Silver City.

Mammillaria vivipara var. *arizonica*. 3 inches in diameter.

REMARKS Very wide range; not to be confused with California cactus described under this name; robust, single-stemmed; short, compact tubercles almost completely covered by very numerous, interlocking spines; only var. *neo-mexicana* has such profuse covering of spines, but they are white, much more slender; var. *deserti* has ashy gray radials, brown centrals, all relatively heavy; most resembles var. *arizonica*, but much more squat and compact, with much shorter tubercles, many more, more appressed, stouter spines; form, spines, and general appearance similar to *Echinocactus intertextus* var. *dasyacanthus* Eng.; most distant from typical form of the species.

Mammillaria fragrans (Hester) Weniger

STEMS Single, very rarely with 1–2 branches from base; conical to cylindrical when older; to 8 in. tall by about 3 in. diameter; tubercles ⅜–⅝ in. long, usually about ½ in.; soft and oval, flattened dorsally, somewhat broadened above base to about ⅜ in. wide, tapering toward tips.
AREOLES Monomorphic, lengthening to form grooves extending nearly to bases of tubercles; with white wool when young, later bare.
SPINES 20–30 slender radials to ½ in. long; white; 6–12 centrals to ⅝ in. long, spreading at all angles; mostly purple or very dark brown, only bases gray; with age usually becoming entirely black.
FLOWERS About 1½–2 in. across and tall, cup-shaped or bell-shaped; magenta or reddish-purple; outer petals greenish with pink edges fringed with long white hairs; inner petals narrow, pointed, reddish-purple shading to light pink at edges from greenish bases, edges entire or very slightly ragged near tips; filaments greenish below to pink above; orange anthers; style about same length as stamens or longer; 6–12 pure white to pinkish stigma lobes, long and more or less pointed, rather thick.
FRUITS Greenish, yellow-green when ripe; oval; to 1 in. long; seeds kidney- or bean-shaped, approximately ⅛ in. (2½–3 mm) long; much flattened; translucent, rich red-brown, shiny smooth, with no pitting; minute checks show through from inner layers with microscope; hilum ventral or nearly so, oval or oblong.
RANGE Big Bend, Texas, from Sanderson on east to Rio Grande west of Alpine, not north of southern slopes of Davis and Van Horn mountains.
REMARKS Difficult to distinguish from relatives; much larger than var. *neo-mexicana*, to double its height; almost never branches; tubercles broaden above bases, flattened on upper sides, giving ballooned appearance except with drought or winter shrinkage; centrals very dark, coloring extending farther down than on others except northwestern specimens of *M. vivipara* var. *borealis*; petals shorter; stigmas intermediate in length between eastern *M. vivipara* var. *radiosa* and western var. *neo-mexicana*; pure white to light pink; very fragrant with sweet scent, hence its name; flowers of var.

Mammillaria fragrans. 2¼ inches in diameter.

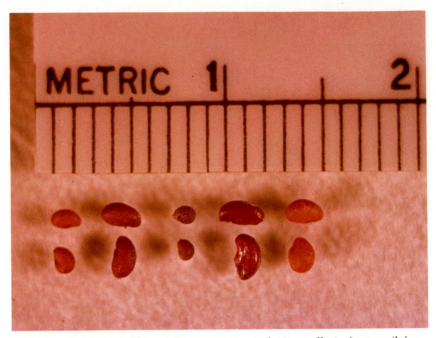

Seeds of some *Mammillaria vivipara* varieties and *Mammillaria fragrans* (left to right): *Mammillaria vivipara* var. *vivipara*, var. *radiosa*, var. *neo-mexicana*, *Mammillaria fragrans*, and *Mammillaria vivipara* var. *borealis*.

neo-mexicana have almost no scent; those of eastern *M. vivipara* forms have very strong, pungent, very green scent; differs almost as completely from var. *radiosa* as from other *M. vivipara* varieties; range of var. *radiosa* stops just northeast of its range. Rare; restricted to lower Big Bend, Texas.

Mammillaria tuberculosa Eng.
(Benson: *Coryphantha strobiliformis* var. *strobiliformis* only in part)

STEMS Globular to egg-shaped, becoming upright cylinders 1–2 in. thick, said to reach 7 in. tall, often much shorter; single until large, then forming small clusters; dull gray-green; many separate tubercles, usually about ⅜ in. long, sometimes not over ¼ in.; tubercles practically cylindrical when young; bases broaden horizontally, somewhat rhomboid and about as wide as tall when old; somewhat crowded; mature tubercles turning upward and overlapping.

Mammillaria tuberculosa. Main stem 3⅝ inches tall.

Mammillaria dasyacantha (left) and *Mammillaria tuberculosa* (right), growing together.

AREOLES Small and round on immature stems; when mature, groove runs to base of each tubercle on upper side as linear extension from spinous portion at tip of tubercle to floral part in axil; when young, filled with white wool; when old, only tuft remains in axillary end of groove.

SPINES 20–30 radial spines, slender but stiff, white, radiating in all directions around areole; varying in size; at top very small bristles, around sides and bottom to ⅜ in. long, rather firm; 4–9 centrals, gray-white with purplish ends; 4 much heavier than radials; 3 spreading upward, to ⅝ in. long; lowest standing abruptly outward or turning a little downward—the heaviest spine; with age, 3–5 more centrals may be added above others, upright with earlier upper ones; never quite as heavy or long as first, intermediate between those and radials; spines tend to be shed from older part of stem, leaving base bare.

FLOWERS ¾–1⅜ in. across, ¾–1 in. tall; opening widely; very delicate lavender-white or extremely pale purple; 16–18 outer petals, greenish-brown with almost white, fringed edges; to ¾ in. long, ⅛ in. wide; 10–15 inner petals, ¾–1 in. long, ⅛ in. wide; very pale lavender fading to almost white at edges; cream-colored filaments; cream-colored or pale yellowish anthers; white style, the same length or just longer than stamens; 5–6 white stigma lobes to 3⁄16 in. long.

FRUITS Egg-shaped to oblong, about ¾ in. long; bright red; very small brown, pitted seeds, usually about ½ mm long.

RANGE Mountains of Big Bend, Texas, southward into Mexico, westward into southern New Mexico.

REMARKS Much less common than usually thought; small size, many spines, small flowers; naked, corky bases are not reliable distinguishing characters; easily distinguished from *M. dasyacantha* when in bloom by larger and much more delicately colored flowers; arrangement of central spines—particularly stout lower central standing out—is best criterion when not in bloom; in general, smaller than *M. dasyacantha*; spines with purplish ends instead of brown and not obscuring stem as completely.

Mammillaria dasyacantha Eng.
(Not Benson: *Coryphantha dasyacantha*)

STEMS Practically spherical when young, elongated and cylindrical when older; usually single but occasionally sprouting at bases to form small clusters; to 8 in. tall, 3 in. thick; tubercles cylindrical, straight in young plants; flattened, somewhat overlapping, ⅜–½ in. long on old plants; oldest tubercles on bases usually bare of spines, discolored, dead-appearing.

AREOLES Spine-bearing portions at tips of tubercles, floral part in axils; tubercles grooved to bases; woolly when young; nearly naked when old; immature areoles merely small, rounded spinous portion.

SPINES 25–35+ radial spines around areole; white, not brittle, usually about ½ in. long, sometimes to almost 1 in.; very slender, upper almost bristle-like; 7–17 centrals, filling center of each areole, spreading irregularly; some almost as slender as radials; ⅜–1 in. long; lower parts white, tips reddish-brown.

FLOWERS 1 in. tall, ½–¾ in. across, not opening widely; whitish to pale pink; 8–10 outer petals ½–⅝ in. long, 3/16 in. wide, pointed; edges fringed; midlines greenish-brown, fading to whitish at edges; 13–16 inner petals, same width and length, tapering gradually to pointed tips; brownish midlines; edges tan, whitish, or pink; pale pink or cream-colored filaments; bright yellow anthers; bright green style, ending in 4–5 very short, very green stigma lobes, deeply grooved on ventral sides.

FRUITS Egg-shaped to somewhat elongated, ½–¾ in. long; dark red or scarlet; small seeds, practically round, about ½–1 mm long, deeply pitted, shiny black.

RANGE Mountains of lower Big Bend, Texas, extreme southern New Mexico, south into Mexico.

REMARKS In extreme southwestern Texas this is the commonest species of group often called Escobarias, also largest of group; found on slopes and ledges in mountains, even on summits, on exposed rock surfaces. Without flowers, *M. dasyacantha* recognized by comparatively thick stems, numerous slender centrals spreading irregularly, without conspicuous, heavier

Mammillaria dasyacantha. Plant pictured, 3 inches in diameter.

central standing outward or downward in areole; flowers not opening widely; with conspicuously green stigmas, fewer outer petals, more and broader inner petals than *M. tuberculosa*; shiny black seeds different from those of *M. tuberculosa*. Juvenile plants markedly different in almost all characters from adults; spherical, sometimes with depressed tops; when very young, tubercles have no grooves, 18–22 white, translucent radial spines ⅛ in. long; 2 centrals per areole, 1 pointing directly upward, 1 downward, each ³⁄₁₆ in. long; at about 1 in. diameter, new tubercles develop short grooves, radials to ¼ in. long, 4 centrals per areole, arranged as points of cross, to ½ in. long; at about 1¾ in. diameter and height, more centrals appear, plants lengthen to adult appearance.

Mammillaria duncanii. Showing root formation. Spiny portion of the stem 1 inch tall.

Mammillaria duncanii (Hester) Weniger
(Benson: *Coryphantha duncanii*)

ROOTS 1 to several fleshy, carrotlike taproots ¼–1 in. diameter; sometimes to 1 ft. long before tapering.

STEMS Practically spherical to broadly ovate or somewhat conical, to about 2 in. tall by 1¼ in. diameter; usually single, a few double or triple; covered by small tubercles about ⅛ in. long.

AREOLES Monomorphic, elongated into groove from spinous portion on tips of tubercle to floral portion in axil; some white wool in axillary portion at first.

Mammillaria duncanii. Same plant, with fruit, after 3 months' cultivation.

SPINES 24 to about 40 radial spines, slender, straight, ³⁄₁₆–³⁄₈ in. long; white or with very slightly brownish tips; 3–16 centrals, usually about 8; spreading very widely; about ³⁄₈ in. long; white, tipped with light brown.

FLOWERS ⁵⁄₈–³⁄₄ in. long, about ½ in. wide, not opening widely; pale pink or whitish with pinkish zones; ovary smooth and rounded; outer perianth segments pointed, outermost with a few cilia on margins; pinkish with whitish edges; inner segments entire, pointed, midlines pink, edges whitish; whitish filaments; pale orange anthers; 4–6 yellow or almost chartreuse stigma lobes.

FRUITS Club-shaped, ½–³⁄₄ in. long, about ³⁄₁₆ in. wide, not including persistent perianth; bright red when ripe; black seeds, practically spherical, pitted; basal hila.

RANGE Small area of Brewster County, Texas, near Terlingua.

REMARKS Extremely rare; spines, flowers, fruits, and especially seeds very close to *M. dasyacantha*; might pass for dwarf form of that cactus except for unusual fleshy taproot, smaller size, yellow stigma lobes; inconspicuous.

Mammillaria albicolumnaria (Hester) Weniger
White Column, Silverlace Cactus

STEMS Oblong or cylindrical almost from beginning; nearly always single, very rarely 2–3 stems; to 10 in. tall but rarely over 5 in.; to about 2½ in. diameter; tubercles about ⅜ in. long, tapering to points from rhomboid bases about as wide as tall; bases of old plants usually naked of spines.

AREOLES Monomorphic, but elongated on mature stems to run whole length of tubercle, spinous part at tip, floral part in axil; narrow groove connects them; when young, areoles usually only partway down tubercles; white wool in grooves when young, most disappears with age.

SPINES 25–35+ radial spines, fine, some almost bristlelike, very rigid and brittle; to ⅜ in. long; very white, somewhat translucent; 11–17 centrals to ⅝ in. long; heavier than radials; fill up center of areole, spreading in all directions; pink or very light red when growing, then translucent white with red-brown tips; all very brittle.

FLOWERS Small, not opening widely, but remaining funnel-shaped; pink, usually ⅜–⅝ in. wide, ¾–1 in. tall; 16–26 outer petals, greenish-brown in midlines with whitish edges fringed to pointed tips; 25–26 inner petals, pale pink to whitish, narrow, pointed, edges not fringed, about ⅛ in. wide; white filaments; yellow anthers; pink style shorter than stamens; 3–7 white or pale pink stigma lobes, short and thick.

FRUITS Oblong or club-shaped; to ⅝ in. long, ¼ in. thick; lower half remains greenish when ripe; upper half pale yellowish or apricot; brown, pitted seeds, about 1 mm long.

RANGE Extreme southwestern corner of Brewster County, Texas, near Terlingua and Lajitas.

REMARKS Spines and flowers most like *M. dasyacantha*; seeds like *M. tuberculosa*; in general, plant and spine characters very much like *M. dasyacantha*, but never as large, usually does not cluster; differs in translucent whiteness and brittleness of spines, which break easily, rather than by numbers or arrangement; many more numerous petals; white stigmas, greenish-apricot fruits, brown, differently shaped seeds.

Mammillaria varicolor (Tieg.) Weniger
(Benson: *Coryphantha dasyacantha* var. *varicolor*)

STEMS Single except when injured, then may branch to form several heads; egg-shaped, to 5 in. tall, nearly as broad; tubercles to about ½ in. long, conical from broadly flattened bases, turning upward to overlap greatly when old.

AREOLES On mature stems, elongated to narrow grooves from spinous portions at tips of tubercles to floral portions in axils; naked except for large tufts of white wool at floral region, growing tips very fuzzy, persists on old

Mammillaria albicolumnaria. Plant pictured, 2⅞ inches in diameter.

Mammillaria varicolor. Largest stem 1⅔ inches in diameter.

tubercles, making axils woolly.

SPINES 15–20 very slender, white, semitranslucent radial spines; some to ¼ in. long, but many, especially uppers, weak bristles ⅛ in. long; usually 4, occasionally 5 centrals, to about ½ in. long, heavier than radials; yellowish at bases; upper part brownish or purplish; semitranslucent and hornlike; lower central standing out perpendicular or downward; 3–4 uppers spreading fanwise in front of upper radials.

FLOWERS Almost pure white, pink, or very pale rose; ¾ in. long, 1¼ in. diameter; 11–12 outer petals, ¾ in. long, fringed on edges, brownish with pinkish edges; 26–27 inner petals, 1 in. long, ⅛ in. wide, pointed, edges smooth, various colors, as above; bright yellow filaments and anthers; white style a little longer than stamens; 5–6 white stigma lobes, about ⅛ in. long, slender.

FRUITS Ellipsoidal or slightly curved club-shaped, wilted perianth persistent; approximately ½–⅝ in. long by ³⁄₁₆–¼ in. diameter; medium bright rose-red when ripe (in August).

RANGE Marathon, Texas, to about 12 miles north of Alpine.

REMARKS Obscure, often mistaken for other forms; flowers white to very pale rose, unlike magenta or purple of similar forms; also distinguished by yellow filaments and fewer stigma lobes.

Mammillaria hesteri. 4 inches tall.

Mammillaria hesteri (Wright) Weniger
(Benson: *Coryphantha hesteri*)

STEMS Spherical to egg-shaped; to 3 in. tall, nearly as wide; single or usually clustering very rapidly to form irregular clumps to 1+ ft. across; covered by tubercles, cylindrical when young, then tapering and turning upward from broad, flattened bases; to ½ in. long when old.

AREOLES Roundish on immature stems; elongating to form grooves almost to axils when mature; flowers produced at ends of grooves; all degrees of lengthening; very small tuft of wool in base of groove at first, usually soon disappears.

SPINES 14–20 even radial spines on mature heads, uppers much longer and heavier than others, lowers ⅛–¼ in. long; uppers often ¼–½ in. long; 1 spine in each areole markedly heavier, standing upright against more slender uppers behind it; sometimes mistaken for central; on young stems 12–13 short, equal, radiating spines; in type locality all very white and translucent at first, later opaque gray with tips of red or purplish-brown; specimens from near Sanderson, Texas, all have gray or tan bases, upper two-thirds red or purple-brown; all more or less flattened.

FLOWERS Mauve, 1–1½ in. across and tall; about 8 outer petals, to about ³⁄₁₆ in. wide; greenish to pinkish, fringed with long white hairs; about 22–27 inner petals, to about ½ in. long, ³⁄₁₆ in. or less wide; bluntly pointed, edges

Mammillaria nellieae. Blooming plant, 1 inch in diameter.

smooth or slightly ragged; mauve, darkest at tips; white to rose filaments; orange-yellow anthers; greenish or yellowish style, slightly longer than stamens; 4–6 short, stout, rough, cream-colored or white stigma lobes.

FRUITS Remaining greenish until drying, spherical or nearly so, about ¼ in. diameter; seeds very small, brown, pitted.

RANGE Small area southeast of Alpine, Texas; another small area west of Sanderson.

REMARKS This and next species are 2 of several diminutive cacti in very limited areas south and southeast of Marathon, Texas. Could easily become an endangered species.

Mammillaria nellieae (Croiz.) Croiz.
(Benson: *Coryphantha minima*)

STEMS Egg-shaped or cylindrical, very small, usually under 1 in. tall, to ¾ in. diameter; occasionally to 1¾ in. tall; usually single, sometimes branching above base; covered with conical tubercles to about ¹⁄₁₆ in. long.

AREOLES Each tubercle has broad, deep, naked groove running full length of upper side, which is the linear monomorphic areole from spinous portion at tip of tubercle to floral portion in axil.

SPINES 13–15 definite radial spines, ¹⁄₁₆–⅛ in. long, lying flat against plant all around areole; rather slender to fairly heavy; 3 other spines, much heavier, to about ¼ in. long, upright in front of and curving slightly backward to lie directly on upper radials; 2 heavy and spreading upward, forming rather distinct V; third somewhat smaller, bisecting V formed by first 2; some consider these centrals, others radials; all pinkish when growing, then yellowish fading to gray; all round, maintain full thickness from bases to very tips, sharp-pointed; somewhat club-shaped.

FLOWERS Rose-purple, about ¾ in. tall, ⅝–1 in. diameter; outer petals short and greenish with pink, fringed edges; inner petals about ⅜ in. long, about ⅛ in. wide; rose-purple; bluntly pointed, with smooth edges; greenish filaments; pale orange anthers; short style; 5–8 green stigma lobes.

FRUITS Egg-shaped, very small, usually ⅛–¼ in. long; green; sometimes with faint yellowish blush; dried perianth persists; blackish seeds, about ½ mm long.

RANGE Only in type locality, south of Marathon, Brewster County, Texas.

REMARKS Dwarf cactus found in Brewster County, Texas, in crevices of limestone ledges, often covered with moss; beautiful purplish flowers. Needs very good drainage to avoid rot but also needs frequent waterings, heat but some shade. Easily recognized by remarkable appearance of spines, lying right against surface, preserving thickness to points, very thick for length; more like tiny clubs than ordinary spines. An endangered species.

Mammillaria roberti (Berger) Weniger
(Benson: *Coryphantha roberti*)
Runyon's Escobaria, Junior Tom Thumb Cactus

STEMS Spherical, becoming oblong; to about 3 in. tall by 1¼ in. thick; branching very fast and irregularly; large, low clumps of dozens of stems; covered with tubercles tapering from cylindrical bases, ³⁄₁₆–¼ in. long.

AREOLES Round, at tips of tubercles on immature stems; on mature stems, develop from oval to almost linear by being prolonged from spinous portion at tip of tubercle into very narrow, very woolly groove running halfway to all the way down upper side of tubercle; flowers and new branches produced from end of groove, at or near axil of tubercle.

SPINES 20–30 slender radial spines, ³⁄₁₆–¼ in. long, white, usually barely tipped with brown; 5–10+ centrals filling center of each areole, spreading in all directions; ⅜–⅝ in. long; upper ones much longer, slender; centrals have white bases, upper three-fourths dark brown, red-brown, or black.

FLOWERS Inconspicuous color; ¾ in. diameter, ⅝ in. tall, opening widely; petals slender and pointed, buff or tan, with midlines of reddish-brown; outer ones fringed, inner ones with or without fringe; pink filaments; yellow anthers; style about ⅛ in. longer than stamens, reddish-brown; 5–6 short, thick stigma lobes, green, yellow-green, or brownish-green.

FRUITS Spherical to egg-shaped, ¼–⅜ in. long, scarlet.

Mammillaria roberti. Largest stem 1⅜ inches in diameter.

RANGE Rio Grande Valley from McAllen, Texas, to mouth of Pecos River and along west side of lower Devil's River.

REMARKS One of most perfectly camouflaged; only a few inches high; dark-tipped spines blend with rocky soil and grasses; flower color also blends; scarlet fruit; fairly common near Rio Grande City and lower Falcon reservoir.

Mammillaria sneedii (B. & R.) Cory.
(Benson: *Coryphantha sneedii* var. *sneedii*)

STEMS To about 2 in. long, ¾ in. thick; small, cylindrical, branching and clustering to form masses of up to 100 heads on old specimens; composed of many tiny, cylindrical, green tubercles 1/16–3/16 in. long.

AREOLES Round or nearly so on immature stems, lengthening on mature stems to form short grooves from spinous portion at tips of tubercles to at most one-third toward axils; flowering or branching at ends of short grooves; a little white wool in groove.

SPINES Tubercles almost entirely obscured by many white spines; 24–45 radiating outer spines, about ⅛ in. long, very slender, rigid; 13–17 centrals, slightly heavier, ⅛–5/16 in. long; centrals all spreading to lie against radials,

Mammillaria sneedii. Blooming stem, ¾ inch in diameter.

except for middle 1 out of center of areole, which often stands outward and downward; all white when mature; pinkish when growing.

FLOWERS Small, about ½ in. tall and broad, not opening widely; pink to pale rose; outer petals narrow, with fringed edges; midlines rose, edged in very pale pink; inner petals paler, edges fringed at least halfway to pointed tips; sometimes notches in otherwise entire margins of petal ends; pink filaments; bright orange anthers; style longer than stamens; 3–4 slender white stigma lobes.

FRUITS About ¼ in. thick, almost spherical, a little longer than thick; deep pink when ripe; brown, pitted seeds, less than ¹⁄₁₆ in. (about 1 mm) long.

RANGE Franklin Mountains between El Paso, Texas, and Las Cruces, New Mexico.

REMARKS Clumps up to 1+ ft. diameter; seems well on way to extinction.

Mammillaria leei (Rose) Weniger
(Benson: *Coryphantha sneedii* var. *leei*)

ROOTS Fibrous when young, when older usually with single definite taproot, which runs some inches before reducing.

STEMS Almost spherical at first, later mostly club-shaped, sometimes cylin-

Mammillaria leei. Plants in garden cultivation. Clusters 4 to 6 inches in diameter.

drical, to about 3 in. long, about 1⅛ in. thick; branching and proliferating very rapidly, forming irregular clumps of up to several hundred very tightly packed stems covered with cylindrical tubercles up to about ³⁄₁₆ in. long, often smaller.

AREOLES Often only circular or elliptical areoles on ends of tubercles; may elongate into grooves from spinous portions at ends of tubercles to about halfway to tubercle bases; flowers and branches come from ends of grooves; at first very woolly, wool remains in grooves; center of spinous part often very convex, bulging outward, with spines mostly pushed back, radiating and framing convex areole center, giving unique, knobby appearance.

SPINES About 40–90+ very tiny white radial spines, appressed against surface, often recurving between tubercles; 6–7 stouter centrals, white or with pale brownish tips, usually about ⅛ in. long, a few may be longer; 1 central perpendicular to plant in center of areole, may be very short; others radiating in front of radials.

FLOWERS Not opening widely; about ¾ in. long, ½ in. wide; deep pink suffused with brownish; outer petals brown or greenish-brown with light edges fringed by white cilia; inner petals deep pink in midlines, edges lighter and entire; 4–6 short white stigma lobes.

FRUITS Oblong or somewhat club-shaped, about ½ in. long by ⅛–¼ in. thick; remain greenish tinged with brownish or faintly pinkish when ripe;

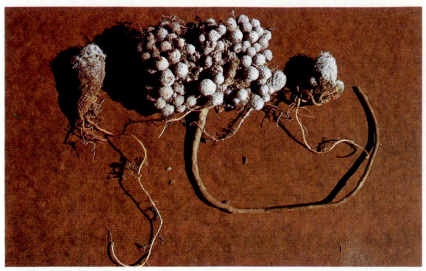

Mammillaria leei. Typical root formation. Large clump, 4¼ inches across.

seeds more or less pear-shaped, dark brown, less than ¹⁄₁₆ in. (1+ mm) long.
RANGE Canyons about 30 miles southwest of Carlsbad, New Mexico.
REMARKS Many stems remain with unelongated areoles, sometimes throughout life of stem; close to *M. sneedii,* ranges not far apart; population not large; very limited area. *Escobaria sandbergii* Castetter et al. from San Andres Mountains of New Mexico seems to vary from *M. leei* in no major character except that it attains a larger size.

Mammillaria bella (B. & R.) Weniger
(Description adapted from Britton and Rose)

STEMS Clustering, heads about 2⅜–3¼ in. long, cylindrical; tubercles ⅝– almost ⅞ in. long, marked by hairy groove, with brownish gland near center.
AREOLES Not stated.
SPINES Several radial spines, whitish, less than ½ in. long; 3–5 centrals, brown, to at least ⅞ in. long.
FLOWERS To ¾ in. across, petals pinkish with pale margins, narrow and pointed, outer ones fringed; reddish filaments; green stigma.
FRUITS Not known.
RANGE "Hills of Devil's River, Texas."
REMARKS Collected by Rose and Fitch before 1914 (described by Britton and Rose in 1922); no subsequent record.

Mammillaria pottsii Scheer

STEMS Cylindrical, to about 1¼ in. diameter, to 8+ in. tall, usually only 4−5 in. high; single or sometimes branching above ground to form small, irregular clusters of 3−4 heads; covered with conical to egg-shaped tubercles, ⅛−¼ in. long, rather closely crowded, somewhat overlapping.

AREOLES Dimorphic; spinous portion on tip of tubercle small, round, especially filled with spines because of enlarged bases of centrals; at first contains much rather long, white wool, later bare; flower develops in or near axil of tubercle, together with long wool and 1−2 bristles, remaining as axillary tuft.

SPINES 30−40 radial spines; white, very slender, straight, rigid; about ³⁄₁₆ in. long, entirely equal in size around areole; 6−12 centrals, same number on any 1 plant; spreading evenly in all directions from greatly enlarged, bulbous bases; lower and lateral ones ¼−⅜ in. long and straight, upper ones ½−⅝ in. long, curving upward; lower ones gray with very tips brownish; upper ones gray with up to outer half dark brown, purple, or bluish; tip of plant purplish.

FLOWERS Small, ⅜−½ in. long and wide, bell-shaped, petals not opening widely, but recurving toward tips; deep red, maroon, or rust-red; develop around upper sides of stem instead of at summit; outer petals very broad, with pointed tips, margins usually ragged or irregularly toothed, not fringed; outer segments red or maroon with pale cream-colored edges; inner petals have red to rust midstripes with rose to pinkish, smooth margins, pointed tips; cream-colored stamens; reddish style; 4−5 cream-colored or yellow stigma lobes.

FRUITS Club-shaped, to ⅝ in. long, pale or light red; blackish, pitted seeds, almost oval, less than ¹⁄₁₆ in. (1 mm or less) long.

RANGE Mountains of Big Bend, near Terlingua, Texas; widely distributed in Mexico.

REMARKS Distinctive, readily distinguished from other Mammillarias found in United States by small, bell-shaped, red blossom; similar to Mammillarias found in Mexico; 1 to several whitish columns with peculiar bluish cast due to unusual coloring of upper centrals; most nearly resembles *M. tuberculosa*, but has more regular and tidy spines, greatly enlarged bases of centrals. Grows successfully in well-drained limestone soil; often used in gardens; desert species; needs much sun, cannot tolerate much dampness.

Mammillaria lasiacantha Eng.

STEMS Usually single, sometimes forming small clusters of 2−3 heads; spherical, conical, or egg-shaped, small, to about 2+ in. diameter, only slightly taller; covered by many small, cylindrical tubercles to about ³⁄₁₆ in. long, ⅛ in. diameter; axils bare.

Mammillaria pottsii. Largest stem 1⅓ inches across. *Mammillaria lasiacantha* var. *denudata* in foreground.

AREOLES Spinous portions of dimorphic areoles on tips of tubercles, small, somewhat egg-shaped; floral portions remain in axils of tubercles, flowers produced in axils.

SPINES 40–60+ white radial spines, flat, interlocking with those of neighboring areoles, covering surface; so numerous that they lie in several series forming 3–4 concentric rings in areole, 1 layer on the next; about $1/16$–$3/16$ in. long; pubescent because of almost microscopic white hairs or smooth.

FLOWERS $1/2$–$3/4$ in. long and across, opening widely; whitish, each petal marked by conspicuous tan, red-brown, or purplish-red midstripe; outer petals slender, ends rounded or bluntly pointed, margins usually somewhat irregular; inner petals oblong, rather wide, $1/16$–$1/8$ in. wide over most of length, tips smooth and rounded or ragged; long yellowish filaments; yellow anthers; greenish style, slightly longer than stamens; 4–5 small greenish or yellowish stigma lobes.

FRUITS Bright scarlet, club-shaped, $3/8$–$5/8$ in. long; flower remains persist; surfaces naked; oval, black, pitted seeds, less than $1/16$ in. (about 1 mm) long.

RANGE Most of trans-Pecos Texas and extreme south-central New Mexico.

REMARKS One of tiniest cacti; small ball to 1–2 in. diameter; perfectly white due to huge number of white spines entirely covering surface; very rarely clustering, only 2–3 heads. Grows on tops of hills in thin soil, often between limestone rocks, needs much limestone in soil; usually more or less covered by surrounding grasses; does not require shade.

Mammillaria lasiacantha var. *lasiacantha* (Eng.) Weniger

STEMS As the species, except to about 1 in. diameter and height.

AREOLES As the species.

SPINES As the species, except averages in upper range for species; surfaces always roughened by some to very many almost microscopic cilia or trichomes; often wholly pubescent.

FLOWERS As the species, except about $3/4$ in. long and wide; main petals about $1/8$ in. wide; stigmas more yellowish than greenish.

FRUITS As the species.

RANGE Fort Stockton, Texas, and Davis Mountains north in Guadalupe Mountains west of Carlsbad, New Mexico, to near Alamogordo.

REMARKS First called var. *minor* by Engelmann. Spines have almost microscopic "hairs," giving fuzzy appearance under lens; *M. lasiacantha* var. *denudata* lacks hair or has only a few scraggly cilia, leaving spines smooth and shiny; rough-spined form also smaller, to about 1 in.; smooth-spined form commonly 2 in. diameter; flowers of smaller form larger, with wider petals; differences may intergrade and ranges overlap, but seem to be two legitimate varieties.

Mammillaria lasiacantha var. *lasiacantha*. Stem 1 inch in diameter.

Mammillaria lasiacantha var. *denudata* Eng.

STEMS As the species, except to at least 2 in. tall and wide.
AREOLES As the species.
SPINES As the species, except smooth and shiny, usually no cilia or trichomes, at most a few scattered "hairs."
FLOWERS As the species, except to about ½ in. diameter; petals almost linear, about ¹⁄₁₆ in. wide; stigma with more greenish than yellowish lobes.
FRUITS As the species.
RANGE Mexico into mountains of Big Bend, Texas, from Sanderson to just beyond El Paso; also north past Alpine and Marfa into southern part of Davis Mountains.
REMARKS More common southern form of the species; very common in parts of Big Bend; larger when grown, has smaller flowers.

Mammillaria multiceps SD
(Benson: *Mammillaria prolifera* var. *texana*)
Hair-Covered Cactus, Grape Cactus

STEMS Spherical to egg-shaped or short-columnar; when mature, blooming heads ½–2 in. diameter, 2 in. tall, producing offsets extremely rapidly;

Mammillaria lasiacantha var. *denudata*. Stem 2 inches in diameter.

Mammillaria multiceps. Cluster of stems, 4⅛ inches across.

12–20 different-sized heads forming large, low matlike clump; tubercles conical or cylindrical, spreading, up to ⅜ in. long.

AREOLES Dimorphic; spinous portion on end of tubercle round, with white wool at first, later naked; floral or vegetative portion in axil of tubercle produces some wool with flower and usually several long, twisted, white hairlike bristles which persist.

SPINES 30–60+ (said to reach 80) radial spines in several series; outer ones white, hairlike, very fine, entirely flexible, usually curved and twisted; when straightened ¼–⅝ in. long; inner series progressively shorter and heavier; innermost straight, rigid bristles spreading in all directions; white or light yellow, usually somewhat pubescent; in center of areole 4–12 comparatively heavy centrals with bulbous bases; straight, rigid, ¼–⅜ in. long, spreading in all directions; white to yellow or brown at bases, upper parts and tips whitish or light honey-yellow to dark red-brown or almost black; more or less pubescent under lens; outer series lighter in color, more slender than inner ones, sometimes very close to inner radials.

FLOWERS About ¾ in. long and across, brownish-yellow or almost tan, with pinkish to mauve-rose streaks; petals have cream-colored or tan edges shading into pinkish or dull rose midlines; usually unfringed; outer ones occasionally have a few cilia on edges; yellowish or white filaments; yellow anthers; short cream-colored style; 3–8 cream-colored to yellow stigma lobes.

FRUITS About ½–¾ in. long, scarlet, egg-shaped to club-shaped, old flower parts persist; black, pitted seeds, approximately ¹⁄₁₆ in. (about 1½ mm) long.
RANGE From Mexico into south Texas to mouth of Pecos River, almost to Rocksprings, Bandera, and Rockport.
REMARKS Easily recognized by flexible, hairlike radial spines covering surface, hence name hair-covered cactus; individual stems small, 1+ in. diameter and height; multiply very rapidly by branching; form low clumps of many heads to 1+ ft. across. Near Rio Grande Valley grows in rich, deep lowland soil in shelter of thickets or coastal grasses; also grows on crests of rocky hills, in crevices and underneath limestone ledges; susceptible to freezing; flowers small and not highly colored; red fruit; 2 rather distinct growth forms in Texas and northern Mexico; one has outer parts of centrals dark brown, red-brown, or black; other has centrals all whitish or translucent, honey-yellow; much like 2 color phases of *Echinocereus caespitosus*. Can be cultivated, even in small pot.

Mammillaria microcarpa Eng.
(Benson: *M. grahamii* in part; not Benson: *M. microcarpa*)
Fishhook Cactus, Pincushion Cactus, Sunset Cactus

STEMS Single till old, then clustering at base or above to form small clumps of several stems; to at least 6 in., usually only to about 3 in. tall; 1–3½ in. diameter; practically spherical, conical, or somewhat cylindrical; tubercles cylindrical when young, then conical from more or less quadrangular bases, sometimes flattened when old; younger tubercles to about ¼ in. long and wide at bases; old tubercles to nearly ½ in. long.
AREOLES Dimorphic; spinous portion at tip of tubercle small, round, or oval, with some white wool at first, later bare; floral or vegetative part, in axil, without wool; axils bare.
SPINES 20–30 conspicuous, slender, white, even radial spines, lying flat, interlocking with those of neighboring areoles; very slender, stiff; often slightly hairy under magnifying glass; ⅛–½ in. long; upper and lower spines of each areole shortest, usually about ¼ in. long, occasionally ⅛ in.; lateral spines longer; 1–3 dark centrals per areole; lowermost perpendicular to plant; ¼–¾ in. long, red-brown to almost black and strongly hooked; upper centrals upright just in front of upper radials, forming V if 2; never hooked, usually whitish over lower half, upper half red or yellow-brown.
FLOWERS Rose-purple; ¾–1⅛ in. long and wide; usually forming ring around new growth; opening widely; outer petals short, oblong or conical, with brownish midlines and pink, fringed edges; inner petals longer, about ¾ in. long, slender (about ³⁄₁₆ in. wide at widest), with smooth edges, bluntly or sharply pointed tips; solid pink or with deeper midlines fading to almost white edges; pink filaments; pale orange anthers; very long style, ¼+ in.

Mammillaria microcarpa. 2 inches tall.

above stamens, pistil about equal to length of longest petals; 6–10 slender, light green stigma lobes, about ³⁄₁₆ in. long.

FRUITS Scarlet when ripe; oval to club-shaped; ¾–1 in. long; dried flower parts persist; fruits develop rather slowly, with long blooming season; sometimes called dimorphic; black, pitted seeds, almost round, less than ¹⁄₁₆ in. (1 mm or less) diameter.

RANGE Northwestern corner of Presidio County to Franklin Mountains near El Paso, Texas, across southern part of New Mexico into Arizona and Mexico.

REMARKS Dainty little fishhook cactus; rather common; blooms well with perfect drainage and hot sun. Includes and perhaps should be called *M. grahamii* Eng.

Mammillaria wrightii Eng.
(Benson: *M. wrightii* var. *wrightii*)

STEMS Solitary, 1½–3 in. diameter above ground; hemispherical or spherical when moist and growing; when desiccated and dormant, flattened and even depressed on top; prolonged below ground into tapering, top-shaped

Mammillaria wrightii. Stem 1³⁄₁₆ inches in diameter.

base, similar to short taproot; above ground covered by conical or almost cylindrical tubercles ¼–⅞ in. long, with round bases and naked axils.

AREOLES Dimorphic; spinous portion on tip of tubercle round, with short white wool; floral part in axil.

SPINES 8–15 radial spines, lying flat or nearly so; ³⁄₁₆–⅝ in. long; all white or with brown tips; uppermost tend to be darker, sometimes all brown; bases somewhat bulbous; more or less fine, hairy pubescence visible with lens; 1–4, usually 2–3, centrals, red-brown or blackish, slender, ⅜–½ in. long, usually all hooked, although upper 1 may be straight; some fine pubescence.

FLOWERS Bright purple; 1–3 in. across when fully open; about 13 outer segments, somewhat triangular, about ⅜ in. long by ³⁄₁₆ in. wide, pointed, purplish-green, with light, fringed edges; about 20 inner petals, almost linear, about ¾ in. long by ⅛–³⁄₁₆ in. wide, pointed, purple; filaments greenish at bases, pinkish above; pale orange anthers; style greenish, pinkish above; 11 lemon-yellow stigma lobes.

FRUITS About ¾–1 in. long, oval to broadly obovate, ½–1 in. widest diameter; dull purple; seeds about ¹⁄₁₆ in. (1.5 mm) long, almost round, black, pitted.

RANGE Always rare but growing over most of central and western New Mexico.

REMARKS Very similar to *M. wilcoxii*; very rare little cactus of lower mountain slopes in south-central New Mexico.

Mammillaria wilcoxii Toumey
(Benson: *M. wrightii* var. *wilcoxii*)

STEMS Solitary, rounded to nearly spherical without large underground base; to 6 in. diameter, often much smaller; tubercles ⅜–¾ in. long, conical from somewhat flattened bases about ¼ in. wide; naked axils.

AREOLES Dimorphic; spinous portion on tip of tubercle oval, very small, with some short wool; floral portion in axil.

SPINES 14–22 radial spines, ⅜–⅝ in. long, slender and straight, white with light brown tips or light brown, radiating from areole or spreading outward slightly, interlocking with those of neighboring areoles; 1–5 spreading centrals, at least 1 hooked, usually 2–3, all hooked; brown, slender, ½–1¼ in. long; variable amount of downlike pubescence under lens.

FLOWERS Pink, pale rose, or very pale purple; 1–1¼ in. long, 1–2 in. wide when fully open; about 20 outer perianth segments, brownish-green, almost linear, ¾ in. long by about ⅛ in. wide, pointed, fringed with white hairs; to about 40 inner petals in 2 rows, long and narrow, usually to 1¼ in. long by ⅛ in. wide, pointed, with pink midlines and cream-colored edges; white filaments; light orange anthers; greenish style; 5–9 green stigma lobes.

FRUITS Pink to greenish-purple, obovate; ⅝–1 in. long, to about ½ in. thick;

Mammillaria wilcoxii. Stem 1⅞ inches in diameter.

black, pitted, almost round seeds, to ¹⁄₁₆ in. (about 1¾ mm) long.

RANGE Southeastern Arizona and Sonora, into southwestern New Mexico.

REMARKS More southwestern form having no enlarged underground base, more radials, longer centrals, smaller flowers, and green stigma lobes to distinguish it from *M. wrightii.* Some specialists have *M. viridiflora* (B. & R.) Bod. and *M. meridiorosei* Castetter et al. as separate forms, but I have not been able to find consistent characters to place these outside this taxon.

Mammillaria heyderi Muehlenpf.
(Benson: *M. heyderi* only in part)
Nipple Cactus, Biznaga de Chilitos, Little Chilis

STEMS Single flattened hemisphere to 5 in. diameter, to about 2 in. tall; from heavy base underground, not prolonged into taproot, covered by firm tubercles in spiral rows; axils very woolly when young, wool disappears or persists, sometimes even becoming thicker; mature tubercles to about ½ in. long; tips round and conical from pyramidal, quadrangular bases about ¼ in. wide, ventral side definitely keeled; milky sap.

AREOLES Dimorphic; spinous portion on tip of tubercle round, small, with a little white wool at first, then naked; floral portion in axil, with much white wool at first.

SPINES 9–26+ even radial spines per areole; 3/16–1/2 in. long, lower longer and stouter than upper, all slender and weak; small upper ones whitish with red-brown tips; larger lower ones usually red-brown; usually only 1 central, straight out from center of areole, short, 1/8–3/8 in. long; dark reddish-brown or with lighter brown tip in center; rarely 2 identical centrals, 1 upward, other deflexed.

FLOWERS Often several in circle around newer growth at center; 3/4–1 1/2 in. tall and wide; brownish, pinkish, or very pale purple shading to white; outer petals have greenish or brownish midline, shading into whitish, smooth, unfringed edges and pointed tip; inner petals have brownish-pink to pale rose midlines with whitish or pink edges, entire to slightly ragged toward pointed tips; whitish to deep pink filaments; yellow anthers; 5–10 light green, cream-colored, or tan stigma lobes.

FRUITS Bright carmine red; club-shaped; 1/2–1 1/2 in. long; usually ripen about a year after inception; often a ring of them at same time as flowers; reddish-brown, pitted seeds, less than 1/16 in. (about 1 mm) long.

RANGE Northeastern limit from Corpus Christi, Texas, to San Antonio, to Jackson and Greer counties in extreme southwestern Oklahoma, then southwest through southern New Mexico into Arizona.

REMARKS A large, wide-ranging species, with several varieties; more or less flattened hemisphere of very regular tubercles in spirals; never as large in diameter as *M. meiacantha*, nearest relative in our area, but often less flattened, taller. Usually found under partial shade; cannot do well in full sun; can tolerate more water than many cacti; more easily grown out of normal environment. Spanish common name, *biznaga de chilitos* (little chilis) refers to fruits; 2 main flower colors, with pinkish midline fading to white edges or with brownish or greenish-brown midline with white edges.

Mammillaria heyderi var. *heyderi* (Muehlenpf.) (Benson: *M. heyderi* var. *heyderi* only in part)

STEMS As the species.

AREOLES As the species.

SPINES As the species, except 20–26 radials.

FLOWERS As the species, except 3/4 to about 1 in. long and broad, 6–8 stigma lobes.

FRUITS As the species, except 3/4–1 1/2 in. long.

RANGE Out of Mexico north to near Fredericksburg, Texas, then northwest across southern New Mexico.

REMARKS Typical variety of the species; widest range of 3 U.S. varieties; only cactus in Southwest with milky sap and 20+ radials.

Mammillaria heyderi var. *heyderi*. 4⅓ inches across.

Mammillaria heyderi var. *applanata*. 4 inches across.

Mammillaria heyderi var. *applanata* Eng.

STEMS As the species.

AREOLES As the species.

SPINES As the species, except 14–20 radials.

FLOWERS As the species, except to about 1 in.; 5–10 stigma lobes.

FRUITS As the species.

RANGE South Texas to Austin and west into Big Bend; also isolated populations in extreme southwest Oklahoma.

REMARKS Can be separated from typical variety only by number of spines; may grow together in parts of range; var. *applanata* grows farther east in south Texas.

Mammillaria heyderi var. *hemisphaerica*. 3½ inches across.

Mammillaria heyderi var. *hemisphaerica* Eng.

STEMS As the species.

AREOLES As the species.

SPINES As the species, except 9–13 radials.

FLOWERS As the species, except almost always pinkish-white instead of purplish or greenish-white, somewhat larger, 1–1½ in. tall and wide; 5–8 stigma lobes.

FRUITS As the species, except average smaller.

RANGE Eastern Mexico along Texas Gulf Coast to Corpus Christi, northwest to Atascosa County; also Jackson and Greer counties, southwestern Oklahoma, and southern New Mexico.

Mammillaria meiacantha. 4 inches across.

REMARKS Smallest number of radials of *M. heyderi* group; any cactus with milky sap and 9–13 radials in our 5-state area likely to be this variety. Grows to edges of sand dunes along beach; can hardly tolerate full sun. Would seem to include *M. heyderi* var. *bullingtoniana* Castetter et al.

Mammillaria meiacantha Eng.
(Benson: *M. heyderi* var. *meiacantha*)
Biznaga de Chilitos, Little Chilis

STEMS Single, circular, to 12 in. across, greatly depressed, rises to 1–2 in. above ground; top of large underground base which might be interpreted as extremely short taproot; almost flat surface, covered with firm, dark green or blue-green tubercles in spiral rows; tubercles pyramidal from quadrangular bases with ventral angle exaggerated into keel; from about ½ in. long, ⅜ in. wide at base to about ⅞ in. long, ⅝ in. wide; milky sap at wounds.

AREOLES Dimorphic; spinous portion on tip of tubercle nearly round, about

⅛ in. across, with white wool at first, later bare; floral portion in axil of tubercle, with white wool at first, later lost.

SPINES 5–9 stout radial spines, more or less spreading; ¼–½ in. long; lower ones longest and heaviest; pinkish at first, fading to gray or yellowish, always with black or dark brown tips; 1 central, similar to radials except often a little darker, about ¼–⅜ in. long, perpendicular or turned upward almost with upper radials.

FLOWERS Opening widely, 1–1¾ in. long and wide; often a ring of blooms outside newer center; 12–14 outer perianth segments with reddish-brown midlines with pinkish, entire edges; 14–16 inner petals with purplish midlines and pink or white edges; ¼ in. wide, with pointed tips, edges often very lightly notched toward tip; white or pink filaments; cream-colored or yellowish anthers; style longer than stamens; 6–9 light green stigma lobes.

FRUITS Elongated and club-shaped, deep rose or scarlet; about ⅞–1¼ in. long; reddish-brown, pitted seeds, less than 1⁄16 in. (1 mm) or less long.

RANGE Northern Mexico throughout southwestern Texas west of line from Sanderson along eastern edges of Davis and Guadalupe mountains to Carlsbad, New Mexico, throughout lower one-fourth of New Mexico into Arizona.

REMARKS Largest Mammillaria found in United States; most specimens 5–8 in. diameter; old plants to 12 in.; in very dry seasons large fleshy base shrinks and pulls plant into ground; tubercles commonly level with soil or slightly above. Not easily distinguished from close relatives; most characters matched by extreme forms of relatives; flowers and fruits quite similar to other species, except a little larger than western varieties of *M. heyderi*; distinguished by spines; 5–9 stout radials; *M. heyderi*, *M. macdougalii*, and *M. gummifera* have 9–20 slender, almost bristlelike radials; Mexican species *M. melanocentra* has similar number and thickness, but length of spines differs; *M. meiacantha* has radials ¼–½ in. long, centrals ¼–⅜ in. long; *M. melanocentra* has radials ¾–1½ in. long, central ¾–1¼ in. long; more specifically a desert plant than *M. heyderi*; can stand full sun better, often grows totally unshaded except for sparse grasses; rots more quickly if watered too much.

Mammillaria sphaerica Dietrich
(Benson: *M. longimamma* var. *sphaerica*)

ROOTS Thick, soft, fleshy taproot to 1 in. thick.

STEMS Light green, spherical, often depressed at top; new heads usually produced on all sides rapidly; when mature, low mass to nearly 1 ft. diameter composed of irregular clusters; tubercles very soft, spreading loosely, ½–1¼ in. long; cylindrical, usually tapering toward end, not grooved, not broadened at base; with insufficient water or too much sun, tubercles shrink to ¼ in. long, become firm, regular, closely packed.

AREOLES Dimorphic; spinous portion on tip of tubercle small and circular, some short wool at first, becoming bare; floral portion in axil of tubercle has some hairs, which may or may not persist.

SPINES 12–15 even radial spines, slender and weak; usually 3 lower ones $3/16$ in. long to thicker lateral and upper ones, $3/8$–$5/8$ in. long; brownish, enlarged bases; upper parts smooth, hornlike, yellow, becoming gray with age; 1 central perpendicular to plant, similar to radials except slightly thicker, $3/8$–$1/2$ in. long.

FLOWERS Clear lemon-yellow; about 2–$2\frac{1}{2}$ in. diameter and height; cylindrical, light green, naked ovary; about 25 petals; outer ones short, narrow, linear, pointed; next are longest, broadening toward point to about $3/8$ in. wide, with brownish midlines and yellow, smooth edges; innermost petals broaden from very narrow bases to about same width, shorter; lemon-yellow; pale orange, swirled filaments; anthers same color, tucked in around style; 8 long, rough, yellow stigma lobes; fragrant.

FRUITS Seldom seen; egg-shaped, about $1/2$ in. long, persisting as green structures with tubercles, then turning maroon; black, pitted seeds.

RANGE South Texas below line from Laredo to Corpus Christi, on into Mexico.

REMARKS Grows under bushes in thickets of south Texas brush country; low clusters; rather common. Quickly distinguished from other Mammillarias of Texas by color: very light, almost sickly yellow-green; others dark green or bluish-green. Without water or shade, tubercles shrink to less than half size to cluster of small, spherical, compact heads of short, firm tubercles; large numbers of large, beautiful, clear yellow flowers; rather good tolerance of coolness and moisture; better for growing in northern and eastern climates than strictly desert species; cannot stand freezing. Very close relative in northern Mexico, *M. longimamma*, larger, tubercles to 2 in. long, spines to 1 in. long, flowers about same size; easily confused, but *M. sphaerica* has smooth spines, swirled filaments; *M. longimamma* has rough or hairy spines and straight filaments.

Mammillaria sphaerica. Main plant, with offsets, 4¾ inches across.

Genus *Opuntia* Miller

Placed last in this account is the large genus *Opuntia*. Those who deal in matters of primitive versus advanced and theories of development tell us it should really be the first U.S. genus considered. The Opuntias are generally regarded as more primitive than the cacti I have already enumerated, and they also certainly deserve first place for their success. In over half of our states Opuntias are the only cacti found, and it is these cacti which enable us to say that cacti grow over almost the whole of the United States. It is also the Opuntias which have escaped and flourished when introduced in such faraway parts of the world as the Mediterranean and north African countries, where they have become in many places a common part of the scenery, and Australia, where they have become the classic examples of plant invaders.

Usually mentioned characteristics of the Opuntias are the possession of jointed stems; cylindrical or conical leaves on young stems; the presence of glochids; the production of spreading, rotate flowers with more or less sensitive stamens and with areoles, which often produce glochids and spines, on the ovaries; fruits with thick rinds; and seeds comparatively large, rounded in one plane and flattened in the other, while covered by hard, bony, light-colored arils.

There is usually little difficulty in recognizing an Opuntia and telling it from the cacti of the other genera. One or another of the features just listed is almost always so obvious that one could hardly miss it. So we do not need to dwell here on the characteristics of the genus.

But once a person knows it is an Opuntia, the problems have only begun, if he or she wishes to classify it further. This is because the process of sorting out the Opuntias within the group is one of the most difficult in all taxonomy. Several things contribute to this difficulty.

One of these is the fact that the Opuntias seem to react to differences in their environments more quickly and with more drastic growth-form changes than do other cacti. In the Echinocacti or Echinocerei the plant usually grows much the same as any other of its own species as long as the environment is tolerable at all, and then ordinarily, if the environment becomes so changed that it cannot put out typical growth, it just fails to grow at all. On the other hand, the Opuntia in a bad situation will grow on, but grow in a form often so radically different from the typical that one would hardly suspect the environmentally modified specimen to be of the same species as a typical one.

As a result of this fact, where, for instance, in the former genera one can list maximum and minimum spine numbers, spine lengths, and spine characters within definite, rather narrow, and unvarying limits, and often use these to recognize species, one has to list the spines of Opuntias within widely varying limits and one must be very careful in any attempt to delineate species of Opuntias by their spine characters. A simple experiment, if only once carried out, would keep a person from ever again depending on Opuntia spines remaining the same. It is easy to take half a dozen different, typically spiny Opuntias and, by growing them a few years in a very shady, moist situation, end up with half a dozen very nearly indistinguishable spineless or only weakly spined specimens. All too often such an atypical plant has been given a separate name or has been mistaken for a normally weak-spined species. The literature is, therefore, a morass of conflicting reports.

Other characters of the Opuntias, such as stem size or even stem shape, flower and fruit size, and so on, are also capable of being influenced by the environment. Where an Echinocactus or a Mammillaria either puts out a standard-sized flower and fruit or else just waits to make the effort until the environment is more favorable, an Opuntia in a poor situation usually does not mind at all putting out a flower half as big as typical and may go ahead to ripen a fruit also half as big as it should have been. Great care must be taken to allow for this variability.

Perhaps the only effort to approach this problem properly was made by Dr. David Griffiths, who, with U.S. experiment stations at his disposal, once started an ambitious program of growing all the Opuntias of the Southwest in identical situations and of raising seedlings of them all in uniform and differing environments in order to discover what really are the constant characters of these cacti. But this sort of a program would take many years to yield really definite answers, and although Dr. Griffiths was able to gain some hints in the years he carried it on, no one continued his fields of Opuntias, and no such attempt has been made again. We are therefore left to work out indirectly what the solid characters of these species are, and it is no easy task.

To the foregoing must be added the fact that some of the Opuntia species cover huge ranges of territory and within these huge territories show various different forms not directly due to environment. It seems clear, for instance, that the large prickly pears of the United States can only be understood if a few very broad species are recognized. One of these, *Opuntia engelmannii*, with its range running from at least Louisiana—and some would say even from Florida—to California, would be one of the widest-ranging of any U.S. cactus. And within this huge entity are a number of varieties which have caused great confusion, as some have described them as separate species, and others have ignored them entirely, assuming them to be the mere results of local environments. It is hard to find agreement as to how to interpret such a situation, and experimental evidence is so far almost totally lacking.

In this study, when faced with this sort of situation, I have taken the attitude that no described form can be ignored and relegated to the synonymy without investigation. So we have made great efforts to locate and study each one described for this area, no matter how obscure. And wherever we have found a form which exists as a population with a definable range, which does not seem to be due to a local environmental factor, but which does not seem distinct enough to be clearly a separate species, I have listed it as a variety. Only by keeping these forms thus in sight can we keep them available for the biosystematic studies which are long overdue and which will someday give us a clearer understanding of the Opuntias.

Those hardy enough, and possessing enough of the true botanist's curiosity to pass up no plant, however thorny, will find a huge opportunity in the study of the Opuntias. In sheer numbers of their populations and extents of their ranges they excel. Nor does one have the disappointing experience with these, as one all too often has with the other cacti, of traveling to a spot where a species is supposed to grow profusely only to find that some collector or dealer has stripped the area bare of every specimen which once was there. So few bother to bring home Opuntias that one can travel through country most ruthlessly sacked of cacti and still find the Opuntias untouched. Even the inroads of agriculture have not adversely affected the majority of them. Root-plowing, chaining, and most of the other practices used to clear the range of the chaparral have usually, while exterminating the other cacti, merely torn the Opuntias apart and distributed their stems widely, each one of which then rooted, and the Opuntia population has, therefore, multiplied. So the opportunity for studying them is perhaps greater today in our area than ever before. Only a few obscure species limited to very small ranges have been reduced by clearing of fields and other agricultural practices, although in the future the picture will probably be very different. All the big guns of the chemical industry are being aimed at the chaparral, and the mass spraying of the range with some of the newer herbicides clearly could reduce these plants to a vanishing point. But the student of the Opuntias can take heart in knowing that, tough as these plants are, they will be among the last wild plants to go.

The flat-stemmed Opuntias are known almost universally as prickly pears. Tough and thorny as they are, these are the main food-producing cacti. Tons of their stems are fed to cattle, particularly in Texas and Mexico, where sophisticated methods are used to burn the spines off so that the flesh is available to the animals. And these plants are used extensively for human consumption as well. The young pads, before their tissues have hardened or their spines been produced, are relished. Called *nopalitos*, these are eaten widely in Mexico, where they are usually breaded with cornmeal and fried, and in Texas, where they are more often boiled and added to a sort of omelet. In the spring they are often on sale at markets in San Antonio and the rest of south Texas, and in San Antonio they are served in some Mexican restaurants, as well as being sold canned in some supermarkets. But the most widely used part of the Opuntia is probably the fruit, called tuna. Certain species producing large, sweet fruits are cultivated as crops in Mexico, and this was one of the reasons for these plants being introduced into some other parts of the world where they have become such pests.

The large, upright, cylindrical-stemmed Opuntias are known collectively as chollas. I do not know of any use of these chollas for food. They are far too woody and tough, and their fruits are not edible. But certain species of them make very large and beautiful bushes and are widely grown as ornamentals. Almost any inhabited area of the Southwest will have some specimens of these species planted just for their beauty. They may be prized highly in places where almost no other shrubs or trees will grow. And anyone who has looked over the typical curio store knows well the lamp bases and other trinkets made of the curious, reticulated wood of these chollas.

So, whether regarded as friends or enemies, the Opuntias are easily some of the most strange, fascinating, and challenging of plants.

Key to the Opuntias

1a. Joints flattened; spines not covered with papery sheaths (Platyopuntias)—2.

  2a. Plants upright and bushy, 2 to 7 feet tall, sometimes spreading and forming thickets, but with no branches prostrate, and with upright branches attaining a length of 3 pads or more—3.

    3a. Areoles ¾ to 2½ inches apart, with the majority on any pad 1 inch or more apart—4.

      4a. Possessing spines—5.

        5a. Spines all round   —*O. stricta* (in part).

        5b. At least 1 spine of each areole flattened—6.

          6a. Pads conspicuously tuberculate by raised areoles; fruits spiny, with 1 to 5 rigid spines up to 1 inch long on at least each upper areole, and these fruits becoming dry when ripe

                              —*O. spinosibacca.*

          6b. Pads not markedly tuberculate; fruits naked or nearly so—7.

            7a. Spines when mature whitish, yellow, red-brown, or mottled, but with no part of any spine black—8.

              8a. Pads circular or variously shaped, but not over twice as long as broad—9.

                9a. Seeds ¹⁄₁₆ to ³⁄₁₆ inch (1½–4½ millimeters) in diameter—10.

                  10a. Spines on old areoles on old pads not increasing in number beyond the normal 10 or so of mature pads—11.

                    11a. Areoles and glochids normal in appearance and not exaggerated in development when old—12.

                    12a. Fruits spherical, oval, or broadly pear-shaped, with little or no constriction below, with the umbilicus not constricted but flat or nearly so and as broad or nearly as broad as the widest part of the fruit; flowers yellow to red, but never yellow with red centers—13.

13a. Fruits 2 to 3½ inches long, deep burgundy in color when ripe; seeds ⅛ inch or a little more (3–4 millimeters) in diameter; stigmas green—14.

14a. Spines deep brown at their bases, becoming white or whitish toward the tips; leaves ¼ to ⅜ inch long; fruits edible
—*O. engelmannii* var. *engelmannii*.

14b. Spines and glochids all bright yellow or yellow with the bases to sometimes all but the tips red-brown; leaves ¼ to ½ inch long; fruits not pleasant to the taste
—*O. engelmannii* var. *texana*.

13b. Fruits 1 to 2 inches long, bright red to purplish-red when ripe; seeds ¹⁄₁₆ to ³⁄₁₆ inch (1½–4½ millimeters) in diameter; stigmas white to greenish—15.

15a. Spines heavy and rigid, the longest spine usually about 1½ inches long and only rarely reaching 2½ inches; fruits purplish-red—16.

16a. Fruits spherical or nearly so with no constriction below and always spineless; seeds about ³⁄₁₆ inch (4–4½ millimeters) in diameter; spines redbrown or with at least the bases red-brown; flowers small with dark green stigmas
—*O. engelmannii* var. *cyclodes*.

16b. Fruits not spherical, but broadly egg-shaped with some slight constriction below and having numerous glochids and often a few spines ¼ to ⅝ inch long on them; seeds extremely small, being ¹⁄₁₆ inch or slightly more (1½–2½ millimeters) in diameter; spines entirely yellow; flowers large with stigmas light greenish-white
—*O. engelmannii* var. *alta*.

15b. Spines slender and long, as well as somewhat flexible, the main spines being 2 to

3 inches long; fruits not so purplish, but more bright red; stigmas either dark green or white—17.

17a. Pads thick and light or yellowish-green; main central spines all sharply deflexed and very flexible and ½ to 3 inches long; fruit broad egg-shaped to club-shaped, with some constriction below; seeds about ⅛ inch (3–3½ millimeters) in diameter; stigmas dark green

    —*O. engelmannii* var. *flexispina*.

17b. Pads thin and blue-green in color; main spines porrect, 2 to 3 inches long and conspicuously longer than the other spines; fruits spherical to oval with no constriction below; seeds between ¹⁄₁₆ and ⅛ inch (2–3 millimeters) in diameter; stigmas white

    —*O. engelmannii* var. *cacanapa*.

12b. Fruits elongated and club-shaped, with the base definitely constricted and the umbilicus also constricted, much narrower than the widest part of the fruit and deeply to very deeply pitted; stigmas yellowish—18.

18a. Spines bright yellow or yellow with light brown bases; flowers all yellow; fruits purplish or plum in color; seeds ³⁄₁₆ inch or less (3½–4½ millimeters) in diameter

    —*O. tardospina*.

18b. Spines brown below with whitish above, never bright yellow; flowers orange-yellow with red centers; fruits bright scarlet-red in color; seeds ³⁄₁₆ inch or more (4–5 millimeters) in diameter

    —*O. phaeacantha* var. *major* (in part).

11b. Areoles and glochids exaggerated in development when old—19.

19a. Areoles enlarging to ½ inch in diameter on old stems and bulging outward to form a sort of cylindrical projection to ½ inch high, with a compact tuft of short glochids on the summit of it; pads large, mostly round, and blue-green in color   —*O. engelmannii* var. *dulcis*.

19b. Areoles large and bulging outward noticeably,

with glochids very long and scattered loosely throughout the areole, forming starlike clusters almost covering the surfaces of the mature pads; pads smaller and more obovate and with the color more dull dark green than is typical for the species
—*O. engelmannii* var. *aciculata* (in part).

10b. Spines on old areoles on old trunks increasing greatly to 20 or 30 per areole, covering the older parts of the plants with a complete covering of spines   —*O. chlorotica.*

9b. Seeds more than ³⁄₁₆ inch (4½ millimeters or more) in greatest diameter —*O. phaeacantha* var. *camanchica* (when unusually large and ascending).

8b. Pads greatly elongated so that at least some of them on a normal plant are at least twice as long as they are broad
—*O. engelmannii* var. *linguiformis.*

7b. Spines when growing black or bright orange, when mature black or dark blackish-brown, at least at the base—20.

20a. Fruits ¾ to 1½ inches long, oval or ovate, with no noticeable constriction below and the umbilicus rather deeply pitted, yellowish to scarlet when ripe; seeds ⅛ to ³⁄₁₆ inch (3–4½ millimeters) in diameter; spines heavy, rigid, very angular, and 1 to 6 per areole, found on most areoles, but to only 2 inches or less in length; glochids becoming long and average in number on edge areoles; pads thin and blue-green to yellow-green in color, not becoming reddish   —*O. phaeacantha* var. *nigricans.*

20b. Fruits 1¼ to 2 inches long, elongated oval or egg-shaped, with some slight constriction below and a shallowly pitted umbilicus; seeds more than ³⁄₁₆ inch (about 5 millimeters) in diameter; spines heavy, rigid, almost round to somewhat flattened, 2 to 4 per areole in only the upper areoles, but to 3 inches long; glochids few at first, becoming *very* many and *very* long in the edge areoles; pads thick and pale green, often reddish in color or spotted with reddish around the areoles
—*O. phaeacantha* var. *brunnea.*

4b. Spineless—21.

21a. Pads elongated obovate to elliptical or even spindle-shaped; surface of pads smooth and shining, not glaucous; leaves only ⅛ to ¼ inch long; ovaries narrow and elongated; fruits elongated, pear-shaped, constricted at the base and with deeply pitted umbilicus   —*O. stricta* (in part).

21b. Pads round or oval or even broader than long, surface dull and glaucous; leaves ⅜ to ⅝ inch long; ovaries short and stout; fruits spherical to broadly pear-shaped, with little or no basal constriction and umbilicus flat or only slightly concave—22.

  22a. Surface blue-green; areoles small; glochids very few and short   —*O. engelmannii* var. *subarmata*.

  22b. Surface bright green or dark green, but not blue-green; areoles enlarged and bulging; glochids very long in loose, spreading clusters —*O. engelmannii* var. *aciculata* (when spineless).

3b. Areoles ¼ to 1¼ inches apart, with the majority on any pad less than 1 inch apart—23.

  23a. Spineless—24.

    24a. Pads pubescent; glochids very many but very short and minute, hardly exceeding the wool in the bulging areoles; fruits remaining greenish and rather dry when ripe   —*O. rufida*.

    24b. Pads not pubescent; glochids few but larger; fruits bright red or orange-red and fleshy when ripe   —*O. macrocentra* (in part).

  23b. Spines present—25.

    25a. Spines black or brown, sometimes with gray but never with yellow coloring, to 4 per areole in a few of the upper areoles only, 2 to 5 inches long, somewhat flexible, and at least 1 spine flattened; pads usually purplish in color; seeds ³⁄₁₆ to more than ¼ inch (4½–7 millimeters) in diameter

                                    —*O. macrocentra* (in part).

    25b. Spines yellow in their outer zones, with black or brown bases, not flexible, from ¾ to 4 inches, but usually less than 2 inches long; pads sometimes reddish, but not distinctly purplish in color; seeds around ⅛ inch (2½–4 millimeters) in diameter—26.

      26a. Spines 1 to 3 on a few upper areoles only, ½ to 2 inches, but said to have attained 4 inches long; bases of spines brown; spines round; pads usually with reddish coloring; glochids many but very short   —*O. violacea* var. *santa-rita*.

      26b. Spines 3 to 16 on many or all areoles; never over 1¾ inches long; bases black or dark red-brown, at least when young; pads yellow-green without purple or reddish coloring; glochids many and long—27.

        27a. Spines 6 to as many as 15, consisting of 1 to 5 rigid main spines which are either round or flattened and ³⁄₁₆ to ¾ inch long, plus up to 10 lower, bristlelike spines ³⁄₁₆ to ¾ inch long   —*O. strigil*.

        27b. Spines 3 to 6, consisting of about 2 rigid, round main ones ½ to 1¼ inches long and 2 or 3 lower, bristlelike spines ³⁄₁₆ to ⅝ inch long   —*O. atrispina*.

2b. Plants growing prostrate or sprawling or, if ascending, never standing upright over 2 or 3 pads or 12 to 20 inches tall—28.

28a. Pads 6 to 10 inches long in maximum size—29.

29a. Areoles ⅜ to ⅞ inch apart; fruits more or less spiny and becoming dry when ripe—30.

30a. Spines 1 to 10 per areole; fruits 1½ to 2 inches long and broadly club-shaped, spiny above or spineless—31.

31a. Spines 1 to 4 in only the upper areoles of the pads
—*O. rhodantha* var. *rhodantha* (in part).

31b. Spines 4 to 10 in all or nearly all areoles of the pads
—*O. rhodantha* var. *spinosior*.

30b. Spines 10 to 15 in all or nearly all areoles; fruits ⅞ to 1¼ inches long and obovate to broadly club-shaped, spiny
—*O. hystricina* (in part).

29b. Areoles ¾ to 2 inches apart; fruits remaining fleshy and spineless—32.

32a. At least some areoles with more than 1 spine; pads almost circular to broad egg-shaped; seeds thin or average in thickness—33.

33a. Spines 1 to 5, slender to medium thickness, round or nearly so with no lower bristlelike spines present—34.

34a. Fruits 1½ to 3½ inches long, club-shaped, with pronounced constriction at the base and with the top narrow and deeply pitted; seeds about ⅛ inch (2½–4 millimeters) in diameter, with narrow rims and the body of the seed rather thick — *O. leptocarpa*.

34b. Fruits 1¼ to 2⅜ inches long, broadly club-shaped, with the base constricted and the umbilicus somewhat pitted; seeds about ³⁄₁₆ inch (4–5 millimeters) in diameter
—*O. phaeacantha* var. *major* (in part, when stunted).

33b. Spines 1 to 8, main spines heavy to very heavy and flattened, often with lower bristlelike spines present; fruits 1 to 2 inches long, oval to very broadly egg-shaped, with little or no constriction at the base and with broad, flat, or shallowly pitted umbilicus; seeds ³⁄₁₆ to ¼ inch (4½–6 millimeters) in diameter, with wide rims
—*O. phaeacantha* var. *camanchica* (in part).

32b. Spineless or with only 1 spine in a few areoles; pads elongated egg-shaped to spindle-shaped; seeds very thick
—*O. compressa* var. *allairei*.

28b. Pads 2 to 6 inches long—35.

35a. At least some areoles of the pad more than 1¼ inches apart—this is a stunted, abnormally small specimen of some larger species, and it will probably be impossible to identify it with this key.

35b. Areoles $\frac{3}{16}$ to 1¼ inches apart—36.

36a. Pads solidly attached to each other and not detaching to come away from the plant at a touch—37.

37a. Spines to 5 or more per areole and found on half or more areoles of mature pads; stigmas bright green—38.

38a. Fruits remaining fleshy when ripe and oval or oblong in shape; seeds not thick for their diameters—39.

39a. Pads thin with definitely constricted or even attenuated bases; spines round or nearly so, slender and flexible and mostly deflexed; glochids red-brown and short; seeds slightly over ⅛ to ¼ inch (3½–6 millimeters) in diameter, with narrow to medium rims
—*O. phaeacantha* var. *tenuispina.*

39b. Pads thickish, round or nearly so with no definite constrictions at their bases; spines at least somewhat flattened, medium to thick and always rigid, glochids long and yellow or light brown; seeds $\frac{3}{16}$ to just over ¼ inch (4½–6½ millimeters) in diameter, with wide rims
—*O. cymochila.*

38b. Fruits dry when ripe, various in shape—40.

40a. Pads elongated oval to clavate, less than half as broad as they are long, and very thick; roots stolonlike; seeds about ¼ inch (6–7 millimeters) in diameter
—*O. arenaria.*

40b. Pads round or oval to broadly egg-shaped or oblong, always more than half as broad as they are long and not unusually thick; roots normally fibrous—41.

41a. Pads more or less prostrate, sometimes with young pads ascending, but with older ones reclining; at least main spines rigid and stout—42.

42a. Surface of pads noticeably tuberculate and often wrinkled; glochids few to average and short; main spines 0 to 5 per areole and porrect to deflexed, 2 inches or less long, all rigid or often becoming greatly elongated, soft, flexible, and hairlike, particularly toward the bases of the pads
—*O. polyacantha* (in part).

42b. Surface of pads not noticeably tuberculate or wrinkled; glochids many and often long; main spines 1 to 8 per areole, spreading, heavy, but moderately flexible, and to 4 inches long
—*O. hystricina* (in part).

41b. Pads all erect or ascending, with not even old pads reclining; spines slender, to 4 inches long, and moderately flexible
—*O. erinaceae.*

37b. Spines 0 to 4 or rarely 5 per areole on only the upper edge areoles or at most on those of the upper half of the pad—43.

43a. Fruit remaining fleshy; stigmas yellow or whitish—44.

44a. Fruits egg-shaped to club-shaped with the bases noticeably constricted—45.

45a. Pads ascending from a central trunklet, blue-green or gray-green in color, usually with some purplish blotching around the areoles; root a large central taproot ½ to 1½ inches in diameter and 12 inches or longer, not tuberlike enlargements on otherwise fibrous roots; flowers deep red to purple—46.

46a. Plants standing 6 to 12 inches tall; pads medium thickness and to 4 or 5 inches long, glabrous, blue-green in color, the surface flat without raised areoles; glochids numerous and yellow in color; fruits 1½ inches or more long; seeds just over ³⁄₁₆ to ¼ inch (5–6 millimeters) in diameter —*O. pottsii.*

46b. Plants standing less than 6 inches tall; pads thin and to only 2½ inches long, glaucous gray-green in color, the surface tuberculate by raised areoles; glochids numerous and bright red-brown in color; fruits ⅝ to 1 inch long; seeds ⅛ inch or a little more (3–4 millimeters) in diameter —*O. plumbea.*

45b. Pads prostrate or sprawling, not ascending from a central trunklet, thick, yellow-gray or deep green, but not blue-green in color; roots fibrous or fibrous with tubers on them, but with no central taproot—47.

47a. Pads gray-green or yellow-green and glaucous—48.

48a. Pads to 5½ inches long; spines to 2¼ inches long and slender to medium in thickness; glochids greenish-yellow to straw-colored or light brown, average in number, and to ¼ inch or less long; flowers large and yellow in color; fruits 1½ to 2½ inches long; seeds ³⁄₁₆ to ¼ inch (5 millimeters plus) in diameter

—*O. compressa* var. *stenochila.*

48b. Pads to 4 inches long; spines to 2¾ inches long and thick to very thick; glochids bright yellow, very numerous and conspicuous, and to ½ inch long on old pads; flowers small and reddish in color; fruits ¾ to 1 inch long and very slender; seeds ⅛ inch or a little more (about 3½ millimeters) in diameter —*O. ballii.*

47b. Pads deep green, surface shining—49.

49a. Plant entirely prostrate, with all pads reclining by

the end of their first season; pads very thick, very wrinkled when dehydrated, but not tuberculate by elevations at the areoles; spines 0 to 3 per areole on the upper areoles and 1 inch or less long, heavy, straight, and round; inner petals 10 to 14 in number —*O. compressa* var. *humifusa.*

49b. Plants sprawling, with very old pads sometimes reclining, but most pads ascending, pads not so thick as the last, somewhat to extremely tuberculate by raised areoles; spines 0 to 5, often some of them over 1 inch long and often the main spine somewhat flattened; inner petals 5 to 9 in number—50.

50a. Spineless; flowers very large (4 to 5 inches in diameter); fruits 2 inches or more long; pads very tuberculate

—*O. compressa* var. *grandiflora.*

50b. Spines 1 to 5; flowers average size (2 to 3 inches in diameter); fruits 1 to 2 inches long—51.

51a. Seeds about ³⁄₁₆ inch (4–5 millimeters) in diameter—52.

52a. Glochids brown or yellowish; surface only somewhat tuberculate; spines 1 to 5; inner petals 7 to 9 in number

—*O. compressa* var. *macrorhiza.*

52b. Glochids bright red-brown; surface very tuberculate; spines 1 to 3; inner petals 5 to 7 —*O. compressa* var. *fusco-atra.*

51b. Seeds only around ¹⁄₁₆ inch (1½–2 millimeters) in diameter

—*O. compressa* var. *microsperma.*

44b. Fruits oval with no constriction below

—*O. phaeacantha* var. *camanchica* (when stunted).

43b. Fruits becoming dry when ripe; flowers yellow, pink, or rose; stigmas bright green—53.

53a. Stigma lobes 4 to 6; fruits ³⁄₄ to 1³⁄₈ inches long, spineless, and without constriction below—54.

54a. Fruits spherical to oval; seeds slightly over ³⁄₁₆ inch (5 millimeters) in diameter, thickish, with narrow, acute rims —*O. sphaerocarpa.*

54b. Fruits oblong; seeds from ¼ to just over ⁵⁄₁₆ inch (6–8 millimeters) in diameter, flat and not thick for the size, with wide rims

—*O. polyacantha* (in part, when sparsely spined).

53b. Stigma lobes 8 to 12; fruits 1½ to 1¾ inches long, broadly club-shaped with some tapering constriction below; upper areoles spiny or else entirely spineless
—*O. rhodantha* var. *rhodantha* (in part).

36b. Pads loosely attached so that they separate at a touch; pads small, thick, and almost cylindrical when young—55.

55a. Fruits fleshy, elongated, and club-shaped, 1¼ inches or more long; seeds just under ³⁄₁₆ inch (4 millimeters) in diameter; pads to 4½ inches long, stigmas yellowish   —*O. pusilla.*

55b. Fruits dry, oval or broadly egg-shaped, ½ to 1 inch long; seeds just over ³⁄₁₆ inch (5 millimeters) in diameter; stigma lobes bright green   —*O. fragilis.*

1b. Joints not flattened but cylindrical or club-shaped; spines with either conspicuous or rudimentary papery sheaths—56.

56a. Joints club-shaped or egg-shaped and very tuberculate; plants prostrate or ascending but 12 inches or less in height; spine sheaths rudimentary on tips of immature spines only and usually not present on adult spines (Cornyopuntias)—57.

57a. Joints elongated club-shaped, prostrate to ascending, usually curved; spines to more than 1¼ inches long—58.

58a. Main central spine very heavy, flat, wide, and roughly cross-striated—59.

59a. Joints 3½ to 6 inches long; tubercles 1 to 1¾ inches long
—*O. stanlyi.*

59b. Joints 1 to 3 inches long; tubercles ½ to ¾ inch long
—*O. schottii.*

58b. Main spines round or nearly so, slender to medium thickness, not striated   —*O. grahamii.*

57b. Joints short club-shaped or egg-shaped; main spines to only 1¼ inches long   —*O. clavata.*

56b. Joints cylindrical; plants upright or ascending, never prostrate, bushy, and 1 to 12 feet tall; spine sheaths conspicuous, at least on newly matured main spines (Cylindropuntias)—60.

60a. Width of current year's joints ¾ to 2 inches—61.

61a. Tubercles ¾ to 1½ inches long; color deep green at all times—62.

62a. Fruits globose and about 1 inch in diameter, always tuberculate—63.

63a. Main spines ¾ to 1¼ inches long; spine sheaths whitish or straw-colored; fruits spineless when mature—64.

64a. Flowers purple or reddish (reported as rarely yellowish or white); growth treelike and 3 to 8 feet tall
—*O. imbricata* var. *arborescens.*

64b. Flowers pale greenish with lavender shading; a small bush

1 to 3 feet tall   —*O. imbricata* var. *viridiflora* (in part).

63b. Main spines 2 to 2½ inches long, with glistening silvery sheaths; flowers greenish-yellow; growth low, 1 to 2 feet tall; fruits with sheathed spines to 1 inch long

        —*O. tunicata.*

62b. Fruits obovate to globose, 1 to 2 inches in diameter, becoming nearly or entirely smooth when ripe; main spines to no more than ⅝ inch long   —*O. imbricata* var. *vexans.*

61b. Tubercles ⅜ to ¾ inch long—65.

65a. A large bush 3 to 12 feet tall; spines 6 to 25 in number, mostly ⅜ inch or less long and only rarely to ⅝ inch, spine sheaths inconspicuous and soon falling off; color of plant surface often purplish in severe conditions   —*O. spinosior.*

65b. Low spreading or mat-forming bushes 1 to 2 feet tall; spines 3 to 12 in number, maximum spine length ¾ to 1¼ inches, spine sheaths loose, persistent, and conspicuous; color of plant surface light green   —*O. whipplei* (in part).

60b. Width of current year's joints ¾ inch or less—66.

66a. Plants low-growing, 1 to 3 feet tall; width of current year's joints ⅜ to ¾ inch, with distinct tubercles—67.

67a. Largest spines 1¼ inches or less long (usually less than 1 inch)—68.

68a. Erect, more or less trunked plants; joints strictly cylindrical; spine sheaths not conspicuous and shining; flower greenish-purple or lavender with reddish stigma lobes

        —*O. imbricata* var. *viridiflora* (in part).

68b. Ascending or spreading, but without real trunks, often mat-forming plants; joints slightly clavate by being constricted at the bases; spine sheaths conspicuous and shining; flowers pale yellow; stigmas greenish   —*O. whipplei* (in part).

67b. Largest spines 1½ to 2 inches long; tubercles ⅝ to 1 inch long

        —*O. davisii.*

66b. Plants bushy and growing 3 to 6 feet or more tall; width of current year's joints ⅛ to ½ inch; tubercles indistinct or sometimes actually absent—69.

69a. Joints ¼ to ½ inch thick, with tubercles indistinct to distinct, but always present; flowers greenish-purple and 1 to 1¼ inches in diameter; fruit red and with indistinct tubercles or else smooth when ripe, ¾ to 1 inch long; spines to 1 inch long

        —*O. kleiniae.*

69b. Joints ⅛ to ¼ inch thick, with tubercles at best indistinct and often absent; flowers yellow or greenish-yellow and ½ to ⅞ inch in diameter; fruits red or orange-red and smooth when ripe

        —*O. leptocaulis.*

Opuntia stricta Haw.
(Benson: *O. stricta* var. *stricta*)
Pest Pear

STEMS Erect, much branched and diffuse; usually only 2–3 ft. tall in Texas, with elongated, ovate to elliptical or spindle-shaped pads usually 6–9 in. long, sometimes to 14 in.; medium thick, bluish-green and glabrous when young, light green, somewhat glaucous when old; leaves ⅛–³⁄₁₆ in. long.

AREOLES Very elongated in young pads, oval when older; ¼+ in. long, 1¼–2½ in. apart.

SPINES Often entirely spineless, may have 1–3 per areole; porrect or spreading, ⅜–1¾ in. long, straight, stiff, medium thick; round cross-section, yellow, sometimes slightly mottled with brown, without brown bases.

GLOCHIDS Few and very short on young pads, more with age, never conspicuous; comparatively short, to about ⅜ in. long; yellow or straw-colored.

FLOWERS About 3–4 in. diameter, clear lemon-yellow; slender, club-shaped ovary, 1½–3 in. long, with a few glochids in areoles; perianth segments pointed, spatulate, greenish at bases, clear yellow above; filaments greenish below, yellow above; yellow anthers; short, greenish-yellow style has 6–8 fat white or very pale greenish-white stigma lobes tipping it.

FRUITS Light pinkish-red to rather bright carmine-red when ripe; elongated, club-shaped, 1½ to about 2¾ in. long by ¾–1 in. thick at broadest part; umbilicus deeply pitted; seeds about ⅛ in. (2½–3 mm) diameter, thin, regular, with very narrow but fairly thick rims.

RANGE Primarily Caribbean, found in Cuba, Haiti, and West Indies, widely spread to South America and Australia; found in United States in south Florida; Houma, Louisiana; and entrance to Galveston Bay, Texas.

REMARKS Ran wild in Australia; may have been brought to United States on early boats from Caribbean. Easily confused with *O. engelmannii* var. *texana* and var. *alta*, but in *O. stricta* fruits elongated club-shaped with deeply pitted summits, light red or carmine-red while in *O. engelmannii* varieties they are broad obovate to almost spherical, deep purplish or burgundy, with umbilici flat or nearly so. When only vegetative characters present, most clear difference is elongated ovate, elliptical, or spindle-shaped pads, contrasting with circular to very broadly ovate pads of all *O. engelmannii* forms in natural growth; *O. stricta* also has many fewer spines which are always completely round, while at least main spines of normal *O. engelmannii* form flattened at least at bases.

Opuntia stricta. Plant pictured, 26 inches tall.

Opuntia engelmannii SD
(Benson: *O. lindheimeri*)
Nopal, Tuna, Engelmann's Prickly Pear, Flaming Prickly Pear

STEMS Upright, compact or open and diffuse bush; commonly to 3–6 ft.; some varieties over 10 ft.; pads thick and circular to broadly egg-shaped; 8–14 in. long when mature; medium green or slightly blue-green, often becoming pale yellowish-green with age; more or less thickly covered with whitish bloom which easily rubs off; leaves about ³⁄₁₆–½ in. long.

AREOLES Small and oval or oblong, usually becoming round and enlarging to ¼+ in. with maturity; sometimes much wool and other tissue forming hemispherically bulging or columnar structure when very old.

SPINES Very variable; typically 1–5 per areole on newly matured pads, sometimes to 10–12 during second year; main spines heavy and rigid on typical forms, on some forms more slender, more or less flexible; larger spines always flattened, often greatly, often somewhat twisted and curved; usually surrounded by smaller spines, round and straight; several main spines heavy, spreading and curving downward and outward, ¾–2½ in. long; on one form porrect, to 3 in. long; others spreading in all directions; shorter, more slender; entirely yellow with slightly brownish bases, mottled with brown, whitish with dark brown bases, or deep reddish-brown and only slightly yellowish above; with more or less annular pattern.

GLOCHIDS Few on sides of pads, rather numerous on edges of old pads; coarse and rigid, almost like smaller spines, ⅛–⅝ in. long, spreading loosely, in one form a large raylike cluster; all yellow, mottled with brown, or all red-brown.

FLOWERS Large and showy, profuse; 2½–4 in. tall and wide, clear yellow, orange, or bright red; whole perianth one color, never variegated; ovary 1–3 in. long, always thick, obovate or inverted cone-shaped, often as wide as long at top; outer perianth segments short, varied shapes; 8–10 inner segments, long, to about 1½ in. wide, tip broadest, entire, blunt, usually with slight point at apex; long cream-colored filaments; anthers same color; stamens very sensitive; style whitish; 5–10 heavy stigma lobes, dark green to pure white.

FRUITS Varying; dark red, usually becoming dull purplish or burgundy when very ripe; completely spherical to broadly pear-shaped, with no or only slight constriction at base; 1–3½ in. long in different forms; umbilicus flat or nearly so; seeds small to tiny, ¹⁄₁₆–³⁄₁₆ in. (1½–4½ mm) diameter, comparatively thin, with narrow rims.

RANGE One of widest-ranging cacti; Gulf Coast to Pacific and deep into Mexico; in our area, Brownsville along Gulf Coast into southwestern Louisiana, back northwest past Dallas, Texas, to extreme south-central Oklahoma, south to Abilene, Texas; northwestward into New Mexico, near

Santa Fe, slightly southwestward into Arizona.

REMARKS Often misunderstood; many local populations different enough to have been considered separate species. Largest and strongest of U.S. prickly pears; straggly bush to 6 or 10 ft. tall; thicket of giant pads like skillets; often takes over rangeland; used to feed cattle. Red flowers common in south Texas, yellow or orange in New Mexico; in southern New Mexico spines very heavy, whitish with dark brown bases; in Texas and California spines more yellow. It is one of the remarkable quirks of cactus history that so many still prefer to call this plant *O. lindheimeri*, a name based on pads of one cactus and fruits of another. When he realized this its author abolished it, saying (Engelmann: *Synopsis*), "*O. lindheimeri* Eng. *Pl. Lindh.* is partly this same plant [*O. engelmannii*, which he had just been discussing], partly a hybrid form between it and perhaps *O. rafinesquii*, with narrow clavate fruit." This supposed hybrid became *O. leptocarpa* Mackensen, and so there is nothing left to be *O. lindheimeri*.

Opuntia engelmannii var. *engelmannii* (SD)
(Benson: *O. phaeacantha* var. *discata* in part)

STEMS As the species, except usually only 3–5 ft. tall.

AREOLES 1–2+ in. apart; larger than in some forms of species, ³⁄₁₆–³⁄₈ in. across, larger when older; oval to round, more or less bulging, with brown wool.

SPINES As the species, except main centrals less than 2½ in. long, heavy, much flattened; at first brown or deep red-brown at bases, shading to lighter above, until outer parts are opaque, chalky white or pale straw-colored, fading to plain gray with age.

GLOCHIDS As the species, except yellow, brownish, or mottled yellow and brown; often increasing greatly to conspicuous, open, spreading clusters on edges of older pads.

FLOWERS As the species, except mostly yellow, occasionally orange or reddish; ovary 1–1½ in. long; 8–10 dark green stigma lobes.

FRUITS 2–3 in. long, globose to broadly pear-shaped, little or no constriction below; flat, wide umbilicus on top; deep, dull burgundy when ripe; pulp juicy; seeds ⅛–³⁄₁₆ in. or less (3–4 mm) diameter, with narrow rims.

RANGE Chihuahua and western Coahuila, Mexico, into western Texas, southern New Mexico, southeastern Arizona, and extreme south-central Oklahoma.

REMARKS Typical form of the species; distinguished by whiteness of spines, usually set off against distinctly brown bases; rarely in young spines shading to straw color near tip.

Opuntia engelmannii var. *engelmannii*. Pad 12 inches long.

Opuntia engelmannii var. *cyclodes* (Eng.) Weniger

STEMS As the species, except spreading bush 3–5 ft. high, usually wider than tall, without well-defined central stem; pads as the species, except 6–8 in. long, usually circular, sometimes very broadly oval or egg-shaped; bright green or yellow-green with some glaucescence.

AREOLES As the species, except not quite as large, only 1–1½ in. apart.

SPINES As the species, but deflexed, relatively slender, pale yellow or straw-colored with or without red or reddish-brown bases; usually 1–2 spines per areole on upper half of pad, sometimes to 6; typically 1 large flattened spine ¾–1¾ in. long, occasionally a shorter spine below, ⅜–1 in. long; sometimes to 4 larger spines spreading downward, 2 lower, shorter ones.

GLOCHIDS As the species, except usually missing on current growth; on older pads side areoles may show a few short ones; edge areoles produce some yellow ones to ½ in. long.

FLOWERS As the species, except smaller, usually about 2 in. diameter and length; bright orange anthers; 6–7 dark green stigma lobes.

FRUITS As the species, except almost completely spherical, 1–1¾ in. diameter, purplish when fully ripe; seeds about ³⁄₁₆ in. (4–4½ mm) diameter, largest in species, with broader rims.

RANGE Chisos Mountains in Texas Big Bend to Anton Chico, New Mexico, to Stein's Pass, where northern limit passes into Arizona.

REMARKS First variety recognized; grows on lower slopes of mountain ranges; large populations.

Opuntia engelmannii var. *texana* (Gr.) Weniger

STEMS As the species.

AREOLES As the species, except with less wool.

SPINES As the species, except usually more slender than typical variety; yellow instead of white; from entirely bright, translucent yellow to yellow with brown bases or almost entirely red-brown with yellowish mottling or yellowish tips; 1–8 per areole on upper areoles of pad.

GLOCHIDS As the species, except perhaps fewer than typical variety.

FLOWERS As the species, except usually about 3–4 in. diameter; 6–9 dark green stigma lobes.

FRUITS Within range of species, but 2–3½ in. long, globose to broadly pear-shaped, little or no constriction below, flat, wide umbilicus; deep, dull burgundy when fully ripe; seeds ⅛–³⁄₁₆ in. or less (3–4 mm) diameter, with narrow rims.

RANGE South and central Texas into western Louisiana; north to Tyler, Texas, and Dallas, southwest to Big Bend and southeastern New Mexico; into Mexico.

Opuntia engelmannii var. *texana*. Largest pads pictured, 8 inches wide.

Opuntia engelmannii var. *alta*. White-flowered. Flower 3⅛ inches across.

REMARKS Differs only slightly from typical *Opuntia engelmannii* var. *engelmannii*; var. *texana* has translucent yellow instead of opaque white spines, more slender; larger leaves; somewhat larger flowers and fruits; pads soft enough to be edible by animals, but also worst pest pear of south Texas. Includes Benson's *O. lindheimeri* var. *lehmannii*.

Opuntia engelmannii var. *alta* (Gr.) Weniger

STEMS As the species, except usually with more definite trunk, averaging taller than typical variety; commonly 3–6 ft. tall, sometimes more than 10 ft.; pad surface more yellow-green, somewhat irregular, often with irregular outline, but not tuberculate.
AREOLES As the species.

Opuntia engelmannii var. *alta*. Red-flowered. Blooming pads, 5½ inches across.

SPINES As the species, except more numerous, 1–6 on most areoles of new pads, 8–10 or 12 on very old pads; pure translucent yellow, no brown at bases; more porrect, not spreading so widely; main spines flattened, but less so than in typical variety; smaller ones usually round; on new growth usually about 1 in. long; on older pads to 2½ in. long.

GLOCHIDS As the species, except bright yellow.

FLOWERS As the species, except more variable in color, very pale cream color through yellow, orange, and red to dark purplish-red; stigma lobes pale green, sometimes almost white; ovary noticeably tuberculate.

FRUITS Purplish-red, as the species; 1–2 in. long; broadly oval or egg-shaped, usually with slight constriction below, umbilici flat to shallowly pitted, narrower than widest part of fruit; usually numerous glochids, often a few slender spines ¼–¾ in. long on fruits till fully ripe; pulp deep red; seeds quite small, less than ¹⁄₁₆ in. or slightly more (1½–2½ mm) diameter, almost no rims.

RANGE From Mexico along Texas Gulf Coast to Sabine River; coastal Louisiana to Florida; Rio Grande Valley to Mission, Texas.

REMARKS Easily confused with more spiny individuals of *O. engelmannii* var. *texana* but clearly different. Grows in huge thickets at mouths of rivers along Gulf, near water on islands, sand dunes, coastal plain; found at Santa Ana and Aransas National Wildlife refuges. Distinct variety; largest and most robust of Texas cacti; strictly coastal; large pads too woody and tough for cattle.

Opuntia engelmannii var. *cacanapa* (Gr.) Weniger (Benson: *O. lindheimeri* var. *tricolor*)

STEMS As the species, except usually more profusely branching; broader, more bushy plant; pads more bluish and glaucous, usually smaller and more round or slightly oval, usually 5–8 in. diameter, rarely to 10+ inches; thinner.

AREOLES As the species, except a little smaller.

SPINES Fewer than typical variety, commonly only 1 on each upper side areole, 1–3, rarely 6, on edge areoles; usually bright yellow, occasionally brown in bases; main spine sharply, rigidly porrect, flattened, 1–3 in. long; other spines ¾–2 in. long, slightly flattened or round, nearly porrect.

GLOCHIDS As the species, except very few, sides often have none; edge areoles have a few.

FLOWERS As the species, except yellow, stigma lobes white or yellowish instead of green; blooms several weeks later than other varieties.

FRUITS Spherical to very broadly obovate with no constriction at either end; small, 1–2 in. long, averaging slightly over 1 in.; dark red, with less purple; umbilicus large, perfectly flat.

Opuntia engelmannii var. *cacanapa*. Largest pad pictured, 7 inches across.

RANGE Small invasions from northern Mexico into Rio Grande in northern Zapata County, western half Webb County, Texas; Chisos Mountains, Brewster County, Texas.

REMARKS More bushy growth of smaller, more bluish pads with long, porrect, bright yellow spines; very common around Laredo, Texas; closest to var. *cyclodes*, distinguished by longer and more slender, more porrect spines, larger flowers with white instead of green stigmas, brighter red fruits with much smaller seeds, thinner blue-green instead of thick bright green or yellow-green pads.

Opuntia engelmannii var. *flexispina* (Gr.) Weniger (Benson: *O. strigil* var. *flexospina*)

STEMS As the species, except smaller, to about 4 ft. tall and spreading, without central trunk; pads mostly yellow-green, with minimum glaucescence, often quite shiny.

AREOLES As the species.

SPINES As the species, except averaging longer, 2+ in., more slender, somewhat flexible; yellow, with or without brown bases; sloping sharply downward or recurving tightly.

Opuntia engelmannii var. *flexispina*. Main pad 10½ inches wide. White spots are cochineal insects.

GLOCHIDS As the species.

FLOWERS As the species, except yellow; dark green stigmas.

FRUITS 1½–2 in. long, broad to rather elongated egg-shaped, some constriction below; seeds about ⅛ in. (3 mm) diameter.

RANGE Webb and Zapata counties, Texas; never common.

REMARKS Occurs in definite area; distinguished from typical *O. engelmannii* only by spine characters: these more slender, longer, to 2–3 in.; somewhat flexible, hence name; markedly deflexed and pressed downward almost against surface on old pads; occasionally found on hills overlooking Rio Grande above and below Laredo; never abundant.

Opuntia engelmannii var. *aciculata* (Gr.)

STEMS As the species, except not over about 4 ft. tall; pads smaller, 5–8 in. long; deep, vivid green.

AREOLES As the species, except more closely set, ½–1¼ in. apart, somewhat more brown wool; young areoles on sides of pads not as small as typical, rounder; edge areoles typical, but more conspicuous because of exaggerated glochid formation.

SPINES Often lacking; sometimes 1–3 on upper and edge areoles; occasionally 3–8 on old stem pads; more slender, more strictly deflexed or spreading downward than typical; brown with yellow tips or mottled.

GLOCHIDS Very conspicuous and formidable; bright red-brown or mottled or bright brown with yellow tips, ⅛–½ in. long in same areole, spreading outward to form large, loose, starlike cluster to ½ in. across on all areoles.

FLOWERS As the species, clear yellow, orange, or brick-red or almost magenta; dark green stigma lobes.

FRUITS Oval to broadly pear-shaped, a little constriction below; umbilici flat or nearly so; deep purplish-red; seeds ⅛+ in. (3–3½ mm) diameter.

RANGE Webb County, Texas, northwestward along Rio Grande to 50 miles above Laredo; also in Nuevo León, Mexico, southwest of Laredo.

REMARKS Much misunderstood; spineless form often cultivated by collectors; spines, when present, like those of *O. engelmannii* complex, nearest to var. *flexispina*; grows on tops of gravelly hills.

Opuntia engelmannii var. *dulcis* (Eng.) Schumann

STEMS As the species, except more low and spreading; to about 3½ ft. tall.

AREOLES As the species at first, becoming very large, often to ½ in. diameter when old; large amount of gray wool in form of raised doughnut with spines and long glochids on edge, tuft of short glochids in center, this becoming columnar growth to ½ in. long which dislodges as unit.

Opuntia engelmannii var. *aciculata*. Largest pad 6⅔ inches across.

Opuntia engelmannii var. *dulcis*. Largest pad 8 inches in diameter. This plant grew for many years in an urn by the entrance to the Old Trail Drivers' Museum in San Antonio.

Opuntia engelmannii var. *subarmata*. Main pad 12 inches across.

SPINES As the species, except usually 1–3, never more than 6 per areole; brown at base, upper parts whitish to pale straw-yellow, fading to dirty tan.
GLOCHIDS Mottled brown and yellow or all yellow in unique arrangement; semicircle of scattered, spreading glochids around lower edge of areole, coarse and formidable, becoming almost bristlelike, to ¼ in. long; with age, upper part of areole also nearly ringed; center has bulging gray wool, at first with mass of short, very fine glochids, later overgrowing depressed center, forming doughnut of gray wool; tight cluster of very fine, short glochids.
FLOWERS As the species; yellow and orange; dark green stigmas.
FRUITS Egg-shaped with slight constriction below; umbilici broad but slightly concave, 1¼–1¾ in. long, purplish; seeds ⅛+ in. (3–4 mm) diameter.
RANGE About 50 miles southeast of Eagle Pass, Texas, on hills overlooking Rio Grande; also Nuevo León, Mexico.
REMARKS Rare; grows in very small areas; areole structure with remarkable wool and glochid formation most striking on old plants.

Opuntia engelmannii var. *subarmata* (Gr.) Weniger
Flap-Jack Cactus

STEMS Large, upright, compactly branching bush to 6+ ft. high, often as broad; pads round to obovate or often broader than long; 12+ in. long and wide; blue-green with much white glaucescence at first; when very old, yellow-green; firm and heavy, to 1 in. thick.

AREOLES As the species, except smaller.

SPINES None on young, active pads; on very old pads, occasionally 1 spine on some areoles; ½ in. or less long, mottled brown or gray, slender, flattened, deflexed.

GLOCHIDS As the species, except very few.

FLOWERS As the species.

FRUITS Very broad egg-shaped, slight constriction below; umbilicus flat or nearly so; 2–2½ in. long; dark red to almost purple; seeds ¹⁄₁₆+ –⅛+ in. (2–3½ mm) diameter, with wider rims than most varieties.

RANGE Never common; occasional along Rio Grande from Laredo, Texas, to Devil's River.

REMARKS Large, robust; huge, smooth pads, totally without spines except on old trunks; broad, round, hence name flap-jack cactus; very tough. Variety distinguished by spinelessness, manner of growth, robustness, firmness of tissue.

Opuntia engelmannii var. *linguiformis* (Gr.)
(Benson: *O. lindheimeri* var. *linguiformis*)
Cow's Tongue Cactus, Lengua de Vaca

STEMS Upright or sprawling, often 3–5 ft. high; pads narrowly ovate to linear, from about 8 in. long by 6 in. wide, sometimes to 36 in. long by 4 in. wide at widest point near base of pad; otherwise as the species.

AREOLES As the species.

SPINES As the species, except often shorter.

GLOCHIDS As the species.

FLOWERS Weak bloomer; sometimes reproduces only vegetatively; sometimes blooms fairly well; identical to species; orange or red; dark green stigmas.

FRUITS As the species, both fruits and seeds.

RANGE Bexar County, Texas.

REMARKS Favorite with gardeners; strange shape of pads striking; seedlings never observed. May represent mutant form of *O. engelmannii*; more damaged by insect pests; more easily killed by frost. Still a few growing wild near China Grove and Sayers, Texas.

Opuntia engelmannii var. *linguiformis*. Blooming pad, 16 inches long. White spots are cochineal insects.

Opuntia chlorotica. Plant about 22 inches tall.

Opuntia chlorotica Eng. & Big.
Clock-Face Prickly Pear

STEMS Erect, bushy, to 6–7 ft. tall in good situations, often smaller; definite, rounded trunk when only 2–3 ft. tall; pads circular to very broadly obovate, little or no constriction below; 6–12 in. long, pale yellowish-green with some whitish glaucescence when young.

AREOLES Small to medium-sized; about 1 in. apart on young pads; to ½ in. on very old pads; trunk almost entirely covered by enlarged areoles; much wool when old, producing thick layer sometimes called tomentum.

SPINES Pure yellow; ½–2 in. long; more or less flattened; medium thick, mostly deflexed; 1–6 per areole on young, growing pads; when old, on main stems and trunk 20–30 per areole; almost wholly covering trunk; formidable mass of spines unique in Platyopuntias.

GLOCHIDS Few and short on new pads, increasing greatly with age to spreading mass of rigid bristles, to ½–¾ in. long in each enlarged areole; yellow or straw-colored.

FLOWERS Clear yellow; 1½–3 in. diameter; ovary 1⅛–1½ in. long, very

Opuntia tardospina. 9 inches tall.

wide, usually 1+ in. diameter; tuberculate, each areole having cluster of short brown glochids; occasionally 1–2 bristles to ½ in. long; yellow stamens; 10–12 fat greenish-yellow stigma lobes.

FRUITS Spherical to ovate, 1½–2 in. long, with shallowly pitted umbilicus; reddish-purple; seeds about ⅛ in. (2½–3½ mm) diameter.

RANGE Mountains of southwestern New Mexico west of Rio Grande on into Arizona, California, and Sonora, Mexico.

REMARKS Very close to some forms of *O. engelmannii*; areoles of *O. chlorotica* closer together on average; growth of areoles and spines beyond *O. engelmannii* forms; flowers practically identical; seeds essentially the same; fruits more consistently round, more areoles with more glochids, a little more deeply pitted umbilicus; grows in high mountains.

Opuntia tardospina Gr.

STEMS Erect, diffuse and spreading instead of bushlike; no central stem or trunk; many ascending branches; thicket 2–3 ft. tall when mature; pads round to broadly pear-shaped, 6–12 in. long, medium thick; glaucous, bright to yellowish-green.

AREOLES Conspicuous, almost round, 3/16+ in. long when young; round, 3/8 in. diameter when old, bulging with much wool; 3/4–15/8 in. apart.

SPINES 1–2 per areole, in only a few upper areoles; main spines 3/4–11/2 in. long, rather heavy and flattened, deflexed or even recurved tightly; second spine, when present, small, also deflexed, 3/16–7/8 in. long; all translucent yellow with or without brown bases; more spiny under cultivation.

GLOCHIDS Few at first, becoming many to very many, 3/16–1/2 in. long; yellow or mottled with brown.

FLOWERS 21/2–3 in. diameter; pure lemon-yellow; ovary 13/4–2 in. long, club-shaped, 3/4 in. wide; a few very short glochids; style shorter than stamens; 7 white or yellow-white stigma lobes.

FRUITS Broadly egg-shaped to club-shaped, rather noticeable constriction of base; umbilici fairly deeply pitted; 11/2–21/4 in. long; purplish-red when ripe; pulp not very juicy, slow ripening; seeds 1/8–3/16 in. (3–41/2 mm) diameter.

RANGE Hills along Colorado River in central Texas from Austin to Llano and Lampasas, southwest to upper Uvalde County.

REMARKS Rare in type locality; remarkable for large, bulging, dark-colored areoles, conspicuous, loose clusters of uneven glochids, yellow and deflexed, late-appearing, soon-discolored spines; clear yellow flowers, fading to pinkish, early in spring; seeds smaller in diameter, very different from *O. phaeacantha* var. *camanchica* and in range of those of nearest relative, *O. engelmannii*; some similarities to *O. atrispina*.

Opuntia spinosibacca Anthony
(Benson: *O. phaeacantha* var. *spinosibacca*)

STEMS Strictly upright, base more or less trunklike by thickening of old pads; many branches; each composed of rows of pads; compact, tidy shrub to 4+ ft. tall; pads usually pear-shaped with rather pronounced constrictions at bases but occasionally almost round; 4–7 in. long, 3–6 in. wide, average thickness; conspicuously tubercled; each areole on summit of small elevation; edge of pad has unusual, slightly notched outline; light green or yellowish-green.

AREOLES 3/4–11/2 in. apart, oval to round, small on faces of young pads, 1/4 in. diameter on edges of older pads.

SPINES 1–8 per areole, all or almost all spiny; as is common in Opuntias, lower areoles have fewer, upper edge of pad has more; fully spined areole has 1–5 main spines 3/4–23/4 in. long spreading in all directions; heavy to very heavy, slightly or greatly flattened, often twisted and curved; red-brown or dark brown over lower two-thirds, gray above, tips yellow and translucent; below these 1–4 lower spines spreading downward, straw-colored mottled

Opuntia spinosibacca. Largest pad pictured, 5¾ inches long.

with brown; ⅜–⅝ in. long, very slender bristles.

GLOCHIDS Very few; none on sides of most pads; 6–12 in each areole of upper edge; to ½ in. long, light brown, often with yellow tips.

FLOWERS About 2 in. tall, not opening widely, 2 in. or less across; bright orange-yellow with red centers; ovary 1 in. long, broadly vase-shaped, slightly tuberculate, ¾ in. across at top, widest point; petals very wide, edges usually somewhat ragged, with tiny point at apex; orange-yellow, bases bright red, may flush up midline most of way to top; stamens very pale yellowish; style long and white; 7–9 light yellow stigma lobes.

FRUITS 1–1¾ in. long, ½–1 in. thick; oval or egg-shaped, slightly tuberculate; no constriction at base, broadly rounded; rather pronounced constriction at top; upper edge flares widely to enclose broad, very deeply concave flower scar; all areoles on edge, a few down on sides have 1–4 spines; ¼–1 in. long, rigid, round to slightly flattened, colored like spines on pads; spreading straight out from upper edge or turning slightly downward, surrounding whole upper part; when mature, very light greenish-yellow; never red or purple shading; dry after yellowing; seeds irregular, round to elongated, 3/16 or less to ¼ in. (4–6½ mm) or more diameter; usually thin or very thin, may be flat or greatly twisted; rim medium wide to very broad, ½–1½ mm wide, varying around seed.

RANGE A few miles from ranger station at Boquillas toward Hot Springs in

Big Bend National Park, Brewster County, Texas.

REMARKS Unique: tall, upright, bushy manner of growth of *O. engelmannii* group, but compact, small pads; very yellow-green color found only in *O. chlorotica* and a few *O. engelmannii*; spines more similar to *O. phaea-cantha*; pads tubercled, unlike all but some small, crawling Opuntias; fruits never red or purple, similar to small, dry-fruited Opuntias and Cornyopuntias: truly spiny, faintly yellowish when mature, then dry, hard, papery.

Opuntia rufida Eng.
Blind Pear

STEMS Erect and bushy with definite trunk, 2–6 ft. tall; pads 4–8 in. long, round to broadly egg-shaped, sometimes wider than long; thick, with flat surfaces, pale gray-green to somewhat yellowish-green; dull, covered with very short pubescence.

AREOLES Conspicuous, round, large, $3/16$–$1/4$ in. diameter, crowded, $1/2$–1 in. apart.

SPINES None.

GLOCHIDS Very many, very short, extremely slender, only about $1/16$ in. long, so crowded as to form dense hemispherical tuft; reddish-brown to light brown, often fading to grayish with age.

FLOWERS 2–$2\frac{1}{2}$ in. diameter; orange-yellow; outer petals almost linear or lanceolate; inner ones obovate, ends erose or notched; whitish stamens; style somewhat longer than stamens; 5–11 dark green stigma lobes; ovary 1–$1\frac{1}{8}$ in. long, about $5/8$ in. across at top, widest part; tuberculate.

FRUITS Almost spherical, about 1–$1\frac{1}{4}$ in. long; greenish-red; pulp greenish; seeds $1/16$–$1/8$ in. (2–3 mm) diameter, irregular, with narrow rims.

RANGE Enters United States from Mexico only in Texas, on rocky mountain-sides along Rio Grande from near Presidio through Big Bend National Park.

REMARKS Large, beautiful, distinctive Mexican species; barely venturing into Texas Big Bend; a truly spineless prickly pear.

Opuntia macrocentra Eng.
(Benson: *O. violacea* var. *macrocentra*)
Purple Prickly Pear

STEMS Upright, small bush to 2–3 ft. high, without trunklike main stem; pads 4–8 in. long, round, broader than long or broadly egg-shaped; comparatively thin, often $1/2$–$5/8$ in. thick; medium green to yellowish-green when shaded and well watered; more often purplish or spotted and streaked with purple, very pronounced in winter and hot summer.

Opuntia rufida. Largest pad pictured, 7 inches long.

AREOLES Small and inconspicuous on sides of pads, to about ¼ in. in edges; spacing varies, ⅜–¾ to ¾–1½ in. apart.

SPINES Few, limited to very upper and edge areoles, long and conspicuous; 1–4, most commonly 1–2 per armored areole; 1–3, 2–5 in. long, upper round, lower flattened or grooved; slender, flexible, usually twisted and bent; black or blackish below with usually gray or brown zones at center and tips, sometimes whitish; often 1 lower deflexed spine ¾–1½ in. long.

GLOCHIDS Very few to average number, short, 1/16–3/16 in. long on sides of pads, not increasing in number, sometimes increasing in length to ½ in. on edges; brown or red-brown.

FLOWERS Approximately 3 in. diameter; light yellowish with red centers; ovary short and egg-shaped, with some glochids; yellow stamens; 5–11 yellow or light greenish-yellow stigma lobes.

FRUITS ¾–1½ in. long, spherical to broadly vase-shaped, no constriction at base, apex deeply pitted; bright red or orange-red when ripe; seeds about 3/16 in. (4–5 mm) diameter, flat but twisted and irregular, with wide, undulating rim.

RANGE Trans-Pecos Texas, southwestern New Mexico.

REMARKS One of most striking Opuntias; beautiful purple pads, extremely long, blackish spines; coloring more vivid in more severe desert climate; bright red and purple pigments shield tender flesh; few spines, among longest of genus, 2–4 in., sometimes to 5 in. long; slender, flexible; at least 1 always flattened, distinguishing it from *O. violacea* var. *santa-rita* (Gr. & Hare) Benson, with which it is often confused. Very common; dominant Opuntia in much of lower Big Bend; grows on rocky slopes; in severe exposures pads smaller with closer areoles; farther north often has larger pads, less purple coloring in summer, less heavy or no spination. Very close to and often confused with *O. phaeacantha* var. *brunnea* Eng., which grows in Big Bend and near El Paso; this form often shows reddish coloring, sometimes almost as purple as *O. macrocentra* and also has long, blackish-based spines.

Opuntia violacea var. *santa-rita* (Gr. & Hare) Benson

STEMS Erect, bushy, 2–5 ft. high with distinct short trunk; pads thin, mostly circular, occasionally very broadly egg-shaped or broader than long; glaucous blue-green, with reddish coloring around areoles and along edges, more pronounced during winter.

AREOLES Oval to round, ⅛+ in. diameter when young, increasing with age to about ¼ in.; bulging when young, with much wool and many short glochids; sometimes elongation of areole structure outward somewhat like that seen to extreme degree in *O. engelmannii* var. *dulcis*; areoles about ½–1 in. apart.

SPINES Not numerous, new pads often spineless or with 1 on only a few edge

Opuntia macrocentra. Largest pad pictured, 6 inches long.

areoles; older pads may have to 3 spines in upper areoles only; brown or red-brown at bases, upper parts yellowish or mottled with yellow; cylindrical, spreading or deflexed, slender, ¾–4 in. long, usually 1½–2 in.

GLOCHIDS Many on all areoles, very short, usually about ⅛ in., forming bulging mass with wool in areole; yellow to brown.

FLOWERS Yellow, with white or yellowish-white stigma lobes.

FRUITS Oval to oblong, often curved, 1–1⅜ in. long, ¾+ in. diameter, little or no constriction below, pitted apex; purple or purplish-red; seeds ⅛ in. (2–3 mm) or less diameter, flat, with narrow, acute rims.

RANGE From Sonora, Mexico, into southeastern Arizona, southwestern New Mexico, in Texas near Rio Grande between Presidio and Big Bend National Park.

REMARKS Similar to several other cacti; reddish pads like *O. macrocentra*, but distinct in almost everything else; arborescent, different shape and color of spines, different color of flowers and fruits, different, much smaller seeds; seeds and growth somewhat like *O. engelmannii*; this and *O. rufida* only other Opuntias in area equaling *O. engelmannii* var. *alta* and var. *tricolor* in smallness of seeds; differs in other ways; seeds almost identical to *O. rufida*, as is appearance; var. *santa-rita* more spiny, not pubescent, different hue of pad, glochids not quite so fine, white instead of green stigmas; different-colored fruits, but may be most closely related to *O. rufida* of any in area. More affected by environmental factors than most large Opuntias, suffering from drought or too much moisture, unusual cold; never common.

Opuntia strigil Eng.

STEMS Erect, diffuse shrub without trunk, usually about 2 ft. tall; pads 3–8 in. long, round to broadly egg-shaped, medium thick with no constriction at base; pale green or yellow-green.

AREOLES ¼–¾ in. apart, appearing crowded on sides, often running together on edges; round or oval, 3⁄16–⅜ in. across, often elevated by addition of much gray wool.

SPINES 5–10 very slender, almost bristlelike, ¼–¾ in. long around lower half of each areole; dark brown at bases, fading to red-brown and finally yellowish or whitish toward tips or all whitish; 0–3 centrals on each upper and edge areole; ¾–1¾ in. long, slender to medium strength, round or somewhat flattened, straight and erect on edges, more or less deflexed and bent in various directions on sides of pads; dark brown below, medium or red-brown, rather translucent in middle zone, translucent yellowish beyond.

GLOCHIDS Each mature areole has loose, spreading cluster of slender yellow glochids in upper part; ⅛–½ in. long, largest ones upward from upper part of areole opposite lower radiating spines, almost equal in length, contrasting color.

Opuntia violacea var. *santa-rita*. 15 inches tall.

FLOWERS Small to medium, 1½–2½ in. across, 1¼–1½ in. tall; ovary short, with leaves, a few long bristles; lemon-yellow to cream-yellow, with slight orange cast to midline; ends 1 in. across, blunt; entirely erose or with very slight point at apex; cream-colored stamens; 6 cream-colored or very pale greenish-white stigma lobes; fading to pinkish or salmon as wilt.

FRUITS Spherical or practically so; very small, usually ½–⅞ in. long; a few very slender brown bristles; broad, flat or slightly depressed umbilici; bright red; seeds ⅛+ in. (3–4 mm) diameter, regular, flat, with narrow, acute rims.

RANGE Small, triangular area of Texas from west of Fort Stockton on northwest to Ozona on northeast, narrowing to vicinity of Longfellow, Sanderson, and Dryden on south.

REMARKS Unusual appearance: compact little upright bushes; fairly common on tops of hills; close-set areoles with numerous, very slender bristles; fruits among smallest of any Opuntia in Southwest; grows in very thin soil overlying limestone outcrops; never forms thickets. Relationship to other

Opuntias not clear; small seeds similar to those of *O. engelmannii* complex, but unlike them in other characters; *O. phaeacantha* var. *nigricans* seeds hardly larger and some specimens approach *O. strigil* rather closely in smaller spines and glochids, but it has very different flowers and fruits.

Opuntia atrispina Gr.

STEMS Ascending, spreading, 2–3 ft. tall; joints round to broadly egg-shaped, 4–7 in. long, 3½–6 in. wide; pads thin to medium thick; areoles usually somewhat raised; rather shiny, bright or yellow-green, occasionally with some red around areoles in severe exposures.

AREOLES Slightly elongated oval, ⅛–³⁄₁₆ in. long when young, to egg-shaped or almost round, ¼+ in. diameter when older; ¼–1¼ in. apart; proliferate when old to contain 2–6 or 8 circular growing centers, glochids in bunches; very big and bulging; edge areoles to ½ in. diameter, almost touching.

SPINES 3–6 on upper half to two-thirds of pad; main ones with black or very dark red-brown bases shading into zone of brown followed by yellow toward tips; smaller ones similar except lighter color; usually 1–2 main spines ½–1¼ in. long, heavy and rigid, round, porrect or deflexed, bent downward, sometimes entirely missing; below, another central ⅜–1⅛ in. long, identical except strongly recurved downward; 1–3 lower, deflexed, spreading, thin bristlelike spines ⅜–⅝ in. long; fade to dull gray-brown or blackish; often brittle, may be broken or missing.

GLOCHIDS Yellowish or brownish or mottled at first, becoming dull blackish-brown when old; average to many on young pads, ⅛–½ in. long; irregular, untidy clusters; very many, filling old edge areoles.

FLOWERS Deep chrome-yellow with somewhat greenish center at first; soon fade to flesh color or apricot; 1–2½ in. diameter; ovary tube small, ¾–1 in. long, slightly tuberculate, with some glochids; cream-colored stamens; white style; 7–8 yellow or slightly greenish-yellow stigma lobes.

FRUITS Bright red or yellowish-red; pulp rather dry and greenish; almost round to broadly pear-shaped, little or no constriction below; umbilici almost flat to quite deeply pitted; extremely variable size; ripe fruits ⅜–1⅝ in. long; seeds ⅛+ in. (3–4 mm) diameter, comparatively thick, with narrow rims.

RANGE Narrow strip of southwest Texas about 20 miles wide from Anacacho Mountains in southwest Uvalde County west past Del Rio, in the mountains of Devil's and Pecos rivers, to Dryden, Texas, and into Mexico.

REMARKS Widely misunderstood because Britton and Rose mistakenly said it had flattened spines; easily recognized in its range by round spines not markedly deflexed, small flowers without red coloring, and small fruits.

Opuntia strigil. Largest pad pictured, 7¾ inches long.

Opuntia atrispina. Largest pad pictured, 6 inches across.

Opuntia leptocarpa. Shown in fruit. Plant 15 inches tall.

Opuntia leptocarpa Mackensen

ROOTS Usually tuberous but fibrous in some populations.

STEMS Large, robust pads, upright at first, too weak to support each other, at length of 2–3 pads falling to ground; low, sprawling, to 1–1½ ft. high; pads broadly oval or egg-shaped or almost spindle-shaped, with gradual, not pronounced constriction at base; 4–10+ in. long, to 7 in. wide, thin; bright, deep green with shiny surface; glaucous, yellow-green with drought or sunburn.

AREOLES Small and oval or round on sides of pads, enlarging somewhat but not conspicuously on edges; ¾–2 in. apart.

SPINES 1–5 per areole, on upper and edge areoles only; occasionally almost spineless; main spines yellow or straw mottled with brown, lower and smaller ones gray; slender to medium thick, round or only slightly flattened; fully armed edge areole has 1 main central ½–1¼ in. long, porrect or slightly deflexed; 1–2 upper spines at any angle; ½–1 in. long; 1–2 slender, deflexed lower ones ¼–1 in. long.

GLOCHIDS Brown to red-brown; few and short, ¹⁄₁₆–⅛ in. long on sides of pads, to medium number, to ¼ in. long, on edges of pads; never conspicuous.

FLOWERS 2½–3 in. across; yellow or orange with maroon to bright red centers; ovary 1½–2 in. long, narrowly club-shaped, tuberculate, with short red glochids; petals with more pronounced point at apex than most Opuntias; cream-colored anthers; 6–8 white or greenish-white stigma lobes.

FRUITS Very large, 2–3½ in. long, 1–1⅝ in. thick; club-shaped with pronounced or exaggerated constriction of base; narrow, deeply pitted umbilici; old red when fully ripe; flesh often remains greenish until late fall; seeds ⅛–³⁄₁₆ in. (2½–4 mm) or less diameter; regular, flat but rather thick-bodied, with narrow, acute rims.

RANGE South Texas, area bounded by Langtry on west, Austin on north, Flatonia on east, Mustang Island near Corpus Christi Bay to Brownsville on southeast, Laredo on southwest.

REMARKS Flowers, fruits, roots essentially different from *O. engelmannii*; pad character and size, glochids, spines, and seeds outside limits of *O. macrorhiza*; few clear differences from *O. phaeacantha* var. *major*: *O. leptocarpa* shorter, more sprawling, almost prostrate; fruits larger, seeds smaller; *O. leptocarpa* usually has tuberous roots; *O. phaeacantha* usually fibrous. Most widespread and common in Comal and Bexar counties, Texas; scattered small populations elsewhere. This is the low spreading cactus common at New Braunfels, "hybrid form between it [*O. engelmannii*] and perhaps *O. rafinesquii*, with narrow clavate fruit," on which Engelmann based his retracted *O. lindheimeri*.

Opuntia phaeacantha Eng.
New Mexico Prickly Pear, Brown-Spined Prickly Pear, Tulip Prickly Pear

ROOTS Almost always fibrous, rarely tuberous.

STEMS Large, robust, ascending 2–3+ ft. high, trunkless, forming dense thickets to 6–8 ft. across, or low, prostrate with pad edges on ground, to 1–1½ ft. high; pads flat, almost spherical to broadly egg-shaped or club-shaped, 4–9 in. long, 3–7 in. wide; glaucous, bluish-green or deep green

Opuntia leptocarpa in foreground; *Opuntia engelmannii* var. *texana* in background.

when young, bright shiny green or yellow-green when older, sometimes purplish cast around areoles and pad edges during winter.

AREOLES Small to medium, oval to round when young, becoming round and enlarged to ¼ in. or so when older; ¾–2 in. apart.

SPINES 1–8 per areole only on very upper areoles or upper three-fourths of pad; ¾–3 in. long; spreading in all directions; upper ones large and heavy; uppermost usually round, at least main porrect or deflexed central flattened; usually some small, weak spines below main ones; yellow, gray, or mottled toward tips, bases brown, red-brown, or black.

GLOCHIDS Few to average in number; short on young pads, usually quite numerous to very many on edges of old pads, ½–⅝ in. long; pale brown to red-brown.

FLOWERS 2–3 in. diameter; bright yellow or orange with red to maroon centers; ovary ¾ in. long in some forms to 1¾ in. in others, always with short red-brown glochids; yellowish or cream-colored stamens; long pinkish or whitish style; 6–10 short, fat, whitish, yellowish, or very pale greenish stigma lobes.

FRUITS Variable: oval or goblet-shaped with little or no constriction at bases, umbilici somewhat pitted to flat, to pear-shaped or club-shaped with pronounced constriction of both bases and umbilici; 1–2½ in. long; yellowish-red to bright scarlet or cherry-red to deep purplish-red; seeds ⅛–¼ in. (3–6 mm) diameter.

RANGE Very large; in our area western halves of Oklahoma and Texas, all of New Mexico.

REMARKS Second major complex of U.S. Opuntias; many different forms, causing much confusion; may equal or exceed *O. engelmannii* in amount of territory in United States; ranges practically to Pacific, north through Nebraska, Colorado, and Montana; extremely hardy, often very conspicuous.

Opuntia phaeacantha var. *major* Eng.
(Benson: *O. phaeacantha* var. *major* only in part)

STEMS Ascending and spreading, without central trunk, to 3+ ft. tall; pads round or nearly so, rarely very broadly pear-shaped, 4–8 in. long; flat, deep green to yellow-green, often with purplish around areoles; very slight glaucescence, usually shiny when older.

AREOLES As the species, except smaller and more elongated oval when young, 1–2 in. apart.

SPINES Fewer, shorter, lighter in color than most forms; typically 1–3 spines on only upper edge areoles, rarely 4 spines on areoles of upper half of pad; 1–2 main spines porrect or spreading, ¾–1⅞ in. long, averaging about 1¼ in.; flat or round, uppermost usually round; lower 1 flattened; gray, whitish, or straw-colored with brown or red-brown bases; may be 1–2

Opuntia phaeacantha var. *major*. Largest pad pictured, 8 inches across.

lower, deflexed, bristlelike spines; ¼–¾ in. long, grayish.

GLOCHIDS Very few and short or none on sides of pads; edges of old pads develop average number to ¼+ in., yellow or brownish.

FLOWERS As the species, except ovary usually 1¼–1¾ in. long.

FRUITS 1½–2½ in. long, club-shaped, with noticeable constriction of bases; constricted, pitted umbilici; light red to purplish-red; pulp juicy; seeds about ³⁄₁₆ in. (4–5 mm) diameter.

RANGE Santa Fe, New Mexico, south and east over southeastern corner of New Mexico into far west Texas from El Paso to Fort Stockton.

REMARKS Range hard to discover because of general tendency to put any brown-spined Opuntia under this catch-all name; in Texas *O. leptocarpa* has almost identical flowers and fruits but is not as robust, usually has tuberous roots and smaller seeds; in western mountains a form rather intermediate between var. *major* and *O. phaeacantha* var. *camanchica* occurs at higher elevations and farther north than var. *camanchica*; spines, fruits, seeds much like var. *major*, but much smaller, lower-growing than this variety farther south; true *major* is rather rare variety.

Opuntia phaeacantha var. *nigricans*. Old 6-inch pad sprawling; new, sprouting 4-inch pads.

Opuntia phaeacantha var. *nigricans* Eng.
(Probably Benson: *O. phaeacantha* var. *wootonii*, *O. atrispina* in part)

STEMS Large bush 2–3 ft. high when mature; branches upright, without central stem; spreading outward to small thickets; pads normally 4–8 in., sometimes to 10 in. long, round to broadly egg-shaped; little or no constriction below; pads thin to medium thick; first very glaucous blue-green; yellow-green when older.

AREOLES ¾–1⅞ in. apart; oval to round, small to medium-sized on sides of pads, to ⅜ in., round on edges.

SPINES 1–6 per areole on upper half to almost all areoles of pad; 1 main central, rarely missing, ½–2 in. long, porrect to deflexed; medium thick to very heavy, very flattened or triangular; mostly black or blackish-brown, usually with zone of gray or purplish-gray above, dark tip; usually 2 very similar lateral spines, spreading, often curving outward; usually 1 upper spine (may be missing) same length, erect or porrect, similar except always round; 0–4 lower, deflexed, slender, often bristlelike spines ¼–¾ in. long, usually gray with bases and tips somewhat blackish.

GLOCHIDS Red-brown, brown, straw-colored, or mottled; very variable in number, 0 to very many on sides of pads, becoming many to very many, ¼–¾ in. long on edges.

FLOWERS As the species, except ovary only ¾–1 in. long.

FRUITS Oval to goblet-shaped, slight constriction at base, rather deeply pitted apex; ¾–1½ in. long; deep purplish-red; seeds ⅛–³⁄₁₆ or less in. (3–4 mm) diameter, flat, usually very irregular.

RANGE Narrow but very long strip entering Texas from Mexico, then far north into New Mexico; eastern and western boundaries between Del Rio on east and Chisos Mountains on west, northward past Fort Stockton on east and Alpine on west, to eastern foothills and western slopes of Guadalupe and Capitan mountains in southern New Mexico, to escarpment just east of Mosquero, New Mexico, in Harding County, its most northeasterly known range, to hills between Albuquerque and Cuba, New Mexico, its most northwesterly penetration.

REMARKS Often forms dense thickets on sides and tops of rocky ridges or steep slopes; pads bluish-green in spring, with smooth, glaucous surfaces, with heat and dryness, yellowish-green; heavy blackish spines. Widely mistaken for *O. atrispina* Gr.; wide-ranging variety of very large and complex species; differs from other varieties: remarkably short ovary (about ¾ in. long) distinctly different from 1¼–1½ in. ovary of others; like others, main central flattened and uppers round; only var. *nigricans* has such dark, heavy, flattened lower centrals; no other form has heavy, flat spreading laterals; grows on tops of limestone ridges, together with *O. strigil*.

Opuntia phaeacantha var. *brunnea* Eng.
(Benson: *O. phaeacantha* var. *major* in part)

STEMS To about 3 ft. tall, upright, without central trunk; pads 4–8 in. long, round or wider than long, usually with no constriction below, sometimes broadly egg-shaped with some lower constriction; slightly blue-green when very young; glaucous yellow-green when older, usually with some purplish-red mottling on edges, often suffused with this color in winter; pads rather thick.

AREOLES Small to medium, elongated to almost round on sides of pads, to about ³⁄₁₆ in., almost round, on edges of old pads; ¾–1⅝ in. apart.

SPINES 1–5 per areole only on upper edge or upper third of pad; main central 1–3 in. long, porrect or deflexed, straight or often twisted and bent, medium to heavy, round to slightly flattened; usually 1–3 upper spines, 1–2½ in. long, erect or spreading upward, medium to very heavy, round to very flat and twisted; all blackish, chocolate-brown or red-brown at bases, upper parts tan or grayish; may be 1–2 lower, deflexed, slender, often bristlelike spines, ³⁄₁₆–1 in. long; round or flattened; gray.

GLOCHIDS Brown to straw-colored, at first almost none to average number; very short on sides of pads; on edges few; later often very many, to ¾ in. long.

FLOWERS As the species.

FRUITS 1¼–2½ in. long, oval to club-shaped with some constriction below, shallowly concave umbilicus above; dull red; seeds ³⁄₁₆+ in. (4½–5½ mm) diameter.

RANGE Southwest Texas from Anacacho Mountains east of Del Rio along Rio Grande through Big Bend to El Paso; northward through Davis Mountains to southern parts of Guadalupe and Organ mountains, a short distance into New Mexico.

REMARKS Recognized by greater glaucescence, thicker joints, purplish-red winter coloring; spines longer than typical for species; upper centrals most greatly flattened instead of lower; seeds larger than most other varieties; sometimes mistaken for *O. macrocentra* because of 3-in. spines and severe weather coloring; *O. phaeacantha* var. *brunnea* never actually purple, but dull, dark, purplish-red; pads of var. *brunnea* thick, others thin; areoles ¾+ in. apart, average over 1 in., others always less than 1 in.; spines long, but not as long as *O. macrocentra*; more brown than black, rigid rather than flexible; *O. macrocentra*'s fruits to 1½ in. long, no constriction below, deeply pitted above, bright red to orange-red; var. *brunnea* 2½ in. long, some constriction below, shallow umbilicus, dull, dark red.

Opuntia phaeacantha var. *camanchica* (Eng.)

ROOTS Usually fibrous, occasionally have tubers.

STEMS Low, semiprostrate, spreading; large pads, usually lying on edges by second season to form chains, which by rooting form clumps sometimes 3–5 ft. across; pads perfectly round through egg-shaped, to occasionally broadly club-shaped with constricted bases; 3–9 in. long, slightly less wide; average about 6 in. long by 5 in. wide; flat, ½ in. or less thick; rather deep green with some glaucescence; sometimes with reddish cast around areoles and edges during winter.

AREOLES Oval or oblong to round; about ³⁄₁₆ in. across on sides of pads, to about ¼ in. on edges; ¾–1½ in. apart.

SPINES 1–8 on upper three-fourths or more of areoles, only lowest spineless; lowermost spine-bearing usually have 1, increasing upward, very upper and edge areoles have 3–8; fully armed areole has 1–5 straight uppers ¾–3 in. long, spreading in all directions upward and outward, medium thick, entirely round on some, flattened on others; bases and usually lower half brown, red-brown, or blackish-brown, followed by zone of tan, gray, purplish-gray, or whitish, ending in yellowish, semitranslucent tips; 1–5 lower spines turning or spreading downward from lower part; largest to 1¼ in. long, flattened, rather heavy; rest smaller in size and thickness, to hardly more than

Opuntia phaeacantha var. *brunnea*. Wide-open flowers, 3 inches across.

deflexed bristles; lower spines whitish or gray with brown tips; plants growing in shade deficient in spines; commonly only upper third has 1–3; 2
lower, deflexed spines ⅜–¾ in. long, gray with lighter tips on most armed
areoles; only occasional areole on very edge has 1 heavier brown upper spine
to about 1¼ in. long.

GLOCHIDS Somewhat variable, none to average number; sometimes very
conspicuous on old pads; ⅛–⅜+ in. long on edges of old pads; straw-
colored, tan, or brownish.

FLOWERS As the species, except longer; ovary 1¼–1¾ in. long.

FRUITS Bright cherry-red to dull plum-red when ripe, with juicy flesh; oval,
not constricted at base, 1–2½ in. long by ¾–1½ in. wide; umbilicus rather
narrow, flat or very shallowly concave; seeds 3/16–¼ in. (4½–6 mm) largest
measurement; very irregular, perfectly flat and thin or twisted and thicker,
round to square or almost triangular; conspicuous rims 1–1½ mm wide,
sharp, usually wavy and irregular.

RANGE Kansas and Colorado through western Oklahoma, Texas, and eastern
New Mexico; in Oklahoma west of line from Blackwell to Ardmore, in
Texas west of line from Fort Worth south to Balcones Fault near San An-
tonio; not found south of there; rather common east of central mountains in
New Mexico, seldom if ever west of central New Mexico.

REMARKS Smallest, most prostrate, most spiny form of species; occurs primarily east of more upright, bushy varieties, on high plains and hills; in immature, stunted, atypical conditions often impossible to distinguish; prostrate growth, smaller, more spiny, fruit shape differs. Wide range, many
minor variations; largest Platyopuntia in high plains; often a pest.

Opuntia phaeacantha var. *tenuispina* (Eng.) Weniger

ROOTS Fibrous, although previously described as sometimes tuberous.

STEMS Low, semiprostrate, spreading; occasionally to about 1 ft. high; pads
3–8 in. long, to 4 in. wide, pear-shaped, bases noticeably constricted; pads
rather thin, smooth, dark blue-green or bright, shiny green.

AREOLES Oval to practically round, ⅛+ to about 3/16 in. across; closely set,
⅜ in. apart low on pad, to 1 in. higher up; some full-sized pads have no
areoles over ¾ in. apart.

SPINES 1–6 on all but very lowest areoles; to about middle of pad 1–3
slender, whitish spines from fraction of inch to 1 in. long; all growing downward, spreading almost against pad; most fully armed areoles around upper
edge have 1–2 main spines 1–2½ in. long, usually white or gray, always
with brown tips, often with pale brownish bases; usually turned severely
downward, occasionally fairly erect on edge; main spines straight, slender,
round or nearly so, firm, not bristlelike but flexible; below, 1–4 shorter, deflexed spines like those found lower.

Opuntia phaeacantha var. *camanchica*. Largest pad pictured, 4⅓ inches long.

Opuntia phaeacantha var. *tenuispina*. Pads 9 inches long.

GLOCHIDS Bright reddish-brown fading to dirty brown; rather numerous, forming dense tuft in center of areole; very slender and short, ⅛+ in. long; hardly extending beyond brown wool.

FLOWERS As the species, except 2½–3 in. across; when old, fading to pale pinkish; 6–8 green stigma lobes.

FRUITS Bright red, oblong or elliptical, little or no constriction at base, very deeply pitted umbilicus; 1–1⅝ in. long, about ¾ in. thick; usually brown glochids on areoles of fruits, sometimes upper edge areoles have 1–3 slender, whitish spines, tipped brown, to ⅜ in. long; seeds very irregular, sometimes round, almost even, more often elongated, twisted, or uneven; ⅛–¼ in. (3–6 mm) greatest diameter; average thickness.

RANGE Dona Ana, above Las Cruces, New Mexico, to San Elizario below El Paso, Texas.

REMARKS Has been confused with other Opuntias due to incomplete spination when immature or in poor conditions; true *O. tenuispina* one of rarest prickly pears, very near extinction.

Opuntia cymochila Eng.

ROOTS Usually fibrous, occasionally tuberous.

STEMS Prostrate, spreading mat of small pads rooting where lie flat on ground or on edges; height of clump is height of most upright pad, 6–8 in.; width of clump usually 1–4 ft.; pads usually round or sometimes wider than long; occasionally slightly egg-shaped; rather thick for size, averaging about ½ in.; 2½ to occasionally 6 in. long, to 4 in. wide; in dry season or in winter much shrunken, wrinkled; in moist growing season, filled out, flat, deep glossy green; when dry or with freeze, lighter green often suffused with reddish.

AREOLES Oval or round, small or medium, usually ⅜–¾ in. apart, occasionally 1 in.

SPINES 1–7 on almost all areoles or only upper half; 1–3 main centrals, 1–2¾ in. long, fairly heavy, round to flattened, often twisted, but straight; most spreading downward, sometimes 1–2 straight out from areole or ascending; from lower part of areole 1–5 small spines ³⁄₁₆–1 in. long spreading downward; slender, almost bristlelike to fairly stout, very slightly flattened; white or gray with very tips light brown and translucent, bases brownish; occasionally brownish coloring extends most of length; in overly dry or exposed places or on immature pads main upper spines absent; only lower, deflexed spines, ¼–1 in. long, slender, bristlelike, pure white with brownish tips.

GLOCHIDS Yellow, straw-colored, or dirty brownish-yellow; not too numerous in young areoles; usually very many in old areoles; compact cluster in middle of areole, comparatively long, ³⁄₁₆ in. at first, often ½ in. long on old pads.

FLOWERS About 3 in. diameter, 2½ in. tall; usually all chrome-yellow, sometimes with center golden-brown; outer petals short and pointed; inner ones broad at ends with tiny point at apex; very pale yellow stamens; long pale green style; 9 green stigma lobes.

FRUITS Purplish-red, oval or broadly egg-shaped, 1–1½ in. long, ¾–1 in. diameter at thickest point; base not constricted or slightly so; umbilicus narrow, forming deep pit; seeds large, ³⁄₁₆+ –¼+ in. (5–6½ mm) diameter, medium thick, irregular; round, elongated, almost triangular, greatly twisted on same plant; depressed in center with ridge around edge; rim wide to very wide (1–2 mm), very sharp; often undulating; no notch at hilum.

RANGE Oklahoma and Texas panhandles and adjacent New Mexico west to mountains and south into west Texas, east to Cheyenne, Woodward, Alva, and Manchester, Oklahoma, north into west and central Kansas and eastern Colorado; south in Texas to line from Abilene to Big Spring and Pecos, south past Fort Davis to just south of Marfa, its southernmost known limit; northward into New Mexico east of Sacramento Mountains.

REMARKS Mature, robust *O. cymochila* easily distinguished from *O. compressa* varieties, some of which grow in its range, by having spines on all or

Opuntia cymochila. Largest pad pictured, 4 inches across.

nearly all areoles; *O. compressa* has spines only on upper parts of pads. Young or stunted specimens of *O. cymochila* often lack major spines, thus appearing almost identical to some forms of *O. compressa*, but fruits of *O. cymochila* are oval with little or no constriction of bases, very large, relatively thin seeds, different from narrow, clavate fruits of the other, with much smaller, very thick seeds. Stunted form can approximate dry, spiny-fruited *O. polyacantha*, but distinct in real spination and purplish, naked, fleshy fruits. Distinct form occurring over vast area of high western plains, usually on flats of valleys.

Opuntia compressa (Salisbury) Macbride
(Benson: *O. humifusa* only in part)
Low Prickly Pear, Smooth Prickly Pear

ROOTS Fibrous, often entirely so, but often with spindle-shaped to spherical tubers; no central taproot.

STEMS Low-growing, pads entirely prostrate or spreading upward at first, then reclining on edges with age; usually 1 ft. or less high, occasionally to 18 in.; pads round or broader than long to egg-shaped or spindle-shaped, may have constriction below; typically 1–6 in. long, by 1–5 in. wide; occasionally to 7–8 in. long; average thickness to very thick for size; tuberculate by raised areoles or smooth and flat; dark green to pale or yellowish-green, sometimes with purplish spots at areoles in winter.

AREOLES Small and inconspicuous, $\frac{1}{16}$–$\frac{1}{8}$ in. diameter, elongated oval to circular at first, with age more circular, to $\frac{1}{4}$ in. across; $\frac{3}{16}$–$1\frac{1}{4}$ in. apart.

SPINES Spineless or with spines on less than upper half of each pad; areoles of lower half to two-thirds always spineless; armed areoles with 1–5 spines arranged as follows: 1–2 straight main ones porrect, somewhat deflexed or erect, $\frac{1}{4}$–$2\frac{1}{4}$ in. long, rather slender to heavy, round or flattened, almost pure grayish-white to yellowish or mottled above with bases brown or red-brown, occasionally all brown; 0–1 lower deflexed spine $\frac{3}{16}$–1 in. long, slender, similar color; occasionally 1–2 bristlelike, spreading downward, $\frac{1}{8}$–$\frac{3}{8}$ in. long, white.

GLOCHIDS Few, short, fine at first, compact tuft in middle of areole; usually increasing greatly on old pads, to $\frac{1}{4}$–$\frac{3}{8}$ in. long; as numerous or more so on sides as on edges; greenish-yellow, straw-colored, brown, or bright red-brown.

FLOWERS 2–5 in. diameter; pale yellow to orange-yellow, or orange-yellow with red centers; ovary elongated obovate to clavate, 1–2$\frac{1}{4}$ in. long; cream-colored anthers; 4–9 white or yellowish stigma lobes.

FRUITS Clavate with constricted or greatly prolonged bases and narrow, noticeably depressed to deeply pitted umbilici; red-brown; seeds round, flat, thick-bodied, with narrow, acute rims; $\frac{1}{8}$–$\frac{1}{4}$ in. (3–6 mm) diameter, 2–4 mm thick.

RANGE Entire United States except approximately northwest third and Maine.

REMARKS Small, prostrate, inconspicuous; most wide-ranging in United States; adaptable; great confusion because of localized forms and too many names. Since I used *O. compressa* for it, Kalmbacher (*Cactus and Succulent Journal*, Jan. and Feb. 1976) and Benson (C.&S.J., Mar.–Apr. 1976) decided that this name was illegitimate and substituted *O. humifusa* Raf. Then Howard and Touw (C.&S.J., Sept. and Oct. 1981) showed the flaw in this reasoning and so we still have *O. compressa*.

Opuntia compressa var. *humifusa*. Largest pad pictured, 3 inches across.

Opuntia compressa var. *humifusa* (Raf.) Weniger
(Benson: *O. humifusa* var. *humifusa* only in part)

ROOTS Usually fibrous, occasionally with peanut-shaped or spindle-shaped tubers; no fleshy taproot.

STEMS Prostrate, never over 1–2 pads high; pads round to broadly oblong, usually 2–4 in. long, sometimes to 5 in.; thick and flat when healthy; wrinkled when desiccated, never tuberculate by elevations at areoles; dark or bright green, shining, sometimes with purplish coloring at areoles in winter or drought.

AREOLES Small, 1/16–1/8 in. long, enlarging little if any with age; elongated oval to round; usually rather concave, pitlike depressions on surface of flat pad; 1/2–1 in. apart.

SPINES Most often spineless; if present, 1–3 on a few upper edge areoles; 1–2 spreading, to 1 in. long; rarely 1 lower, deflexed, very small; main spines round, straight, heavy; whitish to brownish.

GLOCHIDS Few and short at first, small, compact tuft of minute bristles 1/8 in. or less long in small areoles; often not increasing on old pads, sometimes to 3/16 in. with age; red-brown to yellowish.

FLOWERS Yellow, usually with red centers or streaks; 2–3 in. diameter, 1¾–3 in. tall, including relatively long, slender ovary; with some glochids; 10–14 broad inner petals; orange filaments; cream-colored anthers; short style; 4–8 white or very pale greenish-yellow, fat, grooved stigma lobes.

FRUITS Elongated club-shaped or oval above, always with constricted, slender, markedly elongated base, deeply pitted apex; 1⅛–2 in. long, ½–¾ in. thick at thickest part near top; lower third ¼–⅜ in. thick; greenish, later apricot or plum-red or brownish-red, pulp remaining greenish in poor conditions; seeds ³⁄₁₆ in. or less (3½–4½ mm) diameter, thick to very thick, with narrow rims.

RANGE Entering Louisiana from Mississippi, into Arkansas from Mississippi, Tennessee, and Missouri, throughout Arkansas and northern Louisiana into Texas and probably into Oklahoma; southwestern limit a line from Alexandria, Louisiana, to Silsbee, Texas; then north, east of Trinity River to Dallas; back toward Arkansas, except for occurrence near Madill, Oklahoma.

REMARKS The typical form of this huge species is found only east of our area; the Mississippi Valley form which does enter our area can hardly be considered more than a variety, but it is distinct, and both Rafinesque's *O. humifusa* and Engelmann's *O. rafinesquii* seem to apply to it. It is an inconspicuous little prickly pear, found mostly in sandy places or drier hillsides jutting out of piney woods; sometimes forms mats covering ground; occasionally found on wooded hillsides under trees, more straggling pads somewhat etiolated, larger, more elongated but still small, shiny, dark green, very thick; very wrinkled in winter or drought, often with purple blotches at areoles; smooth-surfaced, never tuberculate by elevation of areoles; more often small areoles in slight depressions; neither areole nor glochids increase noticeably in size with age or on edge of pad; thus like more eastern, typical variety; very prostrate, while var. *macrorhiza*, var. *fusco-atra*, var. *allairei* have arms more or less turning upward from old pads and tuberculate surfaces.

Opuntia compressa var. *macrorhiza* (Eng.) L. Benson (Benson: *O. macrorhiza* in part)

ROOTS Basically fibrous, without central taproot, often with spherical to spindle-shaped tubers, fraction of inch to 3 in. diameter; clusters on branching roots or in series along same root; not uncommonly lacking tubers.

STEMS Prostrate or nearly so; old pads mostly leaning edges on ground, newer pads temporarily upright; plant 6 in.–1 ft. high; pads almost round to elongated obovate, often with some constriction at bases, not pronounced; medium thick to rather thick; surface quite tuberculate by raised areoles when growing, remain more or less so on old pads, may become wrinkled; medium, shining green when young; dull, dark green when old; normally

2–5 in. long; under shading vegetation sometimes etiolated to 6–8 in. long.

AREOLES Oval or almost round, about ⅛ in. across, to ¼+ in. on old pads; ½–1¼ in. apart.

SPINES Present on upper fourth of pad or less; occasionally totally lacking; 2–3 spines per areole most common, to 5 on some edge areoles; on young or weak plants round or with only bases somewhat flattened; main spine may be conspicuously flattened; completely armed areoles have 1 main central, porrect or a little deflexed, slender to medium thick, straight, round if weak, flattened if robust, ¼–1¾ in. long; may be 1–2 upper spines porrect to erect, ⅜–1 in. long, slender, weak, always round; main spines gray or whitish, often bases, sometimes tips brown or red-brown, fading to gray and rough when old; sometimes 1–2 lower spines spreading below, very slender, thin whitish bristles ⅛–⅜ in. long.

GLOCHIDS Bright red-brown to dirty straw color; medium in number; ³⁄₁₆–¼ in. long, compact clump at each areole at first; on old pads to ⁵⁄₁₆ in. long, large clusters.

FLOWERS Orange-yellow with red centers; 2½–3 in. diameter, 3–3½ in. tall; ovary 1¼–2¼ in. long, with some reddish-brown glochids; 7–9 inner petals, very broad from narrow red bases; 4–9 yellowish, fat stigma lobes.

FRUITS Elongated club-shaped, 1¼–2½ in. long, ¾–1 in. diameter at thickest part; base greatly constricted and prolonged; top shallowly to deeply pitted; light red to purplish-red, often remaining greenish very late in season; pulp greenish until fall, then colorless or slightly reddish; seeds ³⁄₁₆–¼ in. or less (4–5½ mm) diameter; thick or very thick, rims medium wide, acute.

RANGE Western Arkansas on east through Oklahoma and Texas, throughout New Mexico, into Colorado and Arizona.

REMARKS Very wide-ranging; small, no unique features; common prostrate prickly pear in grass or under thickets; close to other forms in appearance, name often misapplied; very common in central and north Texas, scattered, usually very sandy localities elsewhere; very common as far west as Alva and Woodward, Oklahoma; quite common in northern mountains of New Mexico. Ranges of var. *macrorhiza* and var. *humifusa* overlap; some specimens apparently intermediate; var. *macrorhiza* has tuberculate surfaces, to 5 spines with main 1 flattened, to 1¾ in. when spination completely developed; 7–9 inner petals; var. *humifusa* has flat surface, to 3 spines, heavier, always round, to 1 in. long; 10–14 inner petals; var. *macrorhiza* is more western member of *O. compressa* complex.

Opuntia compressa var. *microsperma* (Eng.) Weniger non Benson

ROOTS Mostly fibrous with small tubers, sometimes entirely fibrous.

STEMS Prostrate, 6–8 in. high; most pads resting one edge on ground; pads

Opuntia compressa var. *macrorhiza*. Blooming pad, 4 inches long.

Opuntia compressa var. *microsperma*. Largest pad pictured, 3 inches long.

broad to elongated egg-shaped, 1–4 in. long by ¾–2½ in. wide, rather thick, very tuberculate by elevations of areoles; medium green with purplish shading around areoles.

AREOLES Small, round or oval, ¹⁄₁₆–⅛ in. long, on top of distinct elevations; ¼–¾ in. apart.

SPINES Sometimes spineless, more often 1–3 on upper areoles of pad; 1–2 main spines very slender, round, all white or with bases brown, upper parts white; occasionally 1 lower, deflexed, bristlelike, ⅛–¾ in. long.

GLOCHIDS Greenish-yellow or straw-colored; many in all areoles; at first to ³⁄₁₆ in. long; to ¼ in. long when older.

FLOWERS Identical with those of previous variety.

FRUITS Very elongated club-shaped; 1–1¼ in. long by ⅜ in. thick at widest part near top; base very constricted; apex deeply pitted; often remain green through September, then dry; seeds ¹⁄₁₆–⅛ in. or less (1½–2½ mm) diameter, smooth, thick, with almost no rims.

RANGE 10 miles north of Campbellton, Atascosa County, Texas, in deep sand near Atascosa River.

REMARKS Closest affinities to more western *O. compressa* var. *macrorhiza* rather than eastern var. *humifusa*, as shown by tuberculate surface, more numerous glochids, more slender spines; fruit never turns red; var. *macrorhiza* grows in same locality; unknown whether unique small seeds are environmentally induced.

Opuntia compressa var. *fusco-atra*. Two specimens from same locality. Largest pad on stunted plant, 2¼ inches long; largest pad on vigorous plant, 5 inches long.

Opuntia compressa var. *fusco-atra* (Eng.) Weniger

ROOTS Fibrous or with small tubers.

STEMS Prostrate, usually at least one edge of each pad resting on ground; 6−8 in. high; pads almost round to broadly club-shaped, some constriction at base; usually 2−4 in. long, 2−3 in. wide, rarely to 6+ in. long, 4 in. wide; thin or medium thick, noticeably tuberculate by elevations of areoles; surfaces shiny, bright green to deep green or rather blue-green.

AREOLES Small and elongated when young, round and larger, to about ¼ in. diameter on old pads; ³⁄₁₆−1¼ in. apart; varying on same plant.

SPINES Usually 1−3 on only upper areoles, rarely 4−5 with 1−2 very small, bristlelike spines at lower edge; 1 main spine porrect or nearly so, slender to medium thick, round or nearly so, ¼−2 in. long; may be 1−2 uppers above this, similar except ³⁄₈−1 in. long; sometimes 1 lower spine deflexed below, ³⁄₈−⅝ in. long; spreading below occasionally 1−2 very slender bristles ⅛− ½ in. long; yellowish when growing, when hardened dark brown or gray with brownish bases.

GLOCHIDS Many; erect, compact clusters in all areoles; very many, to ¼ in. long when old; very bright, shining red-brown when young, fading to dark, dirty brown when old.

FLOWERS Completely sulphur-yellow or with red centers; vary in size, 1¾−4 in. diameter, 2−3 in. tall; very slender ovaries 1⅛−1³⁄₈ in. long, with

Opuntia compressa var. *fusco-atra*. An abnormal form, known as *Opuntia macateei*. Open flower 2 inches across.

some brown glochids; very few, broad inner petals, usually 4–5; usually 9 perianth segments; 3–5 white stigma lobes.

FRUITS Elongated club-shaped with constricted bases, deeply pitted tops; typically 1–1½ in. long, sometimes to 2 in., ⅝–⅞ in. diameter at thickest point; seeds about ³⁄₁₆ in. (4–5 mm) diameter, fairly thick, with narrow, acute rims.

RANGE Coastal plain, sandy areas near beaches and on islands of Texas coast from Houston to Brownsville; only a few miles inland, except in valleys of Colorado and Brazos rivers, to 75 miles.

REMARKS Extreme form of *O. compressa* complex; very close to *O. compressa* var. *macrorhiza*, which is found in most of range; var. *fusco-atra* recognized by numerous brilliant red-brown glochids, very marked elevation of areoles, extreme reduction in number of flower segments. Very common in type locality west of Houston; in this very arid locale plants stunted, pads usually 2–3 in. long; much larger near beaches; never common elsewhere except around Copano Bay, Texas, in the Rockport area. *O. macateei* B. & R. is a remarkable environmental form found there at Fulton Beach, with elongated, diseased fruits; this abnormal growth, resulting in sterility, is caused by insect larvae tunneling into the fruits.

Opuntia compressa var. *grandiflora*. Largest pad pictured, 5¼ inches long.

Opuntia compressa var. *grandiflora* (Eng.) Weniger
Large-Flowered Opuntia

ROOTS Entirely fibrous; no tubers; to ⅜ in. diameter, somewhat fleshy before branching.

STEMS Spreading, semiprostrate; new pads perfectly erect before falling over, to 12 in. tall; pads egg-shaped to rather spindle-shaped, narrowing at base or above and below, 4–6 in. long by 2½–4 in. wide; medium thick; conspicuously tubercled by elevated areoles, except in very wet seasons usually markedly wrinkled; bright green.

AREOLES Small and elongated, to ⅛ in. long on young pads, becoming round, to ¼ in. on old pads; ½–1 in. apart.

SPINES None.

GLOCHIDS Straw-colored, many, conspicuous, short, in tight bunch at first, to ¼ in. long in spreading cluster on old pads.

FLOWERS Normally very large and beautiful, 4–5 in. diameter, 3–3½ in.

tall; can be stunted and reduced to 2 in. diameter in poor conditions; yellow streaked at random with reddish markings or yellow with reddish centers; about 8 inner petals, 2 in. long by 1½ in. wide; ovary 2+ in. long, slender club-shaped; 5 white, thick, grooved stigma lobes.

FRUITS About 2½ in. long, very elongated club-shaped, ½–¾ in. wide at thickest upper part, prolonged constriction below; top somewhat pitted.

RANGE Originally given as "on the Brazos" in Texas; Bastrop State Park, Bastrop County, on Colorado River about 30 miles southeast of Austin.

REMARKS Largest flowers of any Opuntia in Southwest except *O. compressa* var. *allairei*, in cultivation; uninteresting sprawling prickly pear except in spring when flowering; far from widespread. Very local form of *O. compressa* complex, more robust in size of pads and flowers, totally without spines; seeds not described; may be sterile hybrid.

Opuntia compressa var. *allairei* (Gr.) Weniger

ROOTS Tuberous, with clusters of spindle-shaped enlargements on fibrous roots.

STEMS Spreading, joints only recline on one edge when very old; sprawling branches of 2–4 pads to 12–18 in. high; pads elongated egg-shaped or spindle-shaped, thick and firm, not flabby or wrinkled even when desiccated; often somewhat tuberculate when growing; always smooth and flat when older; blue-green to rather yellow-green; pad 4–8 in. long by 2–3¾ in. wide.

AREOLES Small and oval to round on young pads, to round, ¼ in. across on old pads; ½–1¼ in. apart.

SPINES Often spineless; sometimes 1 spine on each of 6 uppermost edge areoles; straight, ½–1¼ in. long, medium thick, round or slightly flattened, gray or whitish, sometimes slightly annulate above, with brownish base.

GLOCHIDS Yellow, many, conspicuous, to ¼ in. long, in compact tuft, as typical of complex.

FLOWERS Entirely yellow, irregularly streaked with red or with red centers; about 3 in. across by 2½ in. tall; in cultivation to 4½–5 in. diameter, 3 in. tall; 9 inner petals to 2½ in. long, 1½ in. wide; slender ovary, elongated to 2 in. on larger flowers; 4–7 white or cream-colored stigma lobes.

FRUITS 1¾–2½ in. long by ¾–⅞ in. thick, elongated club-shaped, constricted at top and bottom; at first some glochids which soon drop off; when ripe bright rose-plum, pulp light red; seeds about ³⁄₁₆ in. (4–5 mm) diameter, thick, with narrow rims.

RANGE Extreme southeast Texas and southwest Louisiana, along east side of Trinity River from mouth to Livingston, Texas, east into Louisiana to Marksville or possibly Natchitoches.

REMARKS Closely related to var. *grandiflora*, flowers identical in favorable

Opuntia compressa var. *allairei*. Largest pad pictured, 6¼ inches long.

conditions; differs only in details of pads and in sometimes having a few spines; more robust and more upright, with profuse fruits and seeds; respond differently to growing conditions; var. *allairei* largest, most robust form of *O. compressa* complex in our area; large version of small eastern form in nearly every character, but pads always elongated, never as broad; grows in Big Thicket in alkaline soil among coarse grasses.

Opuntia compressa var. *stenochila* (Eng.) Weniger

ROOTS Usually entirely fibrous, sometimes with some spindle-shaped to oval tuberous thickenings.

STEMS Low and prostrate, older pads usually resting on ground, young pads temporarily ascending; in spring often a small clump of young, ascending pads 8–10 in. tall; in winter pads flaccid, prostrate; usually 2½–4, sometimes to 6 in. long, nearly round with slight constriction below to elongated oval or egg-shaped with very pronounced constriction below; medium thick to very thick, often ⅝ in., tuberculate when growing, then nearly smooth, often very shrunken and wrinkled from lack of water or cold; dull, light grayish-green or yellowish-green.

Opuntia compressa var. *stenochila*. Largest pad pictured, 4 inches across.

AREOLES Small and inconspicuous on young pads, to ¼ in. or less diameter on old pads, ½–1 in. apart.

SPINES 1–4 in areoles on upper edge to upper half; 1 main central, porrect or deflexed a little, 1–2¼ in. long, slender to medium thick, round to somewhat flattened; usually 1–2 upper spines porrect or spreading upward, ¾–2¼ in. long, medium thick, round; rarely 1 lower spine, ⅜–1⅛ in. long, deflexed, slender, flattened; entirely white or gray, or gray with light brown or yellowish bases; rarely uppers have darker brown bases or brown mottling.

GLOCHIDS Yellow, greenish-yellow, or straw, few to medium in number, short at first, increasing somewhat in number and length to rather conspicuous, to ⅜ in. long on old pads.

FLOWERS Light sulphur or greenish-yellow; 2½–4 in. diameter; ovary a slender club about 1¼–2 in. long; 10 inner petals; 6 small white stigma lobes.

FRUITS Club-shaped with constricted, more or less elongated bases; umbilicus deeply pitted; 1½–2½ in. long; seeds approximately ³⁄₁₆ in. (4–5 mm) diameter, thick to very thick, with narrow rims.

RANGE Common only in northwestern New Mexico and adjacent Arizona, in very scattered locations over most of northern two-thirds of New Mexico, and in upper Texas Panhandle.

REMARKS Does not quite fit descriptions of *O. cymochila* or *O. compressa*

Opuntia pottsii. 6½ inches tall, exclusive of fruits.

var. *macrorhiza*; obviously one of *O. compressa* complex; fruits almost exactly like those of var. *macrorhiza*; seeds very nearly alike; both have fibrous or tuberous roots; var. *stenochila* has yellow glochids, longer spines; pads gray or yellowish-green and dull; var. *macrorhiza* deep and shining green; flowers different; var. *stenochila* has long fruits with constricted bases and thick, narrow-margined seeds.

Opuntia pottsii SD
(Benson: *O. macrorhiza* var. *pottsii*)

ROOTS Large central taproot ¾–1½ in. diameter and 6 in.–1+ ft. long; smooth and carrotlike or, in rocky ground, contorted and constricted; sometimes subdivides into 2–3 fleshy branches but never has tuberous, spherical, or spindle-shaped, potatolike enlargements; when damaged exudes milky sap.

STEMS Small, basically ascending, pads touching ground only when extremely dehydrated or in winter; not mat-forming; small clump of upright pads 6–12 in. tall from central base, often short, cylindrical trunklet; pads 1½–5 in. long by 1–4 in. wide, almost round to elongated egg-shaped, some constriction at bases; thin or medium thick; flat without raised areoles;

glaucous blue-green, often purplish around areoles when young and healthy, fading to yellow-green when old or unhealthy; leaves extremely tiny, about ⅛ in. long.

AREOLES To ⅛ in. long on young pads, to ¼ in. diameter on old pads; ⅜–1 in. apart.

SPINES Only on upper edge or upper third of pad; 1–3 spines, straight, usually twisted, rather slender; round or flattened or ridged; whitish, gray, or gray mottled with tan, or brownish; 1–2 upper spines 1–2½ in. long, deflexed or spreading; sometimes 1 lower, very deflexed spine ½–1 in. long; said to be occasionally spineless.

GLOCHIDS Greenish-yellow to dirty straw color, usually rather numerous in compact clusters, ⅛–¼ in. long on old pads.

FLOWERS Brilliant purplish or rose-red, 2–2¾ in. diameter, 2½–3 in. tall; ovary very slender, 1–2 in. long, with some glochids; about 7–8 inner petals; filaments green below, yellowish above; bright yellow anthers; pinkish style; 5–7 cream-colored, fat, velvety stigma lobes.

FRUITS 1½–2 in. long, slender club-shaped, ¾ in. diameter at upper, widest part above slender, attenuated base; apex deeply pitted; when ripening, light red; seeds about ³⁄₁₆+ in. (4–5½ mm) diameter; thick; rims medium wide, blunt instead of acute, irregular.

RANGE Chihuahua, Mexico, north past El Paso, through western part of Big Bend into Davis Mountains of Texas, on into southern New Mexico; southern Guadalupe Mountains, extends at least as far north as Caprock and Roswell, New Mexico.

REMARKS Very close to *O. compressa* group, but has distinct differences; more like *O. compressa* var. *macrorhiza* but more blue-green, glaucous; not prostrate but ascending from one center; spination similar; has more slender and usually longer spines, but not as many as var. *macrorhiza*, always lacks lower bristles; root of *O. pottsii* always central taproot extension of thick, trunklike stem with very little taper to at least 1 ft. long; *O. compressa* forms have globular to spindle-shaped tubers on fibrous roots; *O. pottsii* has very tiny leaves, 3–4 times smaller than *O. compressa*; purplish or rose-red flowers. Grows strictly on alluvial flats; large range; far from common; easy to grow; not easily harmed by moisture.

Opuntia ballii Rose

ROOTS Small, spindle-shaped tubers on fibrous roots.

STEMS Prostrate and spreading; pads 2⅜–4 in. long, almost circular to broadly egg-shaped, very thick for size; pale yellowish-green and glaucous; smooth, without raised areoles.

AREOLES Small, nearly round.

SPINES 2–4 on most or all areoles; 1–3 main spines spreading upward or

Opuntia ballii. Pad 2⅓ inches across.

erect; 1½–2¾ in. long, plus 1 lower, deflexed, much shorter; straw-colored or pale brownish; heavy, very rigid, straight, a little flattened.

GLOCHIDS Very conspicuous, each areole with compact mass of bright yellow glochids ¼–½ in. long.

FLOWERS Small, 1½–2 in. across, about 2 in. tall; deep rose-red; ovary about 1¼ in. long; very narrow club-shaped or almost linear, with very few yellow glochids in areoles; outer perianth segments have green midlines; smaller ones shading to flesh-colored on edges; larger ones to burnt-orange/pinkish; about 6 inner segments about 1 in. long and wide, blunt ends notched at apex; base and most of inner segments old red through deep rose-red, edges and tips cerise; filaments green at base, then cream color; cream-colored anthers; short and whitish style; 5 cream-colored, fat, thick stigma lobes.

FRUITS Small and very slender, ¾–1¼ in. long, very narrow club-shaped, ¼ in. thick at center of widest part, greatly constricted bases and rather narrowed, pitted umbilici; spineless; seeds ⅛+ in. (about 3½ mm) broad, thick for size.

RANGE "Dry mesa beyond Pecos, Texas" (Rose).

REMARKS Long, heavy spines, yellow glochids to ½ in. long, very nearly the longest on any Opuntia, very small fruits; different roots distinguish from *O. pottsii* or New Mexico plants. Unique small cactus perhaps restricted to Pecos area of west Texas.

Opuntia plumbea Rose

ROOTS Very unusual underground structure; fleshy rhizome, ½+ in. diameter, horizontal underground to at least 4 ft., sprouting pads 4–8 in. apart; fibrous roots produced from it.

STEMS Ascending at point of sprouting from underground stem, not over 1–2 pads high; pads almost circular to broadly egg-shaped, 1¼–2½ in. long, forming clusters to about 4 in. high, to 8–12 in. across at each growing point, finally forming mat to several feet across; pads rather thin; somewhat tuberculate by raised areoles; very glaucous, dull blue-gray, lead-colored.

AREOLES Large for size of pads, oval, about 3⁄16 in. long, ⅜–½ in. apart.

SPINES 1–4, usually 2, in upper areoles only; gray, more or less mottled with pale brown; 1 main spine porrect or slightly deflexed, 1–1⅞ in. long, slender, straight, round or nearly so, sometimes slightly flattened at base; may be 1–2 uppers porrect or nearly so, 1–2 in. long, slender, straight, round; may be 1 lower deflexed, ½–1¼ in. long.

GLOCHIDS Conspicuous, bright, red-brown in all areoles; compact clusters; ⅛–3⁄16 in. long.

FLOWERS Small, about 1½ in. long and wide; purplish; ovary less than 1 in. long, fairly broad; white stigmas.

FRUITS Small, ⅝–⅞ in. long, broadly pear-shaped with pitted umbilici;

Opuntia plumbea. Pad 2¼ inches long.

seeds ⅛+ in. (3½−4 mm) diameter.

RANGE San Carlos Indian Reservation, Arizona, New Mexico west of Silver City.

REMARKS Very rare; only *O. arenaria* has similar creeping and sprouting underground structure, but differs in almost all other aspects.

Opuntia pusilla (Haworth) Haworth
Crow-Foot Prickly Pear, Cock-Spur Cactus, Cockle-Burr Cactus, Sand-Burr Cactus

ROOTS Entirely fibrous or with several oval tubers to 2½ in. long, 1½ in. thick.

STEMS Very prostrate and diffuse; mats 1−15+ ft. across, 4−5 in. high; all older pads lie on ground; pads broadly oblong to elongated club-shaped, 1−4½ in. long by 1−2¼ in. wide; often ¾−1 in. thick, young joints almost globular; smooth, without raised areoles when well watered; shrink and

Opuntia pusilla. Largest pad pictured, 3 inches long.

wrinkle when dry; deep green with darker, bluish coloring around areoles; lighter green when old; very loosely articulated, coming off easily.

AREOLES Round or oval, ⅛−³⁄₁₆ in. diameter, ⅜−¾ in. apart.

SPINES 1−4 straight on almost all areoles or on upper edge only; 1 porrect spine ½−1½ in. long, flattened, twisted, medium thick; may be 1−2 uppers 1−1⅝ in. long; round; may be 1 lower, ¼−¾ in. long, slender, round or flattened, deflexed or porrect; at first light brown, fading to gray with tips clear yellow or blackish.

GLOCHIDS Greenish-yellow or bright straw color, ⅛−¼ in. long, average number to many, compact clusters.

FLOWERS Clear lemon to greenish-yellow, sometimes with slightly deeper yellow in center; 2½−3 in. diameter; ovary ⅞−1 in. long, with a few short red glochids; 8 inner petals; orange filaments; yellow anthers; stamens very sensitive; 5−6 thick yellow or slightly greenish-yellow stigma lobes.

FRUITS Light red when ripe, club-shaped, some constriction below; shallow to rather deeply pitted umbilicus at top; 1−1½ in. long by ½−⅝ in. thick at thickest; seeds ³⁄₁₆ in. or less (about 4 mm) diameter, regular, rather thick, with rather narrow and blunt rims.

RANGE Beaches of North Carolina through Florida to Alabama; strip about a mile long near tip of Bolivar Peninsula, in front of Galveston Bay; may also grow in Louisiana.

REMARKS Very common on and near beaches of southeastern United States;

Opuntia fragilis. Clump 6½ inches across.

flower, fruit, and seed similar to eastern, typical form of *O. compressa*, also with tuberous roots, but pads thicker. It has often been known as *O. drummondii* Graham.

Opuntia fragilis (Nutt.) Haw.
Brittle Cactus, Fragile Prickly Pear

ROOTS Fibrous.

STEMS Low-growing, almost completely prostrate or with spreading branches to 6−8 in. high; very dense mats to 1−2 ft. across; joints begin as almost globular outgrowths to ½−⅝ in. diameter; elongate to 1−1½ in. without broadening, almost cylindrical; may then broaden to small, very thick pads 1½−2 in. long by ¾−1¼ in. wide by about ⅝ in. thick; joints very loosely attached; often very wrinkled and flaccid.

AREOLES Small to medium, some white wool when young, about ⅜−½ in. apart.

SPINES 1−7+, spreading, fairly stout, round or nearly so, ½−1 in. long; whitish with darker tips or straw-colored when mature, dark brown when growing.

GLOCHIDS Very few and short; yellowish.

FLOWERS Clear yellow, sometimes with orange centers; to about 2 in. diameter; yellowish stamens; 4–6 green stigma lobes; small, almost spherical ovary.

FRUITS Oval or egg-shaped, ½–1 in. long, with pitted flower scars; some short spines on upper areoles, dry when ripe; large seeds, about ¼ in. (5–7 mm) diameter, flat, with broad, irregular rims.

RANGE From Canada into extreme northern New Mexico, tip of Oklahoma Panhandle and extreme northwestern Texas.

REMARKS First of our dry-fruited Opuntias, which possess green stigma lobes; rather hard to recognize just from vegetative parts. Grows in very sandy soil; fragile, will not grow in typical hot desert situation or in heavy soil; not fragile to cold; one of most northern cacti. Loosely articulated joints; when growing well, joints broaden into thick, flattened pads to 2 in. long; flowers and fruits not well known because does not flower unless well situated, often relying on scattering of little joints to propagate; rarely blooms in cultivation. In our area not numerous, very scattered; occasionally found in sandy breaks along Canadian River north of Amarillo. A var. *brachyarthra* is often listed, but I cannot separate it from the typical form.

Opuntia sphaerocarpa Eng.
(Not Benson: *O. polyacantha* var. *juniperina*)

ROOTS Mostly tuberous, with small, oblong, or spindle-shaped tubers on fibrous roots, but sometimes entirely fibrous.

STEMS Low, diffuse, mostly prostrate; only new pads temporarily upright; pads round or wider than long to very broadly egg-shaped, 2½–4 in. long, 2½–3½ in. wide; average thickness to thick; tuberculate by raised areoles; soft, shrinking to very wrinkled when water scarce or in winter; bright green when young, fading to somewhat lighter green when old; often suffused with purplish in winter.

AREOLES Elongated, tiny or very small; ⅛ in. or less long on sides of pads, becoming oval, hardly larger on edges; ¼–¾ in. apart.

SPINES Only upper edge areoles armed; typically 1–3 spines; 1 central, deflexed, ¼–1½ in. long, slender to medium thick, flattened; sometimes 1 upper, porrect, ½–1½ in. long, slender to medium thick, round; occasionally 1–2 lower, much deflexed, slender spines, ³⁄₁₆–½ in. long; larger ones brown or reddish-brown mottled above with tan or whitish; lower, slender ones gray with dark tips.

GLOCHIDS Very few, short; compact clump in each areole on sides of pads; somewhat more numerous, longer, to ³⁄₁₆ in. on edges; yellow to dirty straw color.

FLOWERS Greenish-yellow, sometimes with some brownish in centers; 2 in. diameter by 1½–2¼ in. tall; ovary very broad club-shaped, ¾–1½ in. long,

Opuntia sphaerocarpa. In winter condition. Largest pad pictured, 3¼ inches across.

with some tan glochids; 7–8 inner petals; cream-colored or yellowish stamens; long, greenish style; 5 fat, bright green stigma lobes.

FRUITS Perfectly spherical to somewhat oval; ¾–1⅜ in. long and wide; umbilicus very broad, flat or very shallowly pitted; short white wool and many tan glochids to ⅛ in. long in areoles; spineless; dry, brown, papery when ripened, yellowish-green all summer, drying following winter; seeds ³⁄₁₆+ in. (5 mm) diameter, irregular, rather thick with narrow, acute rims.

RANGE Sandia Mountains east of Albuquerque, New Mexico, through Jicarilla Mountains west of Capitan, New Mexico, to Sierra Blanca Mountains north of Ruidosa.

REMARKS One of most misunderstood of all cacti; almost unknown today; often mistaken for *O. compressa* var. *macrorhiza*, found within its range; distinguished by flowers and fruits; intermediate between dry-fruited species and fleshy-fruited *O. compressa* group; has green stigmas of dry-fruited, but fruits dry tardily; by pads, spines, roots, and seeds much more closely related to *O. compressa* group than to *O. polyacantha*. Found only at comparatively high altitudes, usually in association with forests.

Opuntia rhodantha Schumann
(Benson: *O. erinacea* in part)
Wide Cactus, Cliff Prickly Pear

ROOTS Fibrous.

STEMS Low-growing and spreading, 6 to rarely 18 in. high; pads upright at first, later reclining and rooting; pads almost circular, egg-shaped, or oblong, 2–9 in. long by 2–6 in. wide, ½–1 in. thick; often slightly tuberculate; deep green or glaucous and gray-green.

AREOLES Oval and small to medium, about ⅛–³⁄₁₆ in. long; ½–⅞ in. apart.

SPINES Usually 1–6 per areole, only on upper half or less of pad; to 10 in one variety; 1–4 main, spreading spines ¾–2 in. long, medium to heavy, somewhat to much flattened; whitish, yellowish, or variegated with brown; 1–6 slender, round to slightly flattened, deflexed, whitish spines ¼–¾ in. long.

GLOCHIDS Brown, very few in one variety, quite numerous in another.

FLOWERS Yellow or pink or reddish, 2–3 in. diameter, 2–2¾ in. tall; ovary about 1½ in. long, tuberculate, with white wool, often some glochids; no spines; about 12 inner petals, to 1 in. wide at top; greenish, yellowish, or reddish filaments; cream-colored anthers; 8–12 long, slender, deep green stigma lobes.

FRUITS Broadly club-shaped, tapering below, 1½–1¾ in. long; usually have a few areoles at top to sometimes all areoles with clusters of short, whitish spines; occasionally spineless; dry and brittle when ripe; seeds ³⁄₁₆–¼ in. (5–6 mm), flat, with wide rims.

RANGE Southwestern Colorado and southern Utah into northern New Mexico and Arizona; in New Mexico northwest of line from Taos to Albuquerque to Gallup.

REMARKS Largest of small, dry-fruited Opuntias, with thick, fleshy, deep-colored pads with not too many very rigid and heavy spines; yellow to pink flowers; New Mexican plants tend to mostly yellow, Colorado to pink. Grows at higher elevations (usually 5,000+ ft.); immune to cold but does not grow well in extremes of heat.

Opuntia rhodantha var. *rhodantha* (Schumann) Weniger

ROOTS As the species.

STEMS As the species, except pads to only 7 in. long by 4 in. wide.

AREOLES As the species, except to only ⅞ in. apart.

SPINES As the species, except to only 6 per areole, with lower half or more spineless; largest to only 1⅝ in. long; only 1–4 smaller, bristlelike spines per areole.

GLOCHIDS Very few and inconspicuous.

FLOWERS As the species.

Opuntia rhodantha var. *rhodantha*. Yellow-flowered. 6½ inches tall.

Opuntia rhodantha var. *rhodantha*. Pink-flowered. 8 inches tall.

FRUITS As the species.
RANGE As the species.
REMARKS Varieties based on flower color have no significance.

Opuntia rhodantha var. *spinosior* Boissevain

ROOTS As the species.
STEMS As the species, except pads average larger; in wild 4–8 in. long, typical shape; in cultivation, more spindle-shaped, to 9 in. long by 6 in. wide, to 18 in. tall.
AREOLES As the species, except a little larger, to 1 in. apart.

Opuntia rhodantha var. *spinosior*. Larger pad pictured, 4½ inches long.

Opuntia polyacantha. Typical, heavily spined. Largest pad pictured, 4 inches long.

SPINES 1–10 on almost all areoles of each pad; same 3–4 main spines as the species, except to 2 in. long; 1–6 smaller, bristlelike spines below.
GLOCHIDS As the species, except quite numerous, sometimes to ¼ in. long.
FLOWERS As the species.
FRUITS As the species, except not so spiny; about half have spineless fruits; others have spines only on upper edges.
RANGE Southwestern Colorado to near Albuquerque, New Mexico.
REMARKS Very close to *O. rhodantha*; rather similar to *O. nicholii* Benson.

Opuntia polyacantha Haw.
Hunger Cactus, Starvation Cactus

ROOTS Fibrous.
STEMS Prostrate, spreading, rarely over 6 in. high; rooting on edges of joints, often forming dense mats; pads circular to oval, spindle-shaped or broadly egg-shaped, no real constriction at bases; average thickness to thick; tuberculate by raised areoles; usually wrinkled; pale green or yellow-green, becoming reddish with extreme heat or cold; 1½–5 in. long, 1½–4 in. wide.
AREOLES Oval or elongated, small, ¹⁄₁₆–⅛ in. long on young pads, sometimes increasing in size on old pads; much white wool when young; ¼–⅝ in. apart.

Opuntia polyacantha. With spines few and short. Largest pad pictured, 5⅝ inches long.

SPINES Very variable; typically 1–15 spines on all or almost all areoles; 0–5 main, interior ones; when present, 1 main spine ¼–2 in. long, very slender to medium thick, round to somewhat flattened, porrect or deflexed; plus 0–2 uppers ¼–3 in. long, upright or spreading, slender to medium thick, round; 0–2 laterals; ¼–1¼ in. long, slender, round or slightly flattened; white, yellowish, brownish, red-brown, or variegated; 1–10+ outer, radiating spines ⅛–¾ in. long, slender to very slender and bristlelike, white or gray, often with darker tips; larger, main spines may be missing on all but upper edge areoles; occasionally 1–3 only on upper areoles; 1–2 lower bristles, very short; quite often radials of old pads increase greatly in number, especially toward bases, and become flexible, hairlike, elongated to 2–8 in.

GLOCHIDS Few and short on young pads, compact cluster about ⅟₁₆ in. long, sometimes to ³⁄₁₆ in. long, fairly numerous on old pads; yellow to bright brown.

FLOWERS 2–3½ in. diameter, 1½–2½ in. tall; almost always yellow in our area, often pink, rose, or reddish in Colorado and in north; ovary broadly club-shaped to almost spherical, ¾–1⅝ in. long, about ¾ in. wide; tuberculate by many elevated areoles with much white wool, many yellow glochids plus some very slender spines to ½ in. long; 5–10 bright green stigma lobes.

FRUITS Very variable; spherical to oval or egg-shaped, more or less tuberculate when growing; without tubercles when ripe and dry; ¾–2 in. long by ½–2 in. thick; top usually somewhat pitted, may be entirely flat; when completely ripe becoming dry with thin, papery skin over tightly packed mass of seeds; typically 2–12 slender spines ³⁄₁₆–⅝ in. long on each areole of upper third to three-fourths, wholly spiny to spineless; seeds extremely variable, ⅛–¼+ in. (3–7 mm), typically ³⁄₁₆+ in. (5–7 mm) diameter; rim of seed from narrow to very wide.

RANGE Northwestern United States far into Canada, south through western Nebraska and Kansas across western tip of Oklahoma Panhandle into upper part of Texas Panhandle, through Colorado, New Mexico, south into Hueco and Davis mountains of southwestern Texas, west into Arizona.

REMARKS One of widest-ranging of all cacti; probably most northern, practically to Arctic Circle. Not conspicuous, half buried in sand or lost in grass; mats hold soil from erosion and stabilize sand. Many variations often given names, from a few to 15 white to red-brown spines, fruit spherical to egg-shaped, ¾–2 in. long, seeds about ⅛–¼+ in. diameter.

Opuntia hystricina Eng.
(Benson: *O. erinacea* var. *hystricina*)
Porcupine Prickly Pear

ROOTS Fibrous.

STEMS Low, diffuse, spreading, not prostrate; small clumps of upright pads

Opuntia hystricina. Upright pad, 4 inches long.

6 in.–1 ft. high; pads nearly circular to elongated obovate or oblong; 3–5 in. long, 2½–3 in. wide, medium thick; not tuberculate; not noticeably wrinkled from lack of water; medium or bright green.

AREOLES Large and conspicuous, oval, about ³⁄₁₆ in. long on young pads, round, ¼+ in. diameter on old pads; ¼–½ in. apart.

SPINES 6–15 in each areole; 1–8, 5–8 in fully armed upper areoles; main spines 1½–4 in. long; irregularly arranged, spreading in all directions, including upward; brownish or gray or variegated; slender to average thickness, somewhat flattened, often twisted or bent, somewhat flexible; to 7 lower, very slender, white radiating spines ¾–1 in. long in each areole; sometimes a few very slender, white, hairlike spines 2–3 in. long at bases of pads.

GLOCHIDS Straw-colored or brown, often both in same areole, outer ring of older, longer, darkened; inner cluster of younger, shorter, brighter straw-colored ones.

FLOWERS Ordinarily clear, pale yellow, sometimes orange, rose, red, or purplish; 2–3 in. diameter; ovary has white wool and bristlelike spines; 8–10 green stigma lobes.

FRUITS Egg-shaped to broadly club-shaped, ⅞–1¼ in. long by about ½ in. thick; areoles of upper half have 4–12 bristly spines ½–¾ in. long; flat umbilicus, or nearly so; seeds very large, ¼–⁵⁄₁₆ in. (7+ mm) diameter, with broad rims.

RANGE Rio Grande in New Mexico west to Nevada and California.

REMARKS Differs from *O. polyacantha* by being diffuse and spreading with more upright growth; pads darker green; lacks distinct tubercles by raised areoles or marked wrinkling; has more, longer, more erect main spines, usually bent and somewhat flexible; many more and longer glochids; flattened spines not a distinguishing character; stoutness of spines, larger pads, more widely spaced areoles also not distinctive; not just robust version of hunger cactus; rare in New Mexico; characters in common with *O. ursina* Weber include upright growth, ovate or oblong pads with spreading, often erect spines to 4 in. long, only moderately rigid, many conspicuous glochids; more closely related to *O. ursina* than to *O. polyacantha*.

Opuntia arenaria Eng.

ROOTS Unique among Opuntias in our area: not tuberous, but large, rhizomelike structures to ½ in. thick, sometimes running 3–6 ft. horizontally just under surface; underground structures covered with many large areoles and long glochids like old stems, giving off pads and fibrous roots.

STEMS Prostrate strings to 6 ft. long, buried in sand; if underground structures made up from old pads, separate joints not clearly observable, sometimes interpreted as roots, but have areoles and glochids; ascending and

Opuntia arenaria. Largest pad pictured, 2¾ inches long.

spreading pads 6+ in. high; pads 1¼–4 in. long by ¾–2 in. wide, often ¾ in. thick; when small, almost cylindrical, then widen and flatten to elongated oval to very elongated egg-shaped or clavate; young pads light, shiny green, tuberculate, not wrinkled when dehydrated; older pads on prostrate, more or less covered stems are brown and woody.

AREOLES Small, with a little white wool when young, enlarging somewhat on old stems; ³⁄₁₆–³⁄₈ in. apart.

SPINES Almost all areoles armed with 3–10, white or brownish or white with brownish bases and tips; 1–4 main ones; 1 central ¾–2 in. long, rigid, average thickness, slightly flattened, porrect or turned upward; 0–3 others ³⁄₈–1 in. long, round or slightly flattened, spreading downward; below, 2–6 bristlelike spines ⅛–½ in. long, radiating downward.

GLOCHIDS Straw-colored or brownish, few but rather long on young pads; very many, to ¼ in. long in large, spreading clusters almost completely covering old pads.

FLOWERS Yellow; 2–2¾ in. diameter; egg-shaped ovary, ⅞–1¼ in. long; about 8 inner petals; 5 green stigma lobes.

FRUITS Oblong or club-shaped, usually constricted at both bottom and top, deeply pitted above; 1–1½ in. long by ¼–³⁄₈ in. thick; 1–5 slender spines ¼–½ in. long on each areole of broader central zone; seeds nearly ³⁄₁₆–⁵⁄₁₆ in. or less (5–7 mm) diameter, very thin, irregular, rather elongated, with broad margins.

Opuntia grahamii. Pictured clump, 7 inches across.

RANGE Sandy areas along Rio Grande in southern New Mexico and near El Paso, Texas.

REMARKS Unique little cactus with extremely long, stolonlike root or stem structure adapted to survive in deep and shifting sand; about three-fourths of plant entirely buried; almost extinct; does not do well in cultivation, does not grow successfully in regular soil.

Opuntia grahamii Eng.
(Benson: *O. schottii* var. *grahamii*)
Mounded Dwarf Cholla

STEMS Joints elongated oblong, club-shaped, or spindle-shaped; 1½–2½ in. long, covered with low, oblong tubercles ½+ in. long; sometimes tubercles very indistinct; joints forming dense mats to about 1 ft. across, on edges often prostrate, in center ascending; may mound due to sand; joints only branching once above surface, to about 4 in. above sand, firmly attached.

AREOLES Round, ⅛–³⁄₁₆ in. across, with much white wool at first; on ends of tubercles, about ½ in. apart.

SPINES 8–14 per areole; 4–8 main inner ones spreading in all directions; 1¼–2½ in. long, straight, medium thick, round or nearly so, brown or red-brown, smooth at first, grayish and rough when old; not cross-striated or edged; 4–6 outer spines spreading below, slender, round, whitish, ½–1 in. long.

GLOCHIDS Few at first, quite numerous, to ¼ in. long on old joints; brown.

FLOWERS Yellow, 2–2½ in. across; whitish stigmas.

FRUITS Elongated egg-shaped or oblong, 1¼–1¾ in. long, yellow when ripe; tuberculate, with many areoles, each with white wool, several slender white spines, and 20–30 white glochids; seeds slightly over ³⁄₁₆ in. (5–5½ mm) diameter.

RANGE Small area of west Texas, parts of El Paso and Hudspeth counties from foothills of Franklin Mountains through Hueco Mountains and hills east and southeast of El Paso to Sierra Blanca, Texas; also reported in adjacent Chihuahua, Mexico, and just within New Mexico.

REMARKS Low-growing, more or less club-shaped stems; very common on some sand hills; more compact, joints more ascending than those of relatives except *O. clavata*; typically a little mound 3–6 in. high, to about 1+ ft. diameter; very hard to see; distinguished from all close relatives by having comparatively slender, smooth, round or nearly so main spines; others very heavy, very rough, cross-striated, greatly flattened; thus distinguished from *O. schottii*. Although they are variously reported from Texas Big Bend, I still have not seen specimens from there which I consider this form.

Opuntia schottii Eng.
Devil Cactus, Dog Cholla, Clavellina

STEMS Joints elongated, cylindrical, more often club-shaped, prostrate or with only upper ends turned upward; bases constricted, about ¼ in. thick, broadening to almost 1 in. thick at upper end; joints 1–3 in. long; covered by broad, elongated tubercles about ½–¾ in. long; joints rather loosely attached.

AREOLES Round or nearly so, on upper ends of tubercles, small below to ¼+ in. diameter toward end of joint.

SPINES 8–14 per areole; 1 main central, very heavy, very flat, porrect or a little deflexed; 1–2½ in. long, ¹⁄₁₆–⅛ in. wide for most of length; surface very rough, usually distinctly cross-striated; at first straw-colored to light brown with tip translucent yellow, edged with light yellow or whitish; fading to rough gray when old; 2 lower centrals spreading downward, to 1½ in. long, like main central; 1–4 centrals spreading upward, ¼–1½ in. long, heavy, triangular or round, darker brown or red-brown with translucent yellow tips; 5–7 small, slender, round, whitish radials ¼–¾ in. long spreading below; no sheaths on matured spines.

GLOCHIDS Few; in upper areoles to 12 straw-colored bristles to ³⁄₁₆ in. long at top of areole.

Opuntia schottii. Joints pictured, each 2 inches long.

FLOWERS Yellow, about 2−2½ in. across, 2 in. tall; whitish stamens; whitish or very pale greenish stigmas.

FRUITS 1−1½ in. long by ⅜−½ in. thick, elongated club-shaped, with perianth persistent; very light yellow when ripe; covered with narrow tubercles ¼−⅜ in. long, each ending in areole above; areoles small, each with white wool; 4 main centrals, slender, round, 3⁄16−5⁄16 in. long, arranged cross-wise; 25−35 radials, very slender and bristlelike; seeds 3⁄16 in. (about 4 mm) or less diameter.

RANGE Along Rio Grande from Brownsville, Texas, to Lajitas in Big Bend, common from Zapata to Big Bend near river.

REMARKS Very low, inconspicuous little cactus, practically invisible; strong barbed spines; grows on gravelly hillsides overlooking Rio Grande; below Pecos usually single chains of prostrate joints blooming and fruiting sparingly, propagating mostly by separated pads; not as loosely attached as *O. fragilis* or *O. pusilla*; west of Pecos low, compact mats to 2 ft. across, in season with very many flowers and fruits; westernmost range does not quite reach range of nearest relatives.

Opuntia stanlyi Eng.
Stanley's Cholla, Devil Cholla, Creeping Cholla

STEMS Cylindrical, club-shaped joints, 3½−6 in. long, slender at base, enlarging to 1−2 in. diameter at outer end; many joints, prostrate or with ends

Opuntia stanlyi. Largest joint pictured, 4 inches long.

curving upward or whole joint ascending; dense mats 6–12 in. high, sometimes 15–20 ft. diameter; covered with tubercles as ridges 1–1¾ in. long by ¼–¾ in. tall by ¼–½ in. wide.

AREOLES Round or nearly so, on upper slopes of tubercles; ¼+ in. diameter; some white wool at first.

SPINES 10–20+; 5–9 large inner ones 1⅛–2⅜ in. long, spreading, largest 1 porrect or deflexed, very flat, 1/16–⅛ in. wide; upper surface roughened by tiny pits and irregular cross-striation; other main spines not so heavy or flattened; yellowish or reddish-brown, ashy gray when old; 7–15+ outer spines ⅜–¾ in. long, whitish, round to flattened.

GLOCHIDS Few, to ¼ in. long, robust; yellow.

FLOWERS Pale yellow, 1½–2¾ in. diameter; white stigma lobes.

FRUITS Broadly club-shaped or egg-shaped, 2–2¾ in. long, very spiny; seeds about 3/16 in. (about 5 mm) diameter.

RANGE Entering our area from Arizona and Mexico, southwestern New Mexico to upper edge of Grant County, east to Socorro, near El Paso; in Texas along Rio Grande from El Paso to Candelaria in Presidio County.

REMARKS One of worst pest cacti; forms impenetrable thickets. Most closely related to *O. schottii*, which has its main characters in miniature, but joints of *O. stanlyi* not easily separated; ranges separated by only short distance.

Opuntia clavata Eng.
Club Cholla, Dagger Cholla

STEMS Low mat, often 3–6+ ft. across, 3–6 in. high; joints upright or nearly so, short club-shaped to egg-shaped, some narrowing below, not markedly constricted; 1–2½ in. long, to 1 in. thick above; joints covered with low, broad, rather indistinct tubercles about ¼–½ in. long.

AREOLES Large, usually 3/16–¼ in. across, round.

SPINES 10–20, white and rough when mature, bright pink when growing; 4–7 main inner spines ½–1¼ in. long; upper ones more slender, shorter, only somewhat flattened, erect; lower 3–4 spreading downward, larger, flatter; main central deflexed, conspicuous for flatness and thickness, to 1¼ in. long, about ⅛ in. thick at base, tapering evenly to point; upper surface conspicuously cross-striated, lower surface keeled; 6–13 outer spines radiating in every direction; 3/16–⅝ in. long, slender, round.

GLOCHIDS Few to rather many, white or straw-colored, about ⅛–3/16 in. long.

FLOWERS Yellow, small, to 2 in. diameter, less in length.

FRUITS Elongated club-shaped or almost spindle-shaped, with deep umbilicus; 1¼–2 in. long, to 1 in. thick; when ripe, light yellow surface almost completely covered with large number of very slender white or straw-colored bristles from many areoles; seeds 3/16–¼ in. (5–6 mm) diameter.

RANGE Central and portion of northwestern New Mexico.

Opuntia clavata. Largest joints pictured, 1½ inches in diameter.

REMARKS Often huge mats; appears much like grass; pest to livestock but a soil holder; well-named dagger cholla from largest spine.

Opuntia imbricata var. *arborescens* (Eng.) Weniger (Benson: *O. imbricata* var. *imbricata*)

Tree Cactus, Cane Cactus, Candelabrum Cactus, Cholla, Velas de Coyote (Coyote Candles)

STEMS Upright, bushy, or treelike; 3–8+ ft. tall; round trunk often to 3–4 in. diameter, said to reach 5–10 in.; more or less covered with rough bark and enlarged areoles; current year's joints cylindrical, usually 2–6 in., occasionally to 8 in. long, to about 1 in. diameter; covered with elongated tubercles ¾–1¼ in. long, to about ¼ in. high, upper and lower slopes about equal; old stems have woody skeleton.

Opuntia imbricata var. *arborescens*. Branch with ripe fruits. Main branch pictured, 1¼ inches in diameter.

AREOLES Oval or oblong, about ¼ in. long, enlarging with age; some short, whitish, or yellowish wool.

SPINES Very variable in number; 2–10 on current year's growth, with age to 20–30; 1–8 centrals spreading in all directions; ½–1¼ in. long, slender to medium strength, round, yellow, brownish, or variegated; covered by loose sheaths; remainder radiating exterior spines, ¼–⅝ in. long, slender, white to brownish, at least partly covered with tight, whitish sheaths.

GLOCHIDS Very few, sometimes missing; in upper part of areole, short, inconspicuous in wool.

FLOWERS To 3 in. diameter, 1½–2 in. tall; purplish, lavender, or rose-pink; ovary 1+ in. long, nearly as thick; very tuberculate; often has perianth segments and 2–3 white bristles ¼–⅝ in. long on upper areoles; filaments reddish toward bases, greenish-pink above; cream-colored anthers; reddish style, slightly longer than stamens; 6–8 long, fat, pinkish-white or tan stigma lobes.

FRUITS Spherical or hemispherical, about 1 in. long, often a little wider than long; unarmed; with very deeply pitted umbilici; rest of surface covered with pronounced tubercles about ½ in. long, ⅛–³⁄₁₆ in. high; yellow when ripe, not juicy; usually remaining on branches at least a year; sometimes turning brown and dry; seeds regular, smooth, ⅛+ in. (3–4 mm) diameter.

RANGE Southern Colorado over most of New Mexico on into Chihuahua, Mexico; eastern boundary of range from extreme southwestern Kansas

Opuntia imbricata var. *arborescens*. Section of the main stem pictured, 1¼ inches in diameter.

across western part of Oklahoma and Texas panhandles, southeast to Abilene, Texas, southwest to Fort Stockton, into Mexico between Sanderson and Big Bend.

REMARKS Large cholla common over much of western part of our area; sometimes very numerous in mountains, but individuals not as robust as on prairies. Fruits always covered with large tubercles, with very large, very deep umbilici; ripen slowly, bright yellow by late summer; remain on plants most or all of winter without changing shape; thus distinguished from typical *O. imbricata*, which grows only south of Saltillo and is different form with larger joints, more or less ovate fruits twice as big, perfectly smooth, all tubercles vanishing, umbilici becoming flat.

Opuntia imbricata var. *viridiflora* (B. & R.) Weniger
(Not Benson: *O. whipplei* var. *viridiflora*)

STEMS Upright, 1–3 ft. tall, much branched, with no enlarging trunk; old stems more or less bark-covered, with woody support; current year's joints usually ½–¾ in. diameter, occasionally to 1 in. in cultivation; to 5 in. long; covered with prominent tubercles ¾+ in. long.

AREOLES Circular or oval, with short gray or yellowish wool.

SPINES 2–8 per areole on current year's growth, not increasing much with age; ¾–1 in. long, dark brown, with brownish sheaths.

GLOCHIDS Fairly numerous but short.

FLOWERS 1–2 in. diameter, not opening widely; coral-pink within, yellowish to pale green outside; green filaments; yellow anthers; pistil long, reddish; 8–9 reddish stigma lobes.

FRUITS 1 in. or less diameter, as those of var. *arborescens* in shape, with very prominent, persisting tubercles and deep umbilici; long, deciduous bristles at first, usually naked when ripe.

RANGE Only type locality, hills just north of Santa Fe, New Mexico.

REMARKS Doubtful variety, very close to var. *arborescens*, seems a small, stunted version; flowers differ: bright purplish in var. *arborescens*, pale greenish in var. *viridiflora*; flower color not basis for distinguishing species; does not grow as large as other forms of species.

Opuntia imbricata var. *vexans* (Gr.) Weniger

STEMS Treelike cholla with cylindrical branches from upright, bark-covered trunk; to 16 ft. tall from cylindrical trunk to 12+ in. diameter; current year's branches 4–16 in. long, typically 6–12; cylindrical, ¾–2 in. thick, usually narrowing gradually at bases; tuberculate, tubercles about 1¼ in. long, ³⁄₁₆–³⁄₈ in. tall, upper slope abrupt, lower much longer and more gradual.

Opuntia imbricata var. *viridiflora*. Pictured plant, 15 inches tall.

Opuntia imbricata var. *vexans*. Branch with ripe fruits. Largest fruit pictured, 1⅝ inches in diameter.

AREOLES Oval, ¼+ in. long, with gray wool at first, later enlarging and bulging outward.

SPINES 1–10 in areoles of current growth, to 30 on old stems; spreading in all directions, short, ¼–⅝ in. long, very slender to medium thick; brown, more or less annulate, with lighter tips, covered with rather tight, yellowish, gray, or whitish sheaths.

GLOCHIDS Yellowish; from upper part of areole, always very few, 1/16–⅜ in. long.

Opuntia imbricata var. *vexans*. 15 feet, 6 inches tall.

FLOWERS 2–2¾ in. diameter by 1½–2 in. tall; ovary 1–1⅛ in. long by about ¾ in. thick, very tuberculate, with several long perianth segments on it; outside of flower greenish, inside light pinkish-purple; filaments pink suffused with green or brown; yellow or cream-colored anthers; short style; 6–9 stigma lobes, brownish, tan, or whitish; tends to bloom repeatedly during summer with moisture.

FRUITS When young, egg-shaped, about 1¾ in. long by 1 in. wide, very tuberculate with tubercles ⅝–¾ in. long, about ⅛ in. tall, umbilici deeply pitted; some short glochids and around upper edge about 6 very slender white spines ⅜–1⅜ in. long; when ripening in late fall or winter, yellowish-green, egg-shaped to spherical or wider than long, 1¼–2 in. long, 1½–2 in. wide; spineless, wholly smooth, or with only traces of a few tubercles at base; umbilici flattened or nearly so.

RANGE Growing wild only in extreme southwest Kinney County, Texas; used as an ornamental in Webb, Maverick, and Val Verde counties.

REMARKS First named in 1908 from plants said to have been cultivated and also growing wild in Webb County, Texas; once grown in yards from Laredo to Del Rio. Only one population presently known, this growing in the wild in Kinney County, where individuals have attained trunks to 12 in. diameter. Differs from *O. imbricata* var. *arborescens* in different growth form, larger joints, shorter spines, different fruits. The tallest cactus growing uncultivated in these five states.

Opuntia spinosior (Eng.) Toumey
Cane Cholla

STEMS Large, open-branching shrub or treelike plant 3–8 ft. tall, sometimes to 12 ft.; when large, black, scaly trunk 2–4 in. diameter; young joints 4–12 in. long, cylindrical, ⅝–1¼ in. diameter, covered with conspicuous tubercles ¼–¾ in. long; grayish-green, often purplish in winter.

AREOLES Oval or nearly so, ⅛ in. diameter when young, larger, bulging outward with age.

SPINES 6–12 per areole on current year's growth, to 20–30+ when very old; short, mostly ¼–½ in. long, rarely to ¾ in., spreading in all directions; white, gray, or brownish, fading to gray; at first covered entirely, smaller ones only on upper parts, with thin, comparatively inconspicuous sheaths which usually fall off after a year; gray, sometimes with pinkish tinge.

GLOCHIDS A few short, inconspicuous, white or yellowish at top of areole.

FLOWERS 1½–2¼ in. diameter, variable color: commonly purplish, also red, more or less yellowish, white; ovary tubercled, with very slender white spines; cream-colored or yellowish stigma lobes.

FRUITS Yellow when ripe, 1–1½ in. long, almost spherical to oblong or rather egg-shaped; very tuberculate with deeply pitted apexes; at first have

Opuntia spinosior. Largest stem pictured, 1 inch in diameter.

very slender white spines of ovary; fall off before ripening; seeds ⅛+ in. (about 4 mm) diameter.

RANGE Southwestern New Mexico into adjacent Arizona and Mexico.

REMARKS Treelike, open branching, even covering of short, whitish spines, brilliant flowers.

Opuntia whipplei Eng. & Big.
Whipple's Cholla, Rat-Tail Cactus, Sticker Cactus

STEMS Ordinarily erect but low-growing, 6 to about 24 in. tall; extremely numerous branches, joints 2–10 in. long; current year's joints usually ⅜– ¾ in. diameter, occasionally to 1 in.; covered with conspicuous, broad, short tubercles ⅜–⅝ in. long; light or yellowish-green; rather easily detached.

AREOLES Egg-shaped or elliptical, about ³⁄₁₆ in. long when young; some white wool at first, very soon lost.

SPINES 3–12 per areole; 1–4 main spines spreading from center of areole; 1 lower, rather deflexed, usually longer, often somewhat flattened; uppermost 1 flattened, heaviest; all rigid, not very stout; ¼–1¼ in. long; whitish to brown, covered with conspicuous, loose, straw-colored or whitish sheaths; 2–8 smaller, very slender, unsheathed, ¹⁄₁₆–⅜ in. long, radiating or often recurving.

GLOCHIDS Several, white or pale yellowish, to ⅛ in. long near upper edge of areole.

FLOWERS Pale yellow, not opening widely; usually ¾–1¼ in. wide; ovary tube very tuberculate, with large white areoles, a few slender, white, soon-falling spines; greenish filaments; yellow anthers; about 5–6 greenish or white stigma lobes.

FRUITS Almost round to somewhat obovate, ¾–1¼ in. long; very tuberculate; deep umbilici; without spines; remaining green a long time, then yellowish when ripe; seeds ⅛+ in. (3–4 mm) diameter.

RANGE Western New Mexico into southwestern Colorado and Arizona.

REMARKS Often confused with *O. spinosior*, but *O. whipplei* is much smaller, more northern form with to only 12 spines, these to 1¼ in. long, always with yellow flowers, and green stem surfaces, while the other has to 25 spines only to ⅝ in. long, variable color of flowers, and purplish surfaces in winter.

Opuntia whipplei. In winter condition. 10 inches tall.

Opuntia davisii Eng.
(Benson: *O. tunicata* var. *davisii*)

STEMS Low-growing, very much branched bush, usually 12–18 in. tall, occasionally to 30 in.; main stem very short because of immediate branching, hardly increases in diameter; more or less covered with gray, scaly bark; current year's joints cylindrical, often nearly club-shaped; 3–6 in. long, ¼–¾ in. diameter; very tuberculate, tubercles laterally compressed, ⅝–1+ in. long; light green; joints easily detached.

AREOLES Elliptical, about ³⁄₁₆ in. long, some yellowish wool.

SPINES 6–13 per areole; 4–7 main spines in all directions from center of areole; ¾–2 in. long, round, heavy; bright brown or red-brown, somewhat annulate when very large, very loose, bright, glistening, straw-colored or light brown sheaths are removed; 2–5 small radials, ¼–½ in. long, slender, brownish, not sheathed.

GLOCHIDS Compact cluster, yellow, ¹⁄₁₆–⅛ in. long at top of areole.

FLOWERS About 2 in. tall, not opening widely, about 1½ in. diameter; deep green to pale green; centers yellowish, upper edges and outsides tinted with brown or reddish; greenish-red filaments, very coarse; yellow anthers; short style, with 4–7 very large, cream-white to pale purplish lobes; ovary conical, about 1¼ in. long by 1 in. wide, very tuberculate, with some yellow areoles; on upper part, some very slender, white, deciduous spines to 1 in. long.

FRUITS Egg-shaped to clavate, 1–1½ in. long by ⅝–¾ in. thick at top; very tuberculate, with deeply pitted umbilici; short yellow glochids, otherwise naked; greenish-yellow, then dry up; sterile.

RANGE Greer and Harmon counties in extreme southwestern Oklahoma, west across Texas Panhandle and eastern New Mexico to near mountains, south across Texas to Gillespie County in south-central part, to Rio Grande in Big Bend.

REMARKS Eastern counterpart of more western *O. whipplei*, distinguished by spine sheath color; *O. davisii* has 4–7 main spines ¾–2 in. long; *O. whipplei* 1–4, none over 1¼ in. long; *O. davisii* has tubercles compressed, ⅝–1 in. long, instead of broader, shorter ones; flowers yellowish-green, others clear yellow. Very large range, widely scattered locations, perhaps because previously more common or because of ability to reproduce from detached joints. Unusual flower: very firm and waxy, similar to stiff, persistent flower petals of *Echinocereus triglochidiatus* group; seeds never described.

Opuntia tunicata (Lem.) Link & Otto
Abrojo, Clavellina

STEMS Erect, more or less definite woody stem, very many crowded, lateral branches; low and spreading, 1 ft. or less to about 2 ft. tall in our area; cur-

Opuntia davisii. Largest branch pictured, 5-8 inch in diameter.

Opuntia tunicata. Plant pictured, 13 inches across.

rent year's joints 2–6 in. long, narrowly oblong or somewhat club-shaped when short, almost cylindrical when longer; covered with prominent tubercles ¾–1½ in. long; medium to light green; joints very easily detached.

AREOLES Oblong, ³⁄₁₆ in. long at first, enlarging considerably with age; bulging outward with very white wool.

SPINES 6–10; white, yellow, rarely reddish; covered with very loose, very thin, papery, translucent, silvery white sheaths; 3–6 spreading centrals 1–2½ in. long; underneath sheaths more or less angular, very heavy; 2–4 radials from lower part of areole, more slender, from bristlelike, ⅜ in. long to fairly stout, to 1¼ in. long.

GLOCHIDS Small cluster, very short whitish or pale yellow, in upper edge of areole.

FLOWERS Pale greenish-yellow, about 2 in. diameter.

FRUITS Spherical to broadly club-shaped, tuberculate, yellowish-green; seeds not described.

RANGE In United States only on southeast slopes of Glass Mountains in southwest edge of Pecos County, Texas, into central Mexico, Ecuador, Peru, and northern Chile.

REMARKS Very isolated population in Big Bend; immense range; one of most difficult chollas to cultivate.

Opuntia kleiniae DC
Klein Cholla, Candle Cholla

STEMS Erect, shrubby, 3–6 ft. tall, openly, sparingly branching from woody trunks 1–1½ in. diameter; covered with brown, scaly bark; current year's joints 4–12+ in. long, cylindrical, ⁵⁄₁₆–½ in. diameter; low, broad, more or less indistinct tubercles ½–1⅜ in. long; lateral branches fairly easily detached but not as loose as on some chollas.

AREOLES Round to egg-shaped or practically triangular, about ³⁄₁₆ in. long; white wool.

SPINES 1–4 per areole, often only 1; main spine ½–1½+ in. long, said to reach 2 in.; reddish to gray, with loose yellowish sheath which usually falls off soon after spine matures; 1–3 shorter ones.

GLOCHIDS Small compact cluster; yellowish or brown; about ¹⁄₁₆ in. long, at upper edge of areole.

FLOWERS 1–1¼ in. diameter; pale greenish-purple, lavender, or pinkish; egg-shaped ovary, ½–¾ in. long, with woolly areoles on indistinct tubercles; pinkish filaments; 6–7 small whitish stigma lobes.

FRUITS Egg-shaped or almost club-shaped, ¾–1½ in. long, red or bright orange, naked or with clusters of brown glochids ⅛ in. long in areoles when ripe; more or less tuberculate when growing, sometimes remaining so, more often almost completely smooth when ripe; seeds ⅛–³⁄₁₆ in. (about 4 mm) diameter.

RANGE From central Mexico into Texas, New Mexico, Oklahoma, and Arizona; northernmost limit: central New Mexico; reported from Kingfisher, Oklahoma.

REMARKS Tall-growing but inconspicuous; potential pest, but found in scattered locations. Probably most closely related to *O. arbuscula* Eng., a cholla with similar slender, much shorter branches from much thicker trunk, more compact, bushy; similar spines; *O. arbuscula*, with yellowish flowers and green fruits, never found in New Mexico; in Mexico identical to northern specimens except spines commonly to 1½ in. long, fruits often to 1½ in.

Opuntia leptocaulis DC
Desert Christmas Cactus, Slender Stem Cactus, Tasajillo, Aguijilla, Garrambullo

STEMS Small, upright bush 2–5 ft. tall; usually compactly and extensively branched from main trunk, when old, covered with scaly bark, to 1–1¼ in. diameter; current year's joints cylindrical, 1–12 in. long, ⅛–¼ in. thick; may have indistinct tubercles ¼–½ in. long, more often smooth; deep green, often with purplish spots around areoles; lateral joints detach very easily.

Opuntia kleiniae. Plant pictured, 4 feet tall.

Opuntia leptocaulis. Main stem pictured, ¼ inch in diameter.

AREOLES Ovate or often almost diamond-shaped; about ⅛ in. long, with short, white wool.

SPINES 0–3 per areole, most commonly 1; main spine porrect, gray, very variable; may be ⅛–2 in. long; when short, usually very slender with close-fitting sheath; when long and well developed, stout, more or less flattened, covered with loose, papery, white, yellow, or tan sheath; may be 1–2 short, slender, bristlelike spines.

GLOCHIDS Few, very short in 1–3 small bunches in upper part of areole; yellowish to brown.

FLOWERS ½–⅞ in. wide by ¾–1 in. tall, opening very widely; greenish-yellow; ovary about ⅝ in. long, egg-shaped to conical, slightly if at all tuberculate; with brown glochids and elongated perianth segments; outer segments greenish-yellow with soft green spines at summits; inner segments oblong, pointed; greenish-yellow stamens; long style; 3–6 short, thick, greenish-yellow stigma lobes.

FRUITS Bright scarlet, orange-red, or yellowish when ripe; almost globular, pear-shaped, or club-shaped, ⅜–1 in. long; smooth, often with brown glochids in areoles, deeply pitted umbilicus; persistent, often proliferous, sometimes with shoots 2–3 in. long when still on plant; usually 12 or fewer seeds per fruit, ⅛+ in. (3–4 mm) diameter.

RANGE South-central Mexico north into Arizona, all but northwestern quarter of New Mexico, all of Texas south of Canadian River east to Dallas and lower Brazos River, into Oklahoma to Harmon and Greer counties in extreme southwestern corner and Arbuckle Mountains in south-central part.

REMARKS Probably the most hated cactus in our area; major pest; very wide-ranging; grows in great numbers. Varies greatly in size, 2–5 ft.; does not increase diameter of terminal branches over about ¼ in., or trunk over about 1½ in.; thus distinguished from *O. arbuscula*, a close relative found in Arizona; fruit color also distinguishes; *O. kleiniae*, a close relative, sometimes found in same thicket; current year's stems of that species larger, with larger, purplish flowers; probably most primitive Opuntia in our area.

Glossary

The terms below are defined as they are used in this work to refer to the cacti described, and the definitions are not intended to be so broad as to cover their usage for all other plant groups.

Anther. The enlarged, pollen-bearing sac at the tip of a stamen.

Apex. The tip or summit of any structure.

Areole. A spot in the form of a pit or a raised area marking an opening through the epidermis from which leaves, spines, or other structures grow.

Ascending. Not standing perfectly upright, but growing upward.

Axil. The angle between a leaf, branch, tubercle, or other outgrowth and the stem.

Basal. At or referring to the base or lower part of any structure.

Berry. A pulpy or fleshy fruit with numerous seeds embedded in the flesh.

Bud. An unopened flower; a growing tip surrounded by its immature perianth segments or leaves.

Caespitose. Forming a cluster or clump of stems by repeated branching of the stem at or near the base.

Central. Positioned at or near the center of an area, as opposed to being peripheral in position. A spine originating in the center of the areole as opposed to those growing around the edge of the areole.

Character. A characteristic or feature unique enough to have value in distinguishing forms and setting up relationships.

Cholla. Any cylindrical-stemmed member of the genus *Opuntia*.

Cilium (pl.: *cilia*). Very fine, hairlike filaments sometimes forming fringes on the margins of perianth segments.

Clavate. Gradually thickening near the distal end.

Confluent. Running together or more or less coalescing.

Deflexed. Curved or bent back, down upon itself, or toward the surface of the plant. Recurved.

Dehiscent. Splitting open at maturity.

Dimorphic. Having two forms.

Distal. Situated opposite the point of attachment or origin.

Entire. Having the margin continuous and not toothed, lobed, indented, or interrupted.

Epidermis. The outer layer of cells on a plant, forming a protective covering. In ordinary usage thought of as including the waxy nonliving layer that overlies the living cells.

Erose. Ragged, with irregular indentations, as though bits were randomly chewed away.

Felt. A very thick covering of hairs, filaments, or fibers.

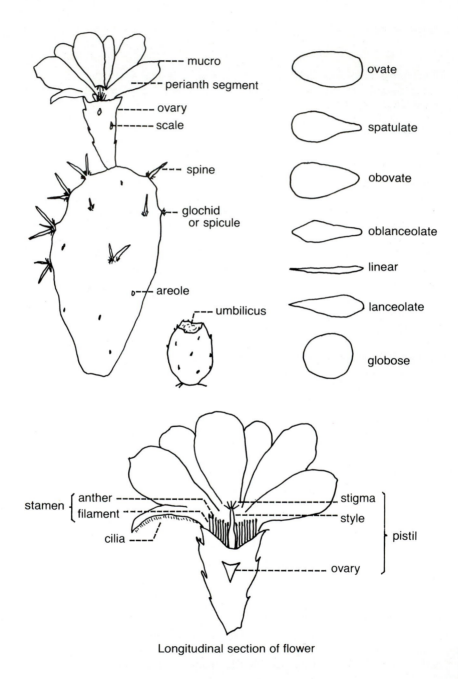

mucro

perianth segment

ovary

scale

spine

glochid
or spicule

areole

umbilicus

ovate

spatulate

obovate

oblanceolate

linear

lanceolate

globose

stamen { anther
filament

cilia

stigma

style

ovary

pistil

Longitudinal section of flower

Fibrous roots. Finely subdivided roots with no obvious thickening or enlarged central root beyond the base of the plant.

Filament. The stalk of a stamen; the threadlike part of the stamen that supports the anther.

Genus. A grouping of species possessing common characters unique enough to be treated as a unit distinct from others.

Glabrous. Smooth and shiny; not pubescent, rough, or hairy.

Gland. A secreting structure, usually in the form of a protuberance or appendage, but sometimes a surface.

Glaucescence. A thin layer of whitish substance, often called the bloom and usually made up of tiny particles of wax, which rub off.

Globose. Spherical or spheroidal in shape.

Glochid. A sharp, hairlike or bristlelike outgrowth equipped with minute and usually invisible barbs so that it resists withdrawal from any tissue.

Hilum. The scar on the seed that marks the point at which the seed was attached during growth.

Intergrading. Not separated by any division into sets, but merging by having an unbroken series of intermediate forms.

Lanceolate. Lance-shaped; much longer than broad, widest just above the base, with a gradual taper from there to the tip.

Lateral. Growing or positioned at the sides.

Linear. Long and narrow, with sides parallel or nearly so, as a blade of grass.

Meristem. A body of tissue with the power to divide and differentiate.

Microgenus. A nonofficial term used here for genera that have been officially described, but seem distinguished by less obvious or significant characters than the major genera.

Midrib. The main or center rib of a leaf or perianth segment.

Monomorphic. Having but a single form and not subdividing.

Mucro. A short, abrupt, and more or less sharp point on the tip of a leaf or flower structure.

Oblanceolate. Reversed lanceolate in shape, with the widest part near the tip.

Obovate. Reversed ovate; the outline of a hen's egg with the broader part above the middle.

Ovary. The enlarged lower part of the pistil containing the ovules.

Ovate. Having the outline of a hen's egg and with the broader part below the middle.

Pectinate. Comblike; used in referring to spines or other structures spread flat like the teeth of a comb.

Perianth segment. One of the parts making up the perianth; a petal or sepal.

Perianth tube. A tubelike arrangement of the perianth segments extending in some forms to some distance above the ovary.

Petal. One of the inner set of perianth segments or corolla.

Pistil. The central, female part of the flower, made up of the ovary, style, and stigma.

Porrect. Positioned outward; standing perpendicular to the surface of the plant.

Prostrate. Lying completely flat upon the ground.

Pubescent. Covered with short, soft, fine, hairlike outgrowths; downy.

Radial. Positioned around the edges of an area; peripheral, as opposed to central. A spine positioned somewhere upon the periphery of an areole.

Radiating. Positioned outward like radii.

Reclining. Sprawling or leaning against something.

Recurved. Curving back upon itself; deflexed.

Reniform. Kidney-shaped.

Rib. A ridge; a raised surface running vertically or sometimes spiraling and bearing areoles in a row along its summit. Often thought of as being composed of more or less coalescent tubercles which may be evident as bulging masses along it.

Rotate flower. Spreading widely rather than remaining bell-shaped or funnel-shaped; wheel-shaped.

Scale. A small, scarcely expanded leaflike structure; also a narrow, triangular, or sometimes spinelike lower perianth segment often found on the ovary or flower-tube surface.

Sepal. One of the outer perianth segments of the calyx.

Spatulate. Spoon-shaped; oblong or rounded above, the base long and narrow.

Species. A population recognizable by characteristics of form and genetic relationship as a unit, often capable of subdivision into varieties all genetically close enough for interbreeding.

Spicule. A very small, fine spine. A glochid.

Spine. A sharp outgrowth, either rigid and woody or sometimes flexible and hairlike. In cacti always arising from an areole and thought of as a modified leaf.

Spreading. Growing outwardly. Used in referring to a series of radial spines projecting obliquely outward around the areole, as opposed to lying flat against the surface of the plant. Used also for plant growth advancing outward by new shoots or by rooting from old, reclining stems.

Stamen. The male part of the flower consisting of the filament and the anther bearing the pollen.

Stem. The main upward axis of a plant.

Stigma. The uppermost part of the pistil, at the tip of the style; the part that receives the pollen; in cacti usually divided into lobes.

Stigma lobe. One of the expanded sections of the stigma.

Stoma (pl.: *stomata*). A microscopic opening through the epidermis of the plant allowing for respiration and transpiration.

Style. The central portion of the pistil, connecting ovary and stigma.

Subgenus. A taxonomic rank sometimes used to divide a large genus into subdivisions above the species level.

Subspecies. A subdivision of the species unit recognizable by certain morphological characters, but not isolated by genetic barriers from others within the species. (No attempt is made in this work to distinguish between the subspecies and the variety.)

Taproot. The primary root axis, when larger and longer than the branch roots, and often thick and used for storage, as a carrot.

Taxon. A formally described category in classification; a series of individuals distinct by some visible characteristics.

Terminal. At the tip or end.

Transpiration. The giving off of water vapor through the stomata by a plant.

Trichome. A hairlike structure found on plants; a slender filament growing from the plant's epidermis by one end.

Tuber. A short, thick, fleshy underground stem or stem branch for storage

Tubercle. A knoblike protrusion from the surface of any structure; a more or less pyramidal knob rising from the stem surface of a cactus and having an areole on or near its summit.

Tuberculate. Having tubercles.

Tuberous root. A root of undistended size overall, a generally fibrous root, but having thick, fleshy sections like tubers scattered upon it. Not a taproot.

Umbilicus. On those species which drop the perianth and upper parts of the flower, the scar left at the summit of the fruit after the floral parts are shed.

Variety. See Subspecies.

Woolly. Covered with long and very thick hairs.

Index of Scientific Names

The number of the page on which the principal description of a form begins is in italics. All other numbers refer to pages on which there is incidental reference to the plant.

Acanthocereus: 7, 82, 85
  Acanthocereus pentagonus: 86
Ancistrocactus: 89, 90
  Ancistrocactus scheeri: 110
  Ancistrocactus tobuschii: 112
  Ancistrocactus uncinatus var.
    wrightii: 102
Anhalonium: 142
Ariocarpus: 7, 88, 142, 153
  Ariocarpus fissuratus: 143, 144
  Ariocarpus fissuratus var. lloydii:
    145
  Ariocarpus retusus: 143, 144
  Ariocarpus trigonus: 143
Astrophytum: 89

Cactus: 155
  Cactus viviparus: 179
Cereus: 79, 82, 85, 155
  Cereus greggii var. greggii: 83
  Cereus pentagonus: 86
Coloradoa: 89
Coryphantha: 146, 155, 156, 157,
    158
  Coryphantha bisbeeana: 184
  Coryphantha clava: 157, 158
  Coryphantha cornifera var. echi-
    nus: 168
  Coryphantha dasyancantha var.
    varicolor: 199
  Coryphantha duncanii: 197
  Coryphantha erecta: 157, 158
  Coryphantha hesteri: 202
  Coryphantha macromeris: 173
  Coryphantha macromeris var.
    runyonii: 175

Coryphantha minima: 203
Coryphantha missouriensis var.
  caespitosa: 176
Coryphantha orcuttii: 184
Coryphantha ramillosa: 170
Coryphantha roberti: 204
Coryphantha scheeri: 165
Coryphantha sneedii var. leei:
  206
Coryphantha sneedii var.
  sneedii: 205
Coryphantha strobiliformis var.
  strobiliformis: 192
Coryphantha sulcata: 168
Coryphantha vivipara: 179
Coryphantha vivipara var. ari-
  zonica: 186
Coryphantha vivipara var. de-
  serti: 188
Coryphantha vivipara var. radi-
  osa: 180
Coryphantha vivipara var. vivi-
  para: 179

Dolichothele: 155

Echinocactus: 7, 88, 89, 137, 153
  Echinocactus asterias: 93, 98
  Echinocactus bicolor: 125
  Echinocactus bicolor var. schot-
    tii: 93, 123, 125
  Echinocactus brevihamatus: 92,
    108, 110, 113
  Echinocactus conoideus: 93, 134
  Echinocactus erectocentrus: 132

Echinocactus flavidispinus: 93, 124
Echinocactus hamatacanthus: 92, 120
Echinocactus horizonthalonius: 94
Echinocactus horizonthalonius var. *curvispina*: 91, 94
Echinocactus horizonthalonius var. *moelleri*: 91, 96
Echinocactus horizonthalonius var. *nicholii*: 96
Echinocactus intertextus: 126
Echinocactus intertextus var. *dasyacanthus*: 93, 128, 190
Echinocactus intertextus var. *intertextus*: 93, 128
Echinocactus longihamatus: 122
Echinocactus mariposensis: 133
Echinocactus mesae-verdae: 91, 92, 107
Echinocactus micromeris: 152
Echinocactus scheeri: 92, 110
Echinocactus setispinus: 114, 120, 122
Echinocactus setispinus var. *hamatus*: 91, 116
Echinocactus setispinus var. *setaceus*: 91, 116
Echinocactus sinuatus: 92, 118, 122
Echinocactus texensis: 92, 96
Echinocactus tobuschii: 92, 112, 113
Echinocactus uncinatus: 89, 90, 104
Echinocactus uncinatus var. *wrightii*: 91, 102
Echinocactus warnockii: 92, 131
Echinocactus whipplei: 105
Echinocactus whipplei var. *heilii*: 93, 105
Echinocactus whipplei var. *intermedius*: 93, 104

Echinocactus wislizeni: 92, 101, 122
Echinocereus: 7, 9, 10, 79
Echinocereus albispinus: 12, 39
Echinocereus baileyi: 12, 37, 40
Echinocereus berlandieri: 15, 74, 77
Echinocereus blanckii: 15, 77
Echinocereus caespitosus: 28, 34, 43, 215
Echinocereus caespitosus var. *caespitosus*: 11, 29
Echinocereus caespitosus var. *minor*: 12, 31
Echinocereus caespitosus var. *perbellus*: 12, 32
Echinocereus caespitosus var. *purpureus*: 12, 32
Echinocereus chisoensis: 12, 41
Echinocereus chloranthus: 18, 22, 26
Echinocereus chloranthus var. *chloranthus*: 11, 23
Echinocereus chloranthus var. *neocapillus*: 11, 24
Echinocereus coccineus: 57, 61
Echinocereus coccineus var. *coccineus*: 13, 58, 59
Echinocereus coccineus var. *conoideus*: 13, 58, 61
Echinocereus dasyacanthus: 43, 47, 50
Echinocereus dasyacanthus var. *dasyacanthus*: 12, 48
Echinocereus dasyacanthus var. *hildmanii*: 13, 49
Echinocereus davisii: 11, 18
Echinocereus dubius: 15, 66
Echinocereus enneacanthus: 62
Echinocereus enneacanthus var. *brevispinus*: 63
Echinocereus enneacanthus var. *carnosus*: 14, 63

Echinocereus enneacanthus var.
  enneacanthus: 14, 63
Echinocereus fendleri: 67
Echinocereus fendleri var.
  fendleri: 14, 69
Echinocereus fendleri var. *rec-
  tispinus*: 14, 69
Echinocereus fitchii: 12, 34
Echinocereus kuenzleri: 14, 70
Echinocereus lloydii: 14, 51
Echinocereus melanocentrus: 12,
  34
Echinocereus mojaviensis: 13
Echinocereus papillosus: 71
Echinocereus papillosus var. *an-
  gusticeps*: 15, 73
Echinocereus papillosus var.
  papillosus: 15, 71
Echinocereus pectinatus: 29, 37,
  43
Echinocereus pectinatus var.
  ctenoides: 12, 45
Echinocereus pectinatus var.
  minor: 48, 51
Echinocereus pectinatus var.
  neo-mexicanus: 48
Echinocereus pectinatus var. *pec-
  tinatus*: 48
Echinocereus pectinatus var.
  rigidissimus: 12, 43
Echinocereus pectinatus var.
  wenigeri: 12, 42
Echinocereus pentalophus: 15,
  74, 76, 77
Echinocereus polyacanthus var.
  neo-mexicanus: 13, 61
Echinocereus polyacanthus var.
  polyacanthus: 13
Echinocereus polyacanthus var.
  rosei: 13, 60, 62
Echinocereus reichenbachii: 28
Echinocereus reichenbachii var.
  albertii: 34

Echinocereus reichenbachii var.
  albispinus: 37, 39
Echinocereus reichenbachii var.
  reichenbachii: 29
Echinocereus roetteri: 13, 14, 50
Echinocereus russanthus: 11, 26
Echinocereus stramineus: 14, 64,
  67
Echinocereus triglochidiatus: 52,
  334
Echinocereus triglochidiatus var.
  gonacanthus: 13, 54, 57
Echinocereus triglochidiatus var.
  gurneyi: 61
Echinocereus triglochidiatus var.
  hexaedrus: 12, 57
Echinocereus triglochidiatus var.
  melanacanthus: 55, 57
Echinocereus triglochidiatus var.
  neomexicanus: 57, 61
Echinocereus triglochidiatus var.
  octacanthus: 13, 55, 61
Echinocereus triglochidiatus var.
  triglochidiatus: 13, 53, 70
Echinocereus viridiflorus: 16, 18,
  21, 22
Echinocereus viridiflorus var.
  correllii: 18
Echinocereus viridiflorus var.
  cylindricus: 11, 18, 22, 26, 43
Echinocereus viridiflorus var.
  standleyi: 11, 18
Echinocereus viridiflorus var.
  viridiflorus: 11, 17, 18
Echinomastus: 89
Epithelantha: 8, 152
  Epithelantha bokei: 154
  Epithelantha micromeris: 153
  Epithelantha micromeris var.
    greggii: 154
Escobaria: 155, 156, 158
  Escobaria orcuttii var. *koenigii*:
    184

Escobaria orcuttii var. *macraxina*: 184
Escobaria sandbergii: 208
Escobaria villardii: 184
Escobesseya: 156
Eu-coryphantha: 155
Eumammillaria: 155
Euphorbia: 156

Ferocactus: 89
  Ferocactus hamatacanthus: 120
  Ferocactus hamatacanthus var. *sinuatus*: 118
  Ferocactus setispinus: 114
  Ferocactus wislizeni: 101

Glandulicactus: 89

Hamatocactus: 89
Homalocephala: 89

Lepidocoryphantha: 158
Lophophora: 7, 88, *137*, 153
Lophophora williamsii: *138*
Lophophora williamsii var. *echinata*: *140*
Lophophora williamsii var. *williamsii*: *138*

Mammillaria: 7, 142, 143, 146, 153, 155, 156
  Mammillaria albicolumnaria: 162, *199*
  Mammillaria bella: 160, *208*
  Mammillaria cornifera: 166
  Mammillaria dasyacantha: 163, *195*, 198
  Mammillaria duncanii: 163, *197*
  Mammillaria echinus: 161, 166, *168*
  Mammillaria fragrans: 162, *190*
  Mammillaria grahamii: 215
  Mammillaria gummifera: 225
  Mammillaria hesteri: 161, *202*

Mammillaria heyderi: *219*, 224, 225
Mammillaria heyderi var. *applanata*: 159, *222*
Mammillaria heyderi var. *bullingtoniana*: 224
Mammillaria heyderi var. *hemisphaerica*: 159, *223*
Mammillaria heyderi var. *heyderi*: 159, *220*
Mammillaria heyderi var. *meiacantha*: 224
Mammillaria lasiacantha: *209*
Mammillaria lasiacantha var. *denudata*: 164, 211, *212*
Mammillaria lasiacantha var. *lasiacantha*: 164, *211*
Mammillaria leei: 163, 164, *206*
Mammillaria longimamma: 226
Mammillaria longimamma var. *sphaerica*: 225
Mammillaria macdougalii: 225
Mammillaria macromeris: 160, *173*
Mammillaria meiacantha: 159, *220*, 224
Mammillaria melanocentra: 225
Mammillaria meridiorosei: 219
Mammillaria microcarpa: *215*
Mammillaria micromeris: 152
Mammillaria multiceps: 164, *212*
Mammillaria nellieae: 21, 163, *203*
Mammillaria pectinata: 168
Mammillaria pottsii: 163, *209*
Mammillaria prolifera var. *texana*: 212
Mammillaria ramillosa: 161, *170*
Mammillaria roberti: 164, *204*
Mammillaria robustispina: 165
Mammillaria roseiflora: 160, *178*
Mammillaria runyonii: 160, *175*

Mammillaria scheeri: 161, *165*, 166
Mammillaria scolymoides: 161, *165*
Mammillaria similis: 160, *176*
Mammillaria similis var. robustior: 170
Mammillaria sneedii: 164, *205*, 208
Mammillaria sphaerica: 159, *225*, 226
Mammillaria sulcata: 161, *168*
Mammillaria tuberculosa: 163, *192*, 196, 209
Mammillaria varicolor: 162, *199*
Mammillaria viridiflora: 219
Mammillaria vivipara: *179*
Mammillaria vivipara var. arizonica: 162, *186*
Mammillaria vivipara var. borealis: 162, *186*, 190
Mammillaria vivipara var. deserti: 162, *188*
Mammillaria vivipara var. neomexicana: 162, *182*, 190, 192
Mammillaria vivipara var. radiosa: 162, *180*, 190, 192
Mammillaria vivipara var. texana: 182
Mammillaria vivipara var. vivipara: 162, *179*, 182
Mammillaria wilcoxii: 159, *218*
Mammillaria wissmannii: 170
Mammillaria wrightii: 159, *216*, 219
Mammillaria wrightii var. wilcoxii: 218
Mammillaria wrightii var. wrightii: 216

Neobesseya: 155, 158
Neocoryphantha: 156, 158
Neoevansia: 82
Neolloydia: 89

Neolloydia conoidea: 134
Neolloydia intertexta: 126
Neolloydia intertexta var. dasyacantha: 128
Neolloydia intertexta var. intertexta: 128
Neolloydia mariposensis: 133
Neomammillaria: 155, 157, 158

Opuntia: 8, 155, *228*
Opuntia arbuscula: 337, 340
Opuntia arenaria: 237, 303, *316*
Opuntia atrispina: 235, 262, *270*, 279
Opuntia ballii: 238, *300*
Opuntia chlorotica: 234, *260*, 264
Opuntia clavata: 240, 319, *322*
Opuntia compressa: 286, *287*, 290, 294, 296, 297, 299, 300, 305, 307
Opuntia compressa var. allairei: 236, 289, *296*
Opuntia compressa var. fuscoatra: 239, 289, *293*
Opuntia compressa var. grandiflora: 239, *295*, 296
Opuntia compressa var. humifusa: 239, 288, 290, 292
Opuntia compressa var. macrorhiza: 239, 289, 292, 294, 299, 300, 307
Opuntia compressa var. microsperma: 239, *290*
Opuntia compressa var. stenochila: 238, *297*
Opuntia cymochila: 237, *285*, 299
Opuntia davisii: 241, *334*
Opuntia drummondii: 305
Opuntia engelmannii: 229, *244*, 245, 254, 258, 261, 262, 264, 268, 270, 274, 276

Opuntia engelmannii var. *aciculata*: 234, 235, *254*
Opuntia engelmannii var. *alta*: 232, *249*, 268
Opuntia engelmannii var. *cacanapa*: 233, *251*
Opuntia engelmannii var. *cyclodes*: 232, *247*
Opuntia engelmannii var. *dulcis*: 233, *254*, 266
Opuntia engelmannii var. *engelmannii*: 232, 245, 249
Opuntia engelmannii var. *flexispina*: 233, 252, 254
Opuntia engelmannii var. *linguiformis*: 234, 258
Opuntia engelmannii var. *subarmata*: 235, *258*
Opuntia engelmannii var. *texana*: 232, *247*, 251
Opuntia erinacea: 237, 308
Opuntia erinacea var. *hystricina*: 314
Opuntia fragilis: 240, *305*, 320
Opuntia fragilis var. *brachyarthra*: 306
Opuntia grahamii: 240, *318*
Opuntia humifusa: 287, 289
Opuntia humifusa var. *humifusa*: 288
Opuntia hystricina: 236, 237, *314*
Opuntia imbricata: 326
Opuntia imbricata var. *arborescens*: 240, *323*, 326, 330
Opuntia imbricata var. *imbricata*: 323
Opuntia imbricata var. *vexans*: 241, *326*
Opuntia imbricata var. *viridiflora*: 241, *326*
Opuntia kleiniae: 241, *337*, 340
Opuntia leptocarpa: 236, 245, 273, 277

Opuntia leptocaulis: 80, 241, *337*
Opuntia lindheimeri: 244, 245, 274
Opuntia lindheimeri var. *lehmannii*: 249
Opuntia lindheimeri var. *linguiformis*: 258
Opuntia lindheimeri var. *tricolor*: 251
Opuntia macateei: 294
Opuntia macrocentra: 235, *264*, 268, 280
Opuntia macrorhiza: 274
Opuntia macrorhiza var. *pottsii*: 299
Opuntia nicholii: 312
Opuntia phaeacantha: 264, 274
Opuntia phaeacantha var. *brunnea*: 234, 266, *279*, 280
Opuntia phaeacantha var. *camanchica*: 234, 236, 239, 262, 277, *280*
Opuntia phaeacantha var. *discata*: 245
Opuntia phaeacantha var. *major*: 233, 236, 274, 276, 279
Opuntia phaeacantha var. *nigricans*: 234, 270, 278
Opuntia phaeacantha var. *spinosibacca*: 262
Opuntia phaeacantha var. *tenuispina*: 237, *282*
Opuntia phaeacantha var. *wootonii*: 278
Opuntia plumbea: 238, *302*
Opuntia polyacantha: 237, 239, 286, 307, *312*, 316
Opuntia polyacantha var. *juniperina*: 306
Opuntia pottsii: 238, 299, 302
Opuntia pusilla: 240, *303*, 320
Opuntia rafinesquii: 245, 274, 289
Opuntia rhodantha: *308*

Opuntia rhodantha var. *rhodantha*: 236, 240, *308*
Opuntia rhodantha var. *spinosior*: 236, *310*
Opuntia rufida: 235, *264*, 268
Opuntia schottii: 240, *319*, 322
Opuntia schottii var. *grahamii*: 318
Opuntia sphaerocarpa: 239, *306*
Opuntia spinosibacca: 231, *262*
Opuntia spinosior: 241, *330*, 332
Opuntia stanlyi: 320
Opuntia stricta: 231, 234, *242*
Opuntia stricta var. *stricta*: 242
Opuntia strigil: 235, *268*, 279
Opuntia strigil var. *flexospina*: 252
Opuntia tardospina: 233, *261*
Opuntia tunicata: 241, *334*
Opuntia tunicata var. *davisii*: 334
Opuntia ursina: 316
Opuntia violacea var. *macrocentra*: 264
Opuntia violacea var. *santa-rita*: 235, *266*
Opuntia whipplei: 241, *332*, 334
Opuntia whipplei var. *viridiflora*: 326

Pediocactus: 7, 88, *146*
Pediocactus knowltonii: *149*
Pediocactus papyracanthus: *150*
Pediocactus simpsonii var. *minor*: 148
Pediocactus simpsonii var. *simpsonii*: *147*
Peniocereus: 7, 79, *82*
Peniocereus greggii: 3, *83*
Pereskia: 155
Platyopuntia: 231
Pseudocoryphantha: 156, 158

Roseocactus: 143
Roseocactus fissuratus: 143

Sclerocactus: 89
Sclerocactus mesae-verdae: 107
Sclerocactus parviflorus: 105
Sclerocactus parviflorus var. *intermedius*: 104
Sclerocactus whipplei var. *reevesii*: 105
Subgymnocarpae: 156

Thelocactus: 89
Thelocactus bicolor var. *flavidispinus*: 124
Thelocactus bicolor var. *schottii*: 123
Theloidei: 146

Wilcoxia: 7, 79, 82
Wilcoxia poselgeri: 3, *80*

Index of Common Names

The spelling of the Spanish names is that of local usage where the plants grow, without correction or standardization.

Abrojo: 334
Aggregate Cactus: 57
Aguijilla: 337
Alicoche: 74, 77
Arizona Coryphantha: 186
Arizona Queen of the Night: 83
Arizona Rainbow Hedgehog: 43

Ball Cactus: 179
Barrel Cactus: 101
Beehive Cactus: 58
Berlandier's Alicoche: 74
Bisnaga de Dulce: 94
Bisnaga Meloncillo: 94
Bisnagre: 94
Biznaga: 101
Biznaga Costillona: 120
Biznaga de Agua: 101
Biznaga de Chilitos: 219, 224
Biznaga de Tuna: 120
Biznaga es Pinosa: 120
Biznaga Ganchuda: 120
Biznaga Limilla: 120
Black Lace: 32
Blind Pear: 264
Brittle Cactus: 305
Brown-Flowered Hedgehog: 102
Brown-Spined Prickly Pear: 274
Bunch-Ball Cactus: 57
Button Cactus: 153

Cabeza del Viejo: 43
Candelabrum Cactus: 323
Candle Cholla: 337
Candy Barrel: 101
Candy Cactus: 96

Cane Cactus: 323
Cane Cholla: 330
Cat-Claw Cactus: 102
Chaparral Cactus: 83
Chautle: 144
Cholla: 323
Claret-Cup Cactus: 52, 54, 55
Classen's Cactus: 28
Clavellina: 319, 334
Cliff Prickly Pear: 308
Clock-Face Prickly Pear: 260
Club Cholla: 322
Cockle-Burr Cactus: 303
Cock-Spur Cactus: 303
Comb Hedgehog: 42
Cow's Tongue Cactus: 258
Coyote Candles: 323
Creeping Cholla: 320
Crow-Foot Prickly Pear: 303

Dagger Cholla: 322
Dahlia Cactus: 80
Deer-Horn Cactus: 83
Desert Christmas Cactus: 337
Devil Cactus: 319
Devil Cholla: 320
Devil's Claw Barrel: 104
Devil's Head: 94, 96
Dog Cholla: 319
Dry Whisky: 138
Dumpling Cactus: 175

Eagle Claws: 94
Early Bloomer: 126
Engelmann's Prickly Pear: 244
Estria del Tarde: 182

Fendler's Hedgehog Cactus: 67
Fendler's Pitaya: 67
Finger Cactus: 168
Fishhook Barrel: 101
Fishhook Cactus: 108, 110, 114,
    116, 215
Flaming Prickly Pear: 244
Flap-Jack Cactus: 258
Fragile Prickly Pear: 305

Garrambullo: 337
Glory of Texas: 123
Golden Rainbow Hedgehog: 47
Grama-Grass Cactus: 150
Grape Cactus: 212
Green-Flowered Pitaya: 16, 22
Green-Flowered Torch Cactus: 16,
    22

Hair-Covered Cactus: 212
Heart Twister: 57
Hedgehog Cactus: 114, 116
Horse Crippler: 96
Hunger Cactus: 312

Junior Tom Thumb Cactus: 204

King's Cup Cactus: 52, 54
Klein Cholla: 337
Knowlton Cactus: 149

Lace Cactus: 28
Lady-Finger Cactus: 74
Large-Flowered Opuntia: 295
Lengua de Vaca: 258
Little Chilis: 219, 224
Living Rock: 144
Long Mamma: 173
Long-Tubercled Coryphantha: 165
Lower Rio Grande Valley Barrel:
    118
Low Prickly Pear: 287

Manco Caballo: 96

Mesa Verde Cactus: 107
Mescal Button: 138
Mounded Dwarf Cholla: 318
Mountain Cactus: 147
Mulato: 153

Needle "Mulee": 165
New Mexico Coryphantha: 182
New Mexico Prickly Pear: 274
New Mexico Rainbow Cactus: 16
Night-Blooming Cereus: 86
Nipple Cactus: 168, 176, 219
Nopal: 244
Nylon Cactus: 16

Organo: 64, 86

Paper-Spined Cactus: 150
Pencil Cactus: 80
Pest Pear: 242
Peyote: 138
Peyote Cimarron: 144
Peyotl: 137
Pincushion: 179, 182, 215
Pineapple Cactus: 168
Pink-Flowered Echinocereus: 67
Pitahaya: 60, 86
Pitaya: 62, 64, 66
Porcupine Prickly Pear: 314
Purple Candle: 28
Purple Hedgehog: 67
Purple Prickly Pear: 264

Rat-Tail Cactus: 332
Red-Flowered Hedgehog Cactus: 57
Red-Goblet Cactus: 60
Root Cactus: 110
Runyon's Coryphantha: 175
Runyon's Escobaria: 204

Sacasil: 80
Sand-Burr Cactus: 303
Sea-Urchin Cactus: 98
Silverlace Cactus: 199

Sitting Cactus: 67
Slender Stem Cactus: 337
Small Papillosus: 73
Smooth Prickly Pear: 287
Sour Cactus: 186
Spiny Star: 179, 182
Stanley's Cholla: 320
Star Cactus: 144
Star Rock: 144
Starvation Cactus: 312
Sticker Cactus: 332
Strawberry Cactus: 52, 55, 62, 64,
    66, 67
Sunami: 144
Sunset Cactus: 215
Sweet-Potato Cactus: 83

Tasajillo: 337
Texas Hedgehog: 102
Texas Night-Blooming Cereus: 83
Texas Rainbow Cactus: 47
Torch Cactus: 67
Toumeya: 150
Tree Cactus: 323
Triangle Cactus: 86
Tulip Prickly Pear: 274
Tuna: 244
Turk's Head Cactus: 57, 94, 102,
    120
Twisted-Rib Cactus: 114, 116

Velas de Coyote: 323
Visnaga: 101, 120
Viznaga: 96

Whipple's Cholla: 332
Whisky Cactus: 138
White Column: 199
White-Flowered Visnagita: 126
Wide Cactus: 308

Yellow-Flowered Alicoche: 71
Yellow-Flowered Echinocereus: 71
Yellow-Flowered Pitaya: 47